CHILDREN OF
THE CAMPS

For Fang Fang and William,
my family

CHILDREN OF THE CAMPS

Japan's Last Forgotten Victims

Mark Felton

Pen & Sword
MILITARY

First published in Great Britain in 2011 by
Pen & Sword Military
an imprint of
Pen & Sword Books Ltd
47 Church Street
Barnsley
South Yorkshire
S70 2AS

ISBN: 978-1-84884-261-8

A CIP catalogue record for this book is
available from the British Library.

Typeset in 11/13pt Palatino by
Concept, Huddersfield, West Yorkshire

Printed and bound in England by
the MPG Books Group

Pen & Sword Books Ltd incorporates the Imprints of Pen & Sword
Aviation, Pen & Sword Maritime, Pen & Sword Military, Wharncliffe
Local History, Pen & Sword Select, Pen & Sword Military Classics,
Leo Cooper, Remember When, Seaforth Publishing and
Frontline Publishing.

For a complete list of Pen & Sword titles please contact
PEN & SWORD BOOKS LIMITED
47 Church Street, Barnsley, South Yorkshire, S70 2AS, England
E-mail: enquiries@pen-and-sword.co.uk
Website: www.pen-and-sword.co.uk

Contents

Acknowledgements

Many individuals and organisations have assisted me in creating this book and you all have my thanks and appreciation. Many thanks to the following: Ron Bridge, AFC, chairman of the Association of British Civilian Internees Far East Region (ABCIFER); David Parker, OBE, Director, Information and Secretariat, Commonwealth War Graves Commission; the historian and expert on the civilian internment camps in China, Greg Leck; Peter Hibbard MBE, President of the Royal Asiatic Society, Shanghai; Jill Durney and her wonderful team of archivists at the MacMillan-Brown Library, University of Canterbury, New Zealand; Ron Taylor and the members of the Far East Prisoners of War Association (FEPOW); The Children Of Far East Prisoners Of War Association (COFEPOW); The National Archives (Public Record Office), Kew, and the National Archives and Record Administration (NARA) in Washington DC. My gratitude and thanks to Brigadier Henry Wilson and all of the team at Pen & Sword Books, and in particular my editor Jan Chamier, as well as Jonathan Wright, Helen Vodden and Jon Wilkinson. To my wife Fang Fang, who has made me the writer that I am today through her love, encouragement, and support, I can only say thank you.

Introduction

I could walk down our barrack past women and children with broken teeth and bleeding gums, hair growing in tufts and faces and stomachs bloated with hunger oedema and beriberi, boils as big as ping pong balls and oozing tropical ulcers and not let myself see *them: pain was pain.*

Ernest Hillen, Dutch child internee
Kampong Makassar Camp, 1944–45

'There must be at this stage be no thought of saving the troops or sparing the population. The battle must be fought to the bitter end at all costs ... Commanders and senior officers should die with their troops. The honour of the British Empire and of the British Army is at stake. I rely on you to show no weakness or mercy in any form.'[1] These words were penned by a British Prime Minister and represent one of the harshest orders ever issued by a British leader in wartime.

The Prime Minister was Winston Churchill and the battle he was referring to was the struggle to defend Singapore from an almost irresistible Japanese military juggernaut which by early 1942 was swallowing up British, American and Dutch overseas territories at a voracious pace. The exhortation from Churchill had arrived on the desk of the hapless British commander in Malaya and Singapore, Lieutenant General Arthur Percival, only two days before the final capitulation. Behind the thin line of British, Australian, Indian and Malay soldiers holding the Japanese at bay was a huge mass of Chinese, Malay and white civilians, all trying

1

to flee Singapore by whatever means at hand, before it was too late. Families crowded the docks and quayside, fighting with army deserters to get aboard the last few remaining ships. No one wanted to fall into the hands of a terrifying Asiatic enemy whom many were comparing, in terms of brutality, to Genghis Khan's Mongol hoard. Frantic mothers, their husbands already lost to the fighting, pulled along terrified and confused children towards what they prayed would be salvation and a ticket to safety. For most, they had left evacuation too late and the women and children were now trapped in a burning and battered Singapore City, the streets littered with rubble from the shelling and bombing and strewn with decomposing bodies, the air rent with the crack of bullets and the crump of mortars and artillery fire, the sky above filled with howling Japanese aircraft that swooped down to strafe at will the long columns of refugees and soldiers.

General Percival's forces had been pushed all the way down the Malay Peninsula since the initial Japanese invasion on 8 December 1941, when enemy troops had first hit beaches in southern Thailand and northern Malaya. By early February 1942 the Japanese were ashore on Singapore Island, the last significant bastion of the British Empire in Asia still resisting the Japanese. Over 70,000 British and Commonwealth troops were trapped with their backs to the sea, the Japanese literally breathing down their necks as they pushed inexorably towards the city centre. Simultaneously, the confused scenes enacted in Singapore were being replicated in almost all of the European colonies in the East. In Hong Kong, the British were also trapped with their backs against the sea, with no hope of reinforcements or relief; in the Philippines American and British nationals tried to stay one step ahead of the Japanese columns cutting through Luzon Island towards Manila; in the Netherlands East Indies, hundreds of thousands of Dutch and British civilians waited with bated breath for the next round of Japanese attacks that must surely soon strike the archipelago once Singapore had fallen; and in Burma, British families had begun to evacuate towards India, sure that the Japanese were about to cross the border and strike for Rangoon.

The maelstrom and confusion at the docks in Singapore was epic as mothers dragged small children through crowds of shouting and fighting whites and Asians, jostling the suitcases containing all they had left in the world towards ship gangplanks, while military policeman yelled at the crowds to stay back and keep order, occasionally firing warning shots into the air from their service revolvers. The deafening detonations of aerial bombs and the shriek and moan of the diving Japanese aircraft was the constant refrain of the evacuation, and the background was the huge black clouds that hung over the city as whole districts burned under the furious bombardment. The women had largely been abandoned to care for their children and get them to safety, as all the able-bodied men were at the front lines or were already dead or prisoners of the Japanese. Rich Westerners even paused to order their chauffeurs to push their expensive cars into the harbour rather than leave them for the conquerors. The clock in the tall, battle-scarred Cathay Building downtown ticked off the minutes as the British Empire in Singapore drew to a violent and ignominious close.

While the desperate scenes of evacuation were played out in Singapore, Hong Kong, Burma and the Philippines, in the city of Shanghai on China's east coast the British population largely sat tight and awaited its fate with a grim stoicism borne of the realization that they literally had nowhere to run to. Hong Kong could have been so different. In 1939, shortly after the outbreak of the war in Europe, Neville Chamberlain's government had drawn up evacuation plans for Hong Kong in the event of a war with Japan. Those to leave would consist of British and other European women and children only. It was felt in London that if the Japanese attacked Hong Kong, and bearing in mind that the Chiefs of Staff considered the colony virtually indefensible, it would have been an embarrassment if large numbers of white women and children were taken prisoner. It was thought that internment would cause not only wholly unnecessary suffering to these non-combatants, but would also allow the Japanese to use the women and children for distasteful propaganda purposes. In July 1940 the Governor of Hong Kong, Sir Mark Young, received orders from the Colonial Office in London to proceed with compulsory evacuations to the American-controlled Philippines. The families of servicemen forming the Hong Kong garrison were evacuated, along with certain registered non-service British women and children. By 3 August 1940 large numbers had been successfully sent away by ship, but not without some controversy. Many in the colony continued to ignore the clear signs of Japanese aggression in the ramp-up to the attack on Pearl Harbor, preferring to believe the myth that the Japanese would not be so foolish as to attack the British Empire or the United States. What many failed to take into consideration was the fact that the British Government had already conceded that Hong Kong was a lost cause before the first Japanese soldier set his cloven-toed boot over the border from occupied China in December 1941. The steady draining away of naval and military assets in Hong Kong had been completed by the time the evacuations were underway. Forces were being diverted to Singapore or the war in Europe and North Africa, leaving only a couple of under-strength and under-trained infantry brigades to delay the Japanese attack and make sure that the colony did not fall without a face-saving show of resistance by the British.

Many of the Hong Kong evacuee women wanted to remain with their husbands, and many husbands believed the government had blundered in ordering the evacuations. Women and children started to return. At the same time the local Chinese were embittered by what they rightly perceived as a racist lottery when it came to evacuations. Even Chinese people who held British passports were denied evacuation – this being reserved for women and children of European descent only – and many white men had married local women. Pressure in the colony led the colonial administration to make the evacuations non-compulsory, with the result that large numbers of white women and children remained in Hong Kong when the Japanese launched their invasion, with terrible results for them all. The evacuees who had already been ordered to leave had been permitted instead to remain in the colony if they volunteered as auxiliary nurses or administrative staff.

Now, it was too late. The ships that had left Hong Kong got no further than Manila, which was about to fall to the Japanese. The ships that had left Singapore stood little chance. Forty out of forty-four would be sunk by Japanese warships or aircraft before they could get to the Netherlands East Indies or Australia, and the survivors were thrown into internment camps. The vast majority of British, American and Dutch civilians living and working in Asia would shortly be swept into a series of camps, where conditions would prove as bad as the concentration camps in German-occupied Europe. They would be starved, beaten and humiliated, have their culture, humanity and dignity steadily stripped away, and they would sicken from a multitude of horrible diseases. The numbers are astounding: 132,895 Western civilians were interned by the Japanese, including 40,260 children under sixteen years of age. Fifteen thousand died. But figures only hint at the misery. Most of today's survivors of the camps were children during their internment, and their childhoods were ruined by what they saw and were forced to do by the Japanese. Over 40,000 children, whose only crime was to have been living in Asia when the war began, received the kind of treatment normally reserved for the most hardened military criminals. That so many survived demonstrated the incredible courage and adaptability of children, who in many ways were better equipped to deal with internment than their parents. Seen through the eyes of children, Japanese internment was the defining experience of the lives of its survivors, a nightmare world in which parents and older children strove to maintain some sense of normality for the little ones cast into this shameful prison camp regime. In this book I shall attempt to tell just some of the stories of the children of the camps.

The effects of imprisonment by the Japanese are still felt by the thousands of people who are alive today and who had the great misfortune to have experienced it. When the Allied prisoners-of-war and internees were released from captivity in September 1945 they were all, to a greater or lesser extent, suffering from the effects of prolonged malnutrition. They had been exposed to the whole panoply of tropical diseases and many had suffered badly with malaria, dysentery, typhus, beriberi, typhoid fever and dengue fever. Some had become infested by parasites that took years to leave their bodies. Many had been physically abused, from being slapped across the face to being beaten with clubs, or subjected to lengthy periods of torture at the hands of the *Kempeitai* military police that had resulted in appalling injuries, and in some cases permanent disability. The psychological effects of Japanese imprisonment were huge, and suggestions have been made by experts that nearly 40 per cent of British internees subsequently suffered from post-traumatic stress disorder as a direct result of the privations they had endured and the violence and death that they had witnessed. Young women had become widows and many of the children died in the camps from starvation or disease. Families had been destroyed, never to be put back together again.

Shanghai, May 2010

1

School's Out

At school we practised getting into slit trenches for air-raids and had to kneel on the rough coco-nut matting, very painful. At home my father kept a rifle in the dining room and wore a pistol at his waist. I remember the frequent earnest discussions, and the packing of bags including tins of food.

Roger Eagle, British child
Singapore, 1942

A long line of Westerners stood huddled in warm winter clothing outside a nondescript office block in downtown Shanghai. A chill wind blew between the tall buildings behind the Bund, coming straight down from frozen Manchuria in the north. Japanese soldiers stood impassively around the queueing Westerners, their dun-coloured uniforms, puttees and forage caps incongruous in the city. Their rifles were topped with razor-sharp bayonets. Many smoked and laughed among themselves to see the whites, who thought themselves so superior to the Japanese, lining up like coolies in the street, waiting to have their details recorded by the *Kempeitai* military police. Their faces wore a hunted, uncertain look – gone was the once-proud jut of the chin, or the ramrod-straight back that shouldered the white man's burden. The Westerners were shell-shocked – their world had collapsed in a few short days. The Japanese had big plans for them all: they were to be reduced from masters to white coolies; men, women and children. If any of the Westerners had glanced aloft at the tall buildings that bracketed the street they would have seen the

Rising Sun flag snapping out in the breeze, where the Union Jack had held dominion for a century.

The outbreak of war in the Pacific on 8 December 1941 had come as a surprise to many Allied civilians, but the warning signs had been in place for weeks and Britain, Holland and the United States had largely ignored them until it was too late. In Shanghai, the Japanese already had the two foreign enclaves in the city, the International Settlement and the French Concession, surrounded since capturing the Chinese areas of the city in 1937. Life had continued relatively unchanged for the Allied civilians living in the 'Settlement' and the 'Concession', though there were restrictions on travelling outside the enclaves into occupied China. The fall of France in June 1940 had meant some Japanese interference in the French Concession, which adopted a Vichy government that collaborated closely with the Germans and the Japanese. Many British and American civilians lived in the French Concession but worked in the International Settlement, which was subdivided into several national concessions, including British and Japanese areas.

The British and the Americans had realized that Shanghai was indefensible should the Japanese move to occupy the enclaves, and the British had pulled out their small garrison of two infantry battalions to Hong Kong in 1940, urging Britons to leave for Australia, the Netherlands East Indies, Singapore or Britain. The United States still had some forces in Beijing and Shanghai, a regiment from the United States Marine Corps whose job was to protect US-owned buildings and diplomatic properties. Many Allied civilians left Shanghai, but many more stayed put – they were used to the comfortable life 'out East', where even whites in relatively minor positions could enjoy servants and private schooling for their children and a vigorous social life in a metropolis variously nicknamed 'Sin City' and 'The Whore of the Orient'.

One family who did not leave after 1940 was the Boseburys, typical British lower-middle-class workers of the Empire. Daughter Rachel Bosebury Beck, who now lives in the United States, recalled that her parents met in Shanghai. Her mother worked for the Shanghai Telephone Company, and her father had been discharged from the British Army after he had met his wife, while he was stationed in Shanghai. He then took a job locally, working as an overseer of Chinese labour. 'We lived in Avenue Hall ... and my daddy worked at the Water Works, and it was just great.' Rachel Bosebury was seven years old when the Japanese took over the foreign sections of the city in 1941. 'I had an amah [Chinese female servant] and ... I remember playing a lot and then we took home leave. That means every four years my Dad had his way paid to go back home to England.'[1] With somewhat questionable common sense, the Boseburys returned from a long leave in Britain and continued with their comfortable, but not wealthy, existence until the Japanese assault – even though the warning signs of Japanese aggression were plainly evident. But Mr Bosebury was not unusual in having complete faith in the strength of the British Empire to defend its citizens; after all, many reasoned, only a very foolish country indeed would attack the world's greatest super power – little realizing that the much-vaunted imperial strength of Britain was slowly dwindling in the Far East, as forces were transferred to Europe and not replaced. Britain was fighting a war for survival right on her doorstep and that was where the main military effort was concentrated.

The colonial lifestyles of the children of empire did not prepare them for the coming storm of war, or for the long period of internment that most of them had to look forward to. Neil Begley, a young boy in Shanghai in 1941, recalled his Chinese nanny, or 'amah', who cared for him. In common with many of the children who were later interned, Begley had a closer relationship with local Chinese people than with his parents:

> My amah smelled like a Chinese, they all smelled the same, not like we 'Foreigners' and, colour apart, I thought that smell was what made them different from us. Taking a nipple in my lips I would suck her warm milk while she ran her fingers through my hair crooning haunting Chinese lullabies. She spoke only Chinese so I was more comfortable with Mandarin that I was with English and quite at home in the servants quarters ... My mother would have been horrified if she'd seen me.[2]

Many Western children developed such bonds with native servants, often because their own parents were too busy with careers or the social whirl of colonial life, to pay much attention to them. 'We children loved to spend time with our cook in the kitchen, squatting next to her on the floor, watching her crush and grind the ''bumbu'' of chillies, coriander, cumin and other spices,' recalled Jan Ruff, a young Dutch girl in Java in 1941. 'She let us take turns at turning the handle of the mincer and fanning the open charcoal stove. In Imah's domain we licked saucepans and scooped our fingers into her delicious dishes ...'[3] Ernest Hillen, a young Dutch boy in the Netherlands East Indies, recalled Manang, the family gardener, who 'smelled of different kinds of smoke. He never hurried and I liked being near him: it was restful ... His large flat feet had spaces between the toes because he didn't have to wear shoes. I felt the bottom of those feet and they were hard and covered with deep, dry, criss-crossed cuts, which he said didn't hurt. I wanted feet like that, his shiny brown skin, and I tried to walk bowlegged like him.'[4]

Soon after arriving back in Shanghai from leave in England, Rachel Bosebury's parents realized that the situation was turning bad for foreigners in the city. This was during the last few weeks before the Japanese bombed Pearl Harbor. 'I remember them saying that the Japanese were bloodthirsty people,' recalled Rachel Bosebury. 'I know I heard stories of babies being thrown up in the air and caught on Japanese bayonets.' Such talk terrified young children, and Rachel and her siblings had little understanding of what was about to change in their stable home life. 'When they were talking I had an imagination. You know, when little children hear the word ''bloodthirsty'', you think they drink blood. So I used to be terribly afraid that they would see me and at night we'd cover ourselves up with our blankets and wouldn't even let a bit of hair show out because we didn't want them to be drinking our blood.' The term 'Japanese' conjured up a ubiquitous bogeyman that haunted the dreams of adults and children alike in Shanghai. 'Kids hear things, but when you're little, you think of it a lot differently, and you get pretty scared,' said Bosebury.[5] The fears Western children harboured after overhearing their parents' conversations were not to prove entirely unfounded, for the war about to be unleashed across Asia was to be marked from the very beginning by acts of almost diabolical barbarity and sadism, changing the world's opinion of Japan forever.

British teenager Heather Burch had returned to Shanghai in 1939, after attending private school in England since the age of eleven. Her father was the chairman of the Shanghai Water Works, where Rachel Bosebury's father also worked as a supervisor. However, there the similarity ended, the Burch family formed part of the British expatriate community's governing class. By 1941 rumours were abounding of Japanese intentions towards the International Settlement. 'It was obvious the situation was getting worse,' recalled Burch. 'People began leaving for Australia and Canada, but few for England.' Going 'back home' was not a very attractive proposition, involving a long sea voyage through waters infested by aggressive German U-boats, and entering a country under constant aerial attack from the *Luftwaffe* and suffering from severe food shortages and rationing. Most people who left Shanghai for England were young single men intent on enlisting and doing their duty. 'In late 1941 my father was told off-the-record by the British Consul that he should leave as quickly as possible. He booked passage for us, but the earliest available was in mid-December.' The Burches had left their escape until it was too late. When the Japanese occupied the Settlement 'we found ourselves trapped.'[6]

Ella Clark was sixteen when the Japanese took over the Settlement, and studying at a local business college. Her father worked for the Chinese Customs Service, and her family lived close to the famous Bund. Early on the morning of 8 December 1941, foreign residents who lived close enough to the Huangpu River were rudely awakened by the sound of gunfire. Japanese troops, supported by light tanks, had begun marching into the International Settlement, and there was nothing effective to stop them. The British-led Shanghai Volunteer Corps (SVC), a part-time militia composed of expatriate men from a dozen different nationalities organized into several infantry companies and cavalry troops, was told to stand down and surrender its weapons. They were a surrounded force and if they had tried to resist would have been quickly overwhelmed by the superior enemy numbers and firepower. The SVC commanders realized that fighting in the densely populated city would have led to thousands of civilian casualties to no avail. Although it opted not to resist, its members

11

were nonetheless imprisoned as military prisoners-of-war by the Japanese, depriving hundreds of families of husbands and fathers.

The only regular military forces in the city were a pair of slightly antiquated Yangtze River gunboats tied up on the Huangpu. The USS *Wake* was taken over by the Japanese without the Americans firing a shot, but the din that awakened the city's foreign residents to danger was the desperate resistance being put up by one lone British gunboat, HMS *Peterel*. Aboard the *Peterel*, the morning watch had stared across the misty river at the bustling city, nursing cups of tea in tin mugs, discerning the first stirrings of a new threat to this quiet and satisfactory morning rhythm. A Chinese laundry boy went about his work unobtrusively as the rest of the small crew of twenty slumbered below. A Japanese gunboat moved in the distance, and a curl of smoke rose from the funnel of the huge Imperial Navy cruiser *Idzumo*, whose guns had been ominously pointing towards the Settlement since early that morning. Japanese soldiers could be seen milling about by the river north of the Bund. Lieutenant Stephen Polkinghorn, the ship's New Zealand skipper, was below when the telephone that had been set up as a direct link with the British Consulate suddenly rang. Since the fall of the Chinese capital of Nanking in 1937, the Consulate had become the temporary British Embassy in China. The voice at the other end was terse and to the point: 'The Japanese have bombed Pearl Harbor in Hawaii, and Britain is consequently at war with Japan!' Polkinghorn was not surprised. 'You can expect a visit from the Japanese at any time,' continued the measured tones of the diplomat. 'Obviously there is nothing you can do with the forces at your disposal. I would suggest that you strike your colours.' Replacing the handset on its cradle after further discussions, Polkinghorn rubbed his chin reflectively for a moment, carefully considering his options. His vessel represented the last regular British armed forces in Shanghai, and naval honour dictated that he could not surrender his ship without some gesture of defiance. Elsewhere in the city, locally recruited agents of Churchill's Special Operations Executive (SOE) had already been activated for nearly a year, and should have formed another arm of British resistance in the city. These brave but amateur spies would be swept into *Kempeitai* prisons within a few weeks.

Lieutenant Polkinghorn did not have long to wait before one of his men called his attention to a small launch coming towards the *Peterel* from the Japanese side. Polkinghorn issued the fateful command 'All hands to battle stations!', and his men manned their two remaining Lewis machine guns, the ship's main armament having unwisely been mothballed some time before. A small group of Japanese army officers, *samurai* swords at their sides, climbed the gangplank and stiffly saluted. Polkinghorn listened impatiently to their interpreter as the Japanese ordered the New Zealander to immediately surrender his ship to them or face dire and, it was hinted, terminal consequences. Polkinghorn drew himself up to his full height, stuck out his chin and hissed 'Get off my bloody ship!' The astonished Japanese officers blinked several times behind their wire-framed spectacles and then turned on their heels and silently filed back into their launch, dumbfounded at the young officer's suicidal boldness.

Grim-faced, Polkinghorn's two dozen ratings took cover behind sandbags piled in the ship's gangways, the men manning the machine guns staring intently at the grey bulk of the *Idzumo* as a klaxon sounded out from across the water and the booming report of the cruiser's massive guns echoed across a city that was just coming to life, rattling windows throughout the Settlement. Children and their parents sat up in bed with a start all over the Settlement, confused by the sudden noise. The little ones called for their amahs or their mothers, while fathers hastily dressed and tried to take stock of what was happening. In the apartments fronting onto the Bund, parents shouted at inquisitive children to stay away from the windows as the loudest pyrotechnic display they had ever heard seemed to shake the buildings to their foundations. Those fathers who were veterans of the trenches of France and Flanders felt a familiar curl of fear wind through their guts at the sound of artillery fire.

Lieutenant Polkinghorn cupped his hands to his mouth and yelled 'Open fire!' through the din of falling shells. The chattering of the machine guns, as they threw long lines of bullets at the monolithic structure of the Japanese cruiser and the gunboat was drowned out by the boom and whoosh of giant naval shells that threw up massive geysers of dirty river water all around the tiny British ship. Amid the flying steel, Polkinghorn bravely directed their fire, his face and uniform streaked with cordite smoke stains and damp with spray, reflexively ducking every time another shell screamed in. The inevitable happened. With a blinding flash and a deafening concussion the *Peterel* was struck, the ship heaving over hard against her cables, flames shooting into the air. Within minutes the whole superstructure was on fire. Bodies littered the blood-soaked deck, and the cacophony of battle intermingled with the high-pitched screaming of the wounded and the copper-stench of blood. The *Peterel* lurched again as another shell found its mark, and the ship began to take on a startling list. 'Abandon ship, abandon ship!' yelled Polkinghorn as the vessel threatened to capsize at any moment. Men plunged into the brown river, casting away their tin helmets as they dove in. Polkinghorn wrenched off a pair of binoculars and dived in after his men.[7]

Ella Clark heard and saw the destruction of the *Peterel* from her parents' riverside apartment. A way of life abruptly ended, as the British warship slid beneath the surface of the river, its cold waters extinguishing the hungry orange blaze with a great hiss of steam. 'We had a wonderful lifestyle before the war,' Clark recalled. 'We never had to go shopping or carrying. Our drinking water came in great big bottles on a stand, and when we were finished we just phoned for another. We had an amah who would look after us while my mother went out to meet her friends.' The solid middle-class childhood enjoyed by Clark was common to most of the British children who were later interned. Another woman remembered, 'We weren't as bad as some children, who would ring for their amah to pass them a book from a cupboard right beside them. But my mother, who was born in Malaya, wouldn't have known how to boil a kettle.'[8]

Living an even more privileged lifestyle was the young James Ballard, later to become world famous as the novelist J.G. Ballard. His father was Chairman of the China Printing and Finishing Company in Shanghai. Ballard was twelve years old when he was sent to an internment camp with his parents and younger sister, and had previously lived in a mansion equipped with nine servants. Being uprooted from such a privileged life and thrown into a camp became the defining experience of Ballard's life, and not an entirely negative one – something commented upon by several other former child internees of the Japanese. 'I remember those years as a time of high interest and activity,' he later recalled.[9]

Valerie Tulloch was a seven-year-old Scot living in the International Settlement when her older brother Ian dragged her out on the street to watch the Japanese victory parade through the city, the day after HMS *Peterel* was sunk. The young boy was fascinated, as young boys often are, by the uniforms, guns and swords, perhaps not realizing the seriousness of the ceremony that he and his little sister witnessed. It was the effective end of a 'foreign' Shanghai that had been in existence since 1842, when the first hardy British traders and merchant adventurers had moved up the China coast from Canton, intent on creating a trading enclave along the muddy banks of the Huangpu River. 'I don't remember being frightened,' said Valerie Tulloch after witnessing the display of Japanese military might. 'Most children are very resilient; they feel safe so long as their parents are around to protect them.'[10]

For Allied civilians still in the International Settlement, their lives began to change quite quickly following the Japanese take-over. Chinese servants were soon dismissed, and access to foreign bank accounts severely limited by order of the Japanese as a way of intentionally reducing the foreigners' living standards to the level of the lowest class of Chinese river coolie. Rachel Bosebury's father was forced to continue working at the Shanghai Water Works under Japanese supervision, as he had been classed as an 'essential worker', one of hundreds of foreigners who kept their posts but not their authority, to keep the city running while the Japanese consolidated their control. In fact, so many British remained in place running everything from the Water Works to the electricity stations, and even the local police force and prison, that questions were raised in London. The word 'collaboration' was noted in reports on more than one occasion, the bureaucrats in Whitehall failing to fully understand the duress under which the Britons worked for the Japanese.

The apartment building where the Bosebury family was living was commandeered by the Japanese, and the family moved into a much less salubrious apartment block in a poorer section of the Settlement. Bosebury's father received no wages from his continued employment by the Japanese, only subsistence. Rachel, who had

15

learned the local Shanghainese dialect, proved a boon to her mother during the hard times before the family was interned. 'When we didn't have hot water my mum would send me into the Chinese settlement, and I knew who to ask. They'd follow me home with water in wooden buckets to pour in our tub.'[11]

Some resistance against the Japanese was mounted by Chinese Nationalist guerrillas. In small groups they instituted an assassination policy against the Japanese garrison. Norman Douglas Shaw was an eleven-year-old British schoolboy when the Japanese occupied the International Settlement. He remembered the guerrilla attacks. 'Many Japanese soldiers and their officers were assassinated by the Chinese underground,' Shaw recalled. 'So at the end of every street there was a barbed wire barricade ready to close off any street to stop assassins escaping, but very few got caught.'[12] For the first few months under Japanese rule some semblance of normality continued. Children still attended school. 'So many sentries were being shot that they had to put steel plates and sandbags around the sentry boxes,' recalled Shaw. 'Many times on the way to school, they would close off the streets because of some shooting, so we were happy not to be able to go to school that day!'[13]

Rachel Bosebury recalled that it was soon abundantly clear from her parent's conversations that the Japanese were waging a race war against Western people. If you were white, it became apparent that you were slated for internment at some point in the near future. Parents and children were suddenly very aware of their skin colour, and of their much diminished status in the city. They had been transformed from masters to an oppressed underclass virtually overnight. 'I'm dark, I'm olive complected, and when I go out in the sun I get dark, and my younger sister's like that too,' recalled Bosebury. 'We'd hear the broadcast about how the Japanese were rounding up all the white people. My little sister said, "Well, Mummy, aren't you glad we're brown?"'[14]

While Rachel Bosebury, Norman Douglas Shaw and thousands of other children tried to adjust to life under the Japanese in Shanghai, in many other places British and Allied children were to suffer through fierce fighting as the Japanese conquered Malaya, Hong Kong, Singapore and Burma. Shanghai had been taken virtually without a shot being fired, but Britain's other Asian territories were fiercely contested, showing great resistance to the invaders, and inevitably children ended up as victims of the fighting. It was not long before some children began to realize that the Japanese posed a serious threat to their lives. 'The first I knew about the war was when we were told the Japanese were coming through the jungle on bicycles and a local gardener had been found with his throat cut,' recalled Catherine Munnoch, whose father was serving with the Argyll and Sutherland Highlanders in Malaya.[15] For other children, the arrival of the war in their lives was slightly more subtle. 'As 1942 approached I became aware of the increasing tension,' wrote Roger Eagle, a toddler when the Japanese assaulted Malaya. His father was also in the army, a captain in the Royal Engineers. 'At school we practised getting into slit trenches for air-raids and had to kneel on the rough coconut matting, very painful.'[16] Eagle was struck by the change that came over his parents. 'At home my father kept a rifle in the dining room and wore a pistol at his waist. I remember the frequent earnest discussions, and the packing of bags including tins of food.'[17]

The Japanese had landed on east coast beaches in southern Thailand and northern Malaya, and after initially fierce resistance by mainly Indian troops and the airforces of Britain and Australia, they had begun to advance steadily down the Malay Peninsula. Although British and Imperial forces outnumbered the Japanese by more than two to one, the British lost air superiority over the battlefields because their aircraft types were largely obsolescent, and they lacked anything effective to stop tanks. Consequently, the Japanese advance was rapid, involving them bypassing and flanking each British attempt to block them, and resulting in countless British units being cut off and surrounded, or dispersed into the jungle and rubber plantations. Most dangerous of all was a growing sense that the Japanese were unstoppable, which deeply affected Allied morale. The Japanese assault, under the overall command of Lieutenant General Tomoyuki Yamashita, was to capture Singapore and its vital naval base.

In Singapore, Robert Brooks, who was six and a half years old in February 1942, found himself swept up in the fighting as the Japanese invaded the island. On 12 February, Brooks, along with his parents and two aunts had abandoned their comfortable home on Bukit Timah Road and moved into the relative safety of Outram Road Jail. Two days later and the Japanese were almost inside the city centre. 'The noise, the dust, the shooting, the smells were quite foreign to a young mind,' he recalled. 'Then the equatorial sky off west Singapore became dark, sinister and smoke-laden as the defending forces had decided to torch the oil storage depots at Pasir Panjang Docks to prevent them falling into Japanese hands.'[18] What Brooks was witnessing was the final act of the Allied defence of Singapore. A monumentally mismanaged British effort to hold Singapore was almost at an end, and for children like Brooks, their options were fast narrowing as the Japanese onslaught began to batter its way through the ring of exhausted British, Indian, Australian and Malay battalions protecting the city. For many families, the docks at Keppel Harbour represented their last avenue of escape.

2

Evacuation

*At last we sailed and I waved and waved to my father until he
became a dot on the horizon. I never saw him again for three
and a half years.*

Catherine Munnoch
Child evacuee, Singapore, 1942

In Singapore the evacuations gained a new urgency by early
February 1942, when it became clear that the Japanese advance on
Singapore City was virtually unstoppable. The colony was going
to fall to the Japanese – the only question that remained was
when? The Allied troops, under the overall command of Lieutenant
General Arthur Percival, doggedly held on to a rapidly thinning
perimeter around the city, but it was only a matter of time before
Japanese tanks breached the defences and were followed by hordes
of infantry into the heart of Britain's most significant colony east of
India. The British and their allies still outnumbered the Japanese
by two to one, but the Japanese had gained and retained air
superiority over Singapore as the RAF had been unable to compete
with the latest Japanese fighters (like the renowned Mitsubishi
Zero), and had been withdrawn to airfields in Java and Sumatra.
The Japanese had tanks; the British had none, and hardly any
weapons capable of stopping them. The Allied soldiers continued
to fight hard, but they were running out of options and with the air
of defeatism and a terrible, debilitating hopelessness permeating
the British high command in their bunker at Fort Canning, a
shameful surrender was already being seriously considered –

regardless of Churchill's exhortations to fight on to the last man and the last bullet.

Upwards of one million Chinese, Malay, Indian, British and Australian civilians had crowded into the remaining areas of Singapore City that were still under Allied control, and they were suffering terribly from the incessant Japanese aerial bombing, food shortages, lack of proper medical facilities and the intermittent artillery fire. The docks at Keppel Harbour were crowded with fleeing civilians and demoralized soldiers from shattered units, including inevitably many hundreds of deserters, all fighting to get aboard the remaining ships sitting alongside the quay, barely controlled by irate military policemen. Looting and lawlessness had broken out across the city as the police force had virtually ceased to function and everyone knew the Commonwealth forces would not be able hold out for many more days against the tightening Japanese pressure.

For all Churchill's belligerent prose, most of the defenders of Singapore were determined to live, especially the civilians trying to board the last handful of evacuation ships. Heartrending scenes were played out on the burning docks, as men placed their wives and children on the ships and then returned to the fighting. Many of the children would not see their fathers again for over three years; in some cases it would be the last time. Catherine Munnoch's father, an Argyll and Sutherland Highlander, had been fighting on Singapore's defence perimeter. He had been wounded and sent to the Alexandra Hospital, the main British Army medical facility in Singapore, but discharged himself to make sure that his wife and family got safely aboard an evacuation ship before the end came. 'We left the house unlocked, packed a small wooden box with items of clothing (my mother panicked and packed garden party frocks, hats, evening dresses – none of which were ever used again!)' recalled Munnoch.[1]

The journey to the docks was hellish. Japanese aircraft constantly milled about overhead, bombing and strafing any large group of people that the pilots spotted moving around in the open. In scenes reminiscent of the Stuka attacks made on columns of fleeing refugees in France in 1940, Japanese aircraft were successfully used to terrorize non-combatants and block the roads, sowing confusion and delay in the enemy rear. As the planes dived down to attack, the hundreds of retreating troops and civilians were forced to take cover in open sewers, nicknamed 'Singapore ditches', that ran beside the roads. Each time the danger passed everyone would emerge, soaked and stinking, to resume their harrowing journey towards the port. Even with the signposts taken down the way to the port was clearly marked by the tall columns of black smoke that reached hundreds of feet into the air and by the detonation of bombs in the distance. Olga Henderson, the ten-year-old daughter of a British builder working in Singapore, recalled that the ditches were awash with human blood when she and her mother had jumped in to take cover.

Catherine Munnoch arrived at the docks early in the morning, but heavy Japanese bombing meant that their ship was unable to leave until about 2 pm. 'The Japs bombed the ship in front and behind. Every time they flew over dropping bombs we would all go below,' recalled Munnoch. 'My father, however, stayed put on the dockside waiting for us to leave. He was very weak but remained standing all the time we were on the deck.'[2] The ships slowly pulled away from the quayside and the families were parted, wives not knowing if they would see their husbands again, and husbands fearful that their wives and children might not even make it out of the harbour alive as the relentless aerial assault continued. 'At last we sailed and I waved and waved to him,' recalled Munnoch of her father, 'until he became a dot on the horizon. I never saw him again for three and a half years.'[3] Munnoch and her family eventually arrived safely in Fremantle, Australia, after a perilous journey during which their ship risked being captured or sunk by Japanese aircraft, or by the warships that moved quickly to try to block the escape routes south and south-east towards the Netherlands East Indies and Australia. Munnoch was among the lucky ones, for huge numbers of evacuation transports were sunk, and many hundreds of women and children were drowned, or were washed ashore on tropical islands and imprisoned by the Japanese in appalling circumstances.

There were few places available on the evacuation ships for couples in mixed-race marriages, or for their children. The wives were local women, either Chinese or Malay, and most did not want to leave their extended families in Malaya and Singapore. The husbands were very often police officers, prison guards, or in other lower status positions filled by working class men from Britain, who had come out East before the war in search of better lives. Many were veterans of the First World War, lured to the Far East by new uniformed careers as the functionaries of Empire, where they would receive a better salary and living conditions than in Britain – nor would they be at the bottom of the social ladder, for their skin colour meant that they became supervisors of native labour rather than labour themselves. The products of unions between Western men and Asian women were known as Eurasians, and some families went back several generations and were well-established in the Far East. The story of Eurasian people in the War has been overlooked in many accounts of the conflict, but many of their experiences were as painful as those of white colonists. They were individuals who were stuck quite literally between East and West, with loyalties in both hemi-spheres and lives shared between or on the margins of disparate cultures. One such was British Eurasian Eileen Harris, who was eleven years old when General Percival surrendered Singapore on 15 February 1942. Her father Tom was British, a prison warder at Outram Road Jail, a place later notorious as a Japanese torture centre and prison camp run by the *Kempeitai* military police during the occupation. Her mother Clara was Malay. Her father faced internment as an enemy alien, but he tried to prevent his wife and mixed-race children from suffering the same terrible fate. 'Shortly before the Japanese arrived in our house, my father told my mother to leave the house and take the children and pretend to be local people.' Harris's mother, who was pregnant and expect-ing her eighth child at the time, did as her husband suggested, 'and in the beginning we were mostly ignored for we had inherited our mother's dark eyes and black hair and easily passed as Singaporeans.'[4] But their liberty was to be cruelly cut short when poverty and desperation forced them to return to their former house searching for possessions and food. The price was denunciation by other locals and swift arrest by the *Kempeitai* and a long imprisonment alongside the white settlers.

In many ways, those women and children who were swept up by the advancing Japanese and interned were better off than those who had tried to escape the net that had fallen over Singapore in early February 1942. The evacuation of British women and children was begun too late by the generals; consequently families like the Munnochs had to run the gauntlet of fire and death in order to reach the last few ships in Keppel Harbour. The figures make sobering reading. In the last few days before General Percival capitulated, forty-four evacuation ships of many sizes and types cast off from the colony heading south to the Netherlands East Indies, and then southeast to Australia. All of these vessels were overloaded with civilians, including thousands of women and children, government employees, the elderly, and the administrators of empire, as well as large numbers of military deserters, many of them armed. The ships formed a loose, and very long convoy. Out of the forty-four vessels, only *four* made it to safety. The Japanese sank or captured all of the rest, and in the process a horrible bloodbath occurred in the seas south of Singapore that took the lives of hundreds of innocent children. The experiences of the Boswell family are one example of the utter turmoil and distress when modern warfare is made upon civilians.

Drina Boswell was sixteen when the Japanese bombed Pearl Harbor. Her father managed a rubber processing plant in the Malay capital, Kuala Lumpur. By January 1942, Japanese forces were fast approaching the city, and Boswell's father was ordered to set fire to the processing plant in order to prevent its use by the Japanese; after completing this task he evacuated his wife and children south to Singapore. By 10 February the Boswell family was to be found sheltering from the incessant bombardment of Singapore City in a rat-infested cellar close to the harbour, as they desperately waited for places on one of the evacuation ships. In the event, places were found for them, but Boswell's father was separated from his family and put aboard the *Mata Hari*, while Drina Boswell, her mother, three sisters, younger brother and three half-brothers, went aboard HMS *Giang Bee*.[5]

The *Giang Bee* was a Chinese-owned 1,646-ton coastal steamer that had been built in Rotterdam in 1908, and had been requisitioned by the British in 1941 for use as a patrol vessel. The Malay crew had been put ashore and replaced by a small contingent of personnel from the Royal Naval Volunteer Reserve, later assisted by some male civilian evacuees. Under the command of Captain Lancaster, the *Giang Bee* sailed at 10.00 pm on 12 February, loaded down with civilians. Lancaster had initially refused to take women and children aboard the vessel, believing that they would be exposed to unnecessary dangers because the ship was a military vessel. But such was the shortage of available craft that he was forced to accept 300 refugees. As well as a large contingent of women and children, including Eurasians, the passengers included YWCA personnel from Malaya and Singapore, jockeys and trainers from the Singapore Turf Club and other racing venues, employees of the Ministry of Information and Malayan Broadcasting Corporation, journalists, solicitors, rubber planters and miners.

As the ship headed out into the open sea under the cover of darkness, Captain Lancaster knew that the odds were not stacked in his favour. Japanese warships were cutting across the British line of retreat through the Banka Strait to the Netherlands East Indies and Australia, and they were sinking any vessel that they encountered. From the air, Japanese war planes dive-bombed or strafed British vessels with impunity, the surviving planes of the RAF having long been evacuated to safer airfields on Sumatra (where they would nevertheless all be destroyed during the next Japanese amphibious invasion). When the sun rose like a burning ball the next morning, the *Giang Bee* was 170 miles south of Singapore, and steaming through the Banka Strait en route for Sumatra. It was not long before dots appeared in the sky in the far distance, slowly resolving themselves into Japanese aircraft. The enemy aircraft repeatedly attacked the vessel, causing some damage, but the *Giang Bee* was still seaworthy and piling on the coal in an attempt to outrun the Japanese blockade. Suddenly, lookouts reported an ominous sight on the horizon – two Japanese destroyers. For the women and children huddled below, already terrified out of their wits by the incessant air attacks, this was a grim new development. Most expected the worst.

The two destroyers advanced at high speed towards the *Giang Bee*, one signalling incomprehensible Morse code, until both vessels stopped half a mile away, their guns pointing ominously towards the helpless evacuation ship. Lancaster reacted by ordering the White Ensign lowered, and the women and children up to the deck so that the Japanese could see that the *Giang Bee* was not a threat, or a viable military target. A launch set out from one of the destroyers, but when the small boat had almost reached the *Giang Bee*, an RAF or Dutch bomber suddenly roared overhead and began circling the area. The Japanese destroyers both opened fire with their anti-aircraft guns, and the bomber flew off, chased by black puffs as flak shells studded the sky. The Japanese launch retreated back to its mother ship, and an ominous waiting period ensued.

As darkness fell the Japanese switched on powerful search-lights, trained on the *Giang Bee*. Suddenly, at 7.30 pm the Japanese ordered Lancaster and his passengers to abandon the *Giang Bee*. The vessel had four lifeboats, each with a maximum capacity of thirty-two people. Lancaster crammed fifty women and children into each. The men were left to fend for themselves, and many passengers remained behind on the vessel, some staying with wounded or sick relatives or friends. The evacuation of the ship was a disaster. The aerial attacks had left two of the lifeboats damaged. When one of them was being lowered, a rope parted company with the davits and the women and children aboard were pitched into the dark sea. 'I shall never forget that as long as I live,' recalled survivor J.V. Miller. 'The sound of little children calling out for their mothers will be forever in my ears, it was simply heartrending.'[6] A second lifeboat was full of holes from bomb fragments, and when it was launched full of passengers it simply sank, leaving the women and children thrashing around in the ocean, a strong tidal current sweeping them behind the stern of the *Giang Bee*. 'When I got into our lifeboat the screams for help were appalling,' recalled another survivor of the sinking of the *Giang Bee*, Gordon Preis. 'Mostly women's voices – obviously from the damaged lifeboats and now struggling in the sea.' Nothing could be done for the unfortunates already in the sea, and nearly all of them drowned. The Japanese ships stood by and did not attempt to help, even when Captain Lancaster sent messages to them asking for assistance. The destroyers pulled further off when a dinghy from the *Giang Bee* containing ship's officers was rowed towards them.

At 9.30 pm, while there were still over 100 people aboard the *Giang Bee*, the Japanese suddenly opened fire, slamming six armour-piercing shells into the steamer. A fire broke out aboard. 'Terrified figures could be seen jumping from the target's deck, soon ablaze from end to end,'[7] recalled a witness. The *Giang Bee* sank shortly afterwards, killing many more refugees. Drina Boswell, her mother, little brother and two of her sisters had made it into one of the two lifeboats that were seaworthy. It contained fifty-six people, and only one small barrel of drinking water that was strictly rationed. Drina and some of the others took to drinking seawater in a futile effort to quench their terrible thirst, but this only made them thirstier, and gave them mouth ulcers. The small children in the lifeboat cried incessantly, as they could not understand why they could not drink. Throughout the two days that Drina Boswell and her family were adrift in the lifeboat, Japanese aircraft constantly prowled the skies above and often dived down to pass over the heads of the terrified occupants of the open boat, who fully expected to be machine-gunned in the water.[8] Boswell's mother was also tortured by uncertainty over the fate of one of her daughters and three of her sons – they had sadly all perished in the sinking.

The Boswells' lifeboat, along with the other boat containing forty-two people, eventually made landfall on Banka Island. The exhausted survivors, which included a large number of children, struggled ashore and found sanctuary in a native village. In return for jewellery, the locals *sold* the shipwrecked survivors water, and a little rice and salted fish. They also told the refugees that Singapore had fallen to the Japanese, that Banka Island had also been occupied and that they must give themselves up. The next day the survivors of the *Giang Bee* presented themselves at the town of Muntok, where the Japanese imprisoned them in the local jail. It was for the survivors of the *Giang Bee*, and several other evacuation ships that had been sunk off the island, the beginning of a nightmare captivity in Muntok Camp, noted by Allied investigators after the war to be among the worst in the entire Japanese prison camp system. As we will see, later in the war the Japanese moved the survivors across the Banka Strait to Palembang in Sumatra, then back to Muntok and finally to Loembok Linggan Camp. The death rate for women and children was an astounding 33 per cent.

3

New Masters

Who were these noisy soldiers wearing strange uniforms,
netted steel helmets or cricket-type caps and rubber shoes with
cloven toe?

Robert Brooks, British child internee
Singapore, 1942–45

The arrival of the Japanese, either as battle-fatigued and often trigger-happy units fighting their way grimly to victory as in Singapore, or simply marching in without firing a shot, as in Shanghai, spelt only suffering and horror for those who fell under their heel. The children of empire would be no exception, and would pay as heavy a price as their parents for being enemy aliens in lost colonies. They would suffer through the battles and suffer even more through the occupation, tiny victims of a heartless and sadistic new regime that ruled not through the exercise of law, but torture and murder. A new Dark Age had dawned, and those children who survived it to emerge into the sunshine of liberation in September 1945 were forever marked and changed by their experiences. Their childhoods, such as they were, had been ruined by the Japanese.

In Singapore, young children like six-and-a-half-year-old Robert Brooks, looked apprehensively at the first Japanese soldiers they encountered. Brooks and his family had taken shelter behind the solid walls of Outram Road Jail during the intense fighting around the outskirts to the city. The day after the surrender of the colony, 16 February 1942, the first Japanese soldiers had arrived at the prison. 'Comments in the prison with regard to the British surrender of 15th February soon became known – except to us kids whose fantasies made our little minds worse than hell,' recalled Brooks. 'Who were these noisy soldiers wearing strange uniforms, netted steel helmets or cricket-type caps and rubber shoes with cloven toe?'[1]

On 16 February, the Japanese *Kempeitai* military police ordered the captured British Governor of Malaya, Sir Shenton Thomas, to make a radio address. Sir Shenton was 'to tell ... that all European civilians were to go to the Padang (City Green) and assemble for registration at the Raffles Hotel,' recalled Brooks. 'Anyone who had contacts with British subjects or their work had to be registered with the Europeans.' This was the first stage in a process of internment for Allied civilians in Singapore that was already underway in Hong Kong and elsewhere in Asia. 'Within a week civilians had been transported to the Seaview Hotel or Katong House in East Coast Road.' Olga Henderson and her family had not managed to escape Singapore by ship and they were soon interned along with the remaining Britons unlucky enough to have been stranded. The Seaview Hotel and Katong House were turned into rudimentary transit camps while the Japanese decided where to send their civilian prisoners.

The Japanese had not been prepared to take so many prisoners and dealing with the over 70,000 Allied troops who surrendered in Singapore was a massive logistical headache for the Japanese Army. Some of the instances of neglect and brutality in the early days were the result of the Japanese being overwhelmed by the sheer numbers of prisoners, and not knowing how to care for them properly. They were also disgusted by the concept of 'surrender' – it was not a part of their military ideology and this reinforced their often brutal attitude towards prisoners. The added pressures of several thousand white civilians only made the burden worse and the administration more inefficient, leading to more neglect by confused and uninterested Japanese authorities. It appeared evident to many of the prisoners that the Japanese had no plan in hand to deal with captives, and were simply making it up as they went along. Brooks said, 'The Katong House soon became too full and adjacent large houses were commandeered. On arrival, men were separated from women and children.' At this point most of the fathers disappeared from their children's lives until liberation in September 1945. For those whose fathers were military personnel many would be shipped out of Singapore and Hong Kong to work as slave labourers in the jungles of Burma and Thailand, or in the mines of Japan and Manchuria. At least one quarter would perish. Depending on which camps they were sent to, some civilian men remained for the duration inside the segregated sections of the internment centre, while others were permitted to see their wives and children during the day but slept separately at night. Others still were permitted to live with their families. All of them were constantly in danger of falling foul of the *Kempeitai* military police, which on occasion murdered several and severely maltreated many more civilian men whom the authorities suspected of espionage and other 'anti-Japanese' activities.

The Japanese moved first to deal with the huge numbers of captured Allied military personnel in Singapore. On the morning of 16 February, General Percival and his senior commanders, who had spent the night after the surrender camped inside their former command bunker at Fort Canning, were told that all military prisoners would be relocated to the modern British barracks complex at Changi, on the island's east coast. Changi Cantonment covered six square miles, and consisted of state-of-the-art three-storey white barrack blocks and smart married quarters bungalows, and had originally been designed for a brigade-sized garrison of 5,500 troops. The Japanese decided to cram in nearly ten times that number of men. The cantonment was sixteen miles from the centre of Singapore City, and to move over 50,000 men and all of their associated kit and rations the Japanese gave the British a grand total of just eighteen trucks and only one day to complete the operation. Thousands of men in a multitude of units began marching towards their new home, filling the roads and filling the air with cheerful First World War marching songs like 'Tipperary', 'Pack up your troubles', and 'There'll always be an England'. Civilians of many races watched the long lines of soldiers trooping past, the once seemingly invincible army of the British Empire disarmed, disorientated and passively taking itself off to prison. Some Indian and Malay spectators jeered and abused the British and Australian soldiers as they marched past, while for the most part the Chinese stood in silence, in dread for their own future under a Japanese occupation force – in previous conflicts the Japanese had murdered thousands of ethnic Chinese everywhere in Asia the moment victory was achieved. The Argyll and Sutherland Highlanders were piped part of the way to Changi, the skirl of the pipes adding to the terrible melancholy of the event.

At Changi, the British were left to organize the camp themselves, divided and run along the original infantry divisions that had fought and lost the Battle of Malaya. As the troops were being moved they witnessed the fate of the white civilian population in transit. Some 2,300 white men, women and children marched through the blistering heat, loaded down with whatever belongings they could carry, prams piled high with children and possessions, and led by the governor. Sir Shenton Thomas had been deliberately identified by the Japanese as a 'special case to be humiliated', and it must have been quite a sight for the Indians, Malays and Chinese lining the road to see the erstwhile governor of one of Britain's richest and most important colonies at the head of this motley collection of Western men and women who had once commanded such power and prestige. Many of the Asians wept as the procession trooped past, and some dashed out with bottles of water or a handful of biscuits, risking the irritation of the Japanese guards who escorted the column with rifles and fixed bayonets. In common with Hong Kong's Governor Sir Mark Young, Sir Shenton 'had felt that it was his duty to stay, and that by not running away he would help redeem British prestige. In this he was right. Sixty years later, in the heart of Singapore's thriving financial centre, there is a Shenton Way.'[2]

As his party approached Kallang Airport, Captain R. M. Horner of the Royal Army Service Corps recalled that 'we passed a long and rather tragic procession of civilians – all men and white – on their way to their internment.[3] A senior British officer, Brigadier Eric Goodman of the Royal Artillery, described what he saw:

They were all ages but many around 60 who had obviously been used to many years of comfortable living. Some were pulling suitcases along on homemade carts, some just had haversacks, one even had only a bottle of whisky as far as I could see, and some had the greatest difficulty in just getting themselves along. The Japanese guards with them appeared to be behaving quite correctly.[4]

Conditions inside the civilian transit camps at the Seaview Hotel and at the Katong House complex had degenerated rapidly. For white colonists who had enjoyed very comfortable pre-war existences, being evicted from their houses and force-marched into an internment camp was an enormous shock. Added to this was the Japanese policy of initially separating husbands and wives, though as already mentioned this practice was not universal among the hundreds of camps set up throughout Asia. For example, in Shanghai families were permitted to remain together as a unit, and they were sent to special family camps; only single men and women were segregated into gender-specific camps. The camps in Shanghai, though not particularly pleasant places to sit out the war, were nonetheless considered the best of a bad lot in the Occupied Territories and, compared with those in Singapore, Hong Kong and elsewhere, they were much more humanely run. 'Singapore, even in February, is still very hot and humid,' commented Robert Brooks, interned at the age of six and a half. 'Electric fans had been switched off and the norm of "two baths a day, at least" had become history. After a couple of days personal hygiene left a lot to be desired and the modern saying "as stinky as a wino's dog" could almost have been assimilated to many of these internees-to-be and their children, and clothes.'[5]

By early March 1942, the two transit camps in Singapore were overflowing with people and the facilities were overloaded. 'Sewerage was failing and the first bore-hole latrines were dug in the garden,' wrote Robert Brooks. 'Sweat and dust, dirt and irritation and hunger became the *modi operandi*.'[6] The Japanese moved quite quickly to sort out the situation, perhaps fearing a dysentery or cholera epidemic that could easily have spread to their troops. On Sunday, 8 March the 'quiet morning was ended at Katong Transit Camp after 10.00 am by Japanese soldiers ordering the women to line up with their baggage. The heavy baggage went by lorry, the women walked.' The destination for the women and children was Changi Internment Camp, formerly Changi Prison, a building constructed by the British in 1936 beside the new military cantonment. 'It was a walk of eleven miles to the infamous Changi

Jail,' recalled Brooks. 'Only the very elderly, frail and children were transported by lorries – all standing up in the back for the native inhabitants to see.'[7]

The march to Changi began under a hot, cloudless sky at 11.00 am. By that stage the macadam road surface was so hot that most people walked along the grass verges. 'Being British, the British spirit was maintained,' said Brooks. 'Walk properly, orderly manner, organised and cheerful. We children left about 1.00 pm and passed the marchers at Bedok Road. There was no loud shouting or waving from the lorry passengers or the marchers. Not surprising really. Would anyone dare do that with an irritable Japanese sentry with a bayonet-fixed rifle?'[8] Like the soldiers who had marched to Changi, the women used songs to try and keep up their spirits during the long trek. 'I was told later by my mother, who had been on the march, that among the songs sung by the women en route was: "There'll always be an England" and "England shall be free" etc. Many of these women did not live to see England again.'[9]

Olga Henderson recalled some of the horrors witnessed by even young children on the long, hot march to Changi. 'On the way, we marched over a bridge. There were ten severed heads on spikes on the side of the bridge, as an example of what might happen if we didn't behave.'[10] Brigadier Ivan Simson, General Percival's chief engineering officer, recalled similar horrific sights that he witnessed in Singapore City shortly after the surrender. He was approached by two young Japanese officers. They took him for a drive around the conquered city, Simson sitting on the back seat between them. For two hours the car trundled along roads littered with bodies, rubble, burnt-out vehicles and assorted detritus, not to mention Allied soldiers wandering about looting army stores and fighting with one another, and huddled civilians wandering the streets in confusion and fear. As the car approached the docks, where only days before frantic escape attempts had been played out, Simson spotted groups of armed Japanese soldiers who were herding local civilians along the smoke-blackened quayside at gunpoint. The brigadier 'saw about fifteen coolies, their arms cruelly trussed behind their backs with barbed wire. They had been caught in the act of looting. Eight were Chinese, who, as the horrified brigadier watched, were pushed forward.'[11]

A Japanese officer drew his *samurai* sword, and with a guttural bellow he sliced off the first coolie's head, a great gush of arterial blood pumping from the crumpled corpse as the detached head rolled across the litter-strewn pavement. The officer moved down the line, decapitating each coolie in succession as the Japanese guards watched in evident admiration. Simson turned away from the scene of what he later called 'medieval culture', sickened and horrified. The other captives, who were Indians and Malays, were released with a stern warning, for the Japanese had made it clear that they had come to 'liberate' the oppressed colonial peoples of Asia. The Chinese were killed because they were considered the blood enemies of the Japanese, and worthy only of enslavement, not liberation. The warning was as much for the benefit of Brigadier Simson and the British prisoners. The new masters had direct methods for dealing with those who disobeyed them, and the punishment was usually terminal.

The British children and the elderly aboard the trucks were the first to arrive at Changi Jail. They were greeted by a forbidding sight. 'The lorries turned into the vast concrete-built prison and its narrow drive at approximately 2.00 pm, through the high *porte cochère* with open steel gates,' recalled Robert Brooks. The women arrived much later, footsore and sunburned. 'We welcomed the 400 tired, hot and dirty women into the main courtyard about 4.00 pm, after their march from Katong, watched by Japanese sentries and the male internees who had already arrived and been incarcerated two or three days before.'[12] Once the prison gates were slammed shut, few of the internees would leave the complex again for three and a half years. For the children, their childhood, their path to adulthood, was the 'camp', and their education was to be heavily influenced by starvation, beatings, and disease.

33

4

Internment

*This sounds extraordinary, but seen from the angle of a child:
here we were in this shack and life was very primitive – but it
did not bother us one little bit. My brother and I were not a bit
put out that one day we had a lot, and the next we had nothing.
We were perfectly comfortable with it.*

Jacqueline Honnor, British child internee
Santo Tomas Camp, Manila

Nearly 40,000 Western children, of all ages from babes-in-arms to
sixteen-year-olds, were interned by the Japanese. The greatest
number were in the Netherlands East Indies, where a complete
failure to initiate an evacuation plan before it was too late resulted
in 29,000 children ending up in camps on Java, and a further 4,700
on the big island of Sumatra. Some 1,500 Western children were
interned in mainland China and a further 315 in Hong Kong, 330
in Singapore and 1,300 in the Philippines.

Olga Henderson, along with her mother, was imprisoned inside
E Block at Changi Prison in Singapore, the women and children's
section, while her father and two brothers went into the men's
section. E Block eventually housed 330 children and 1,000 women
prisoners. They were put to work, the Japanese believing that all
children from eleven upwards should carry out hard physical
labour. Henderson said, 'We were given pieces of land to cultivate
but we weren't allowed to keep the food we grew – that went to
the Japanese.' Food was to play a central role in all the prisoners'
lives from now on, for there was never enough, and finding more
became an all-consuming obsession.

Life soon became a struggle for survival as the Japanese endeavoured not only to arrest and imprison white civilians, but also Eurasian people who held British or other Allied nationalities. The Japanese considered Eurasians 'enemy aliens', and therefore a potential security threat that could best be neutralized by casting them into the internment camps alongside the Westerners. The Harris family, a white British father, Malay mother and Eurasian children, could no longer reside in their house as the *Kempeitai* military police had noted that the address was a British residence. To remain *in situ* would have invited immediate arrest. Eileen Harris's father Tom, a prison warder at Outram Road Jail, had already been interned, but his heavily pregnant wife Clara and their children had attempted to pass themselves off as locals in an attempt to avoid the same fate. 'Two or three times my mother crept back into our house,' recalled Harris, 'now thoroughly wrecked and pilfered and managed to find some of our clothing which she threw into the middle of a table and made a bundle. Food was very scarce and we were always foraging for food.'[1] Clara Harris gave birth to her eighth child in these appalling circumstances; the baby died shortly afterwards. That same day the family were identified as British, arrested by the Japanese and thrown into Changi Prison. Tom Harris was also interned in Changi Prison, but was kept separate from his wife and family in the men's section. 'The chain of events around that time had a very detrimental effect upon my mother who was never to recover to her normal self,'[2] wrote Eileen Harris. The following three and a half years of Japanese imprisonment destroyed the family and left emotional scars in the surviving children that remain open to this day.

At Changi, the British quickly organized a school for the young children. When the camp first opened in 1942, the women's section contained only fifty children. By March 1945 that figure had multiplied to around 330. At Changi, certain groups of prisoners were exempted from working, which left much more time to care for the youngest, and to attend to their educational needs. Harris described how 'the aged, the sick, the infirm, the children and the mothers with families were all exempted from the more exacting camp chores.' The Japanese agreed to the creation of a school in the camp dining room and an experienced teacher, Mrs Betty

Milne, was appointed headmistress. The children, in addition to their regular classes, received daily religious instruction from the ten regular female teachers, which included a Miss Rank, Mrs Nelson, Miss Robinson, and Miss Russel-Davis. A welfare committee was also formed by the internees to make sure that the children were properly cared for in the camp, and this was chaired by a noted paediatrician, Dr Cicely Williams, who had undertaken pioneering work in Africa before the war. It remains a testament to the selflessness of so many of the volunteer teachers, the mothers and the prisoner doctors and nurses that none of the children died during their long captivity. The presence of the children united the adults, and gave them a reason to live. It was noted in all of the camps where education was permitted by the commandant, that schools created a sense of normality and continuity, and gave structure to the lives of the internees. It also allowed the adults to have some precious time, space and privacy when the children were in their classes.

In Hong Kong, the Japanese moved swiftly to concentrate not only the 10,000 military prisoners they had captured when the colony surrendered on Christmas Day 1941, but also the remaining Allied civilians who were living in the territory. The battle had torn the heart out of the colony. Between 8 and 25 December 1941, British, Canadian, Indian and Chinese forces had battled furiously with overwhelming numbers of Japanese troops. Churchill had exhorted the British commander, Major General Christopher Maltby, to fight on for as long as possible with the 10,000 men at his disposal, in order to buy time for the British position in Malaya and Singapore. Outnumbered nearly five to one, Maltby's two gallant brigades had fought hard for almost every inch of the New Territories, Kowloon and finally Hong Kong Island, with absolutely no hope of relief or reinforcement. There had been no mass evacuation of civilians from Victoria Harbour as the end approached. Those civilians still in Hong Kong had done their bit for the defence, donning uniforms in the Hong Kong Volunteer Defence Corps or the Red Cross, and stood by their posts until captured or killed. The rest had retreated with the troops into the Stanley Peninsula, and there awaited their fate once Maltby surrendered the colony at a small ceremony inside the famous Peninsula Hotel in Kowloon on Christmas Day.

On 4 January 1942, a notice had appeared in the English language press that ordered all 'enemy nationals' to assemble at the Murray Parade Grounds on a set date. Although about 1,000 mainly British civilians complied with the Japanese edict, many missed the notice in the confusion following the end of hostilities, and they were slowly gathered up over the coming days and weeks. Those civilians who reported to the parade grounds were marched down to the waterfront and imprisoned for seventeen days in a disgusting collection of flea pit hotel-brothels that had been the pre-war playground of rowdy sailors and soldiers from the local garrison. The accommodation was dirty, over-crowded and the food was poor. During the interim period the new Japanese military administration in Hong Kong had liaised with some of the high ranking British civil servants and diplomats that they had taken prisoner, and through these consultations they had decided upon a permanent camp for the civilian internees. Dr P. S. Selwyn-Clarke, Director of Medical Services, and Frank Gimson, the Colonial Secretary, recommended to the Japanese that the internees, including themselves, should be moved to the Stanley Peninsula into St Stephen's College and the grounds of Stanley Prison. Gimson took the lead in asking for this because the Governor of Hong Kong, Sir Mark Young, had been placed in isolation at the Peninsula Hotel preparatory to being flown north to Shanghai and imprisonment there.

The site of the new camp was at the time slightly over six miles from the centre of Victoria on Hong Kong Island. The Japanese agreed at once and moved the internees by boat to Stanley, but failed to make any provision for their reception there. What the internees discovered on their arrival at Stanley was a camp almost bereft of facilities. There was nowhere to cook, all the furniture had been looted by local Chinese, and there was little crockery or cutlery left. The toilets were dirty, inadequate and lacking water. The camp would become very overcrowded, and initially at least little attention was paid to hygiene or public health.

In Hong Kong, almost 2,800 internees would eventually be living in the Stanley Internment Camp, 2,500 of whom were British. Among them were 286 children below the age of sixteen (ninety-nine under the age of four). The camp was under the control of the Japanese Foreign Affairs Department, and the commandant and his guards were not drawn from the dreaded Imperial Army, but from the Consular Police. However, they dressed like soldiers and carried rifles. They were perhaps slightly more humane than the Imperial Army, but many prisoners later remarked that there was not that much separating the two, or their attitude towards prisoners. The actual organization of the camp was the responsibility of the prisoners themselves, and very soon the British formed committees for housing, food and medical care. This was a pattern followed by the Japanese nearly every-where. They were sensible enough to realise that Anglo-Saxons, and especially the British, enjoyed creating organizations and committees, and fell naturally into this form of democratic govern-ment with its elected leadership positions and strong sense of fair-play and cooperation. The British were for their part canny enough to realize in Hong Kong and elsewhere that the key to surviving the horrors of Japanese internment was in organizing themselves, and in creating order out of what could so easily have degenerated into chaos and anarchy, and a Darwinian 'survival of the fittest' situation. It is a tribute to the selflessness exhibited by the vast majority of Allied civilians who were interned that, among the vulnerable groups such as children, very few deaths were recorded in the camps.

Food was the single most important issue to all prisoners-of-war and civilian internees throughout the Japanese Empire. The Consular Police in Hong Kong provided little food to the Stanley Camp, and it was typically of very poor quality. The rice and other foodstuffs the Japanese issued to the internees often contained such repellent and health-threatening additives as dust, mud, rat and cockroach excreta, cigarettes butts and dead rats. The daily bill of fare could scarcely sustain body and soul for very many months and seemed designed to slowly kill the prisoners off. At 8.00 am, rice congee (a kind of porridge) was served, followed at 11.00 am by rice with stew (which contained very little meat). The evening meal at 5.00 pm was also rice with stew. The internees only survived because the Japanese permitted them some limited contact with friends and family outside the wire who were able to send in food. The Japanese probably tolerated this arrangement as it saved them money and time in procuring supplies. Some Red Cross parcels were also distributed, and the internees took to creating vegetable plots to supplement their meagre rations. They could also buy overpriced food from the camp canteen or obtain things through the thriving black market that existed in occupied Hong Kong. Money equalled survival, and although committees existed that made sure that people could at least be kept alive, the wealthier the interned family, the less they ultimately suffered in Stanley.

Health was the next most important concern after food for the Stanley internees. The Japanese routinely refused to provide medical facilities to prisoners, and they allowed tropical and malnutrition diseases to flourish everywhere throughout Asia. At Stanley, 121 people died before the end of the war, nearly all through illness. There were, however, no major disease epidemics at the camp because there were so many medical staff imprisoned alongside everyone else, including 40 doctors, 2 dentists, 6 pharmacists and 100 trained nurses. A simple hospital was created and drugs were begged from the Japanese or bought on the black market. Malaria was the most common disease at Stanley, closely followed by the usual Japanese prison camp illnesses of malnutrition, beriberi and pellagra.

Many of those who survived Stanley Camp spoke of how important children were to the survival and general wellbeing of the internees. Women and children contributed a sense of normality, a continuation of conventional social, family, and gender relations. Many of the adult internees believed that the presence of so many children made them less selfish, as they were forced to consider the needs and welfare of the little ones first. Children as a motivating force for survival were extremely significant, and as well as giving essential physical support to their parents and to the general camp population through their labour, they 'acted as a barometer by which adults measured their success or failure to retain control and sustain Western values and colonial culture.'[3] Internment completely changed a child's understanding of the world. For many children, internment was not the wholly negative experience that their parents endured, but rather a time of liberation. Internment 'offered the children broader horizons, new experiences, challenges, knowledge and understanding. The multifunctional room with limited amenities, the sudden poverty, sickness, hard labour, responsibility, unchaperoned outdoor life and close proximity to other Western adults and children – all enabled them to mature in ways not offered by the traditional colonial childhood.'[4] One young girl imprisoned in Stanley recalled: 'We children experienced a wonderful sense of freedom with loads of time to idle away, this sounds somewhat paradoxical as we were all prisoners.'[5] The types of experiences depended very much on where a child was interned, and the atmosphere and regime inside a particular camp.

Education at Stanley did not just mean learning the 'three R's', it was also an opportunity for the adults to try to instill some sense of 'Britishness' into the children, and to try to reinforce some of the colonial values that had been undermined by the war and internment. It was also an opportunity to try and educate children about their own culture. Classes were held to tell the children about life in Britain, as most of them had never lived there – many had been born and spent their entire lives in the colonies. The children were taught about trains, travel, the post office, and British villages and towns. But the adults nonetheless discovered that the children were keen on avoiding school and exploring instead their new-found freedoms. 'It was easy to skip school if you wanted and crawl under the wire and wander around,' recalled one young internee.[6]

It was soon recognized by the teachers assigned to the education classes at Stanley that the children had been profoundly changed by what they had experienced during the Battle for Hong Kong. Kathleen Anderson, headmistress of the junior school inside Stanley Camp, recalled: 'At the time of coming into camp, after a fortnight of siege warfare and four weeks of nerve wracking confinement, the children were suffering from shock and anxiety ...'[7] What the children had seen and heard during the battle had been both frightening and confusing. The subsequent weeks that families had spent cooped up in arduous circumstances in the former waterfront brothels had not improved their outlook. 'The children cannot fail to have been adversely affected by the atmosphere of anxiety, irritation and depression,' noted Anderson. During internment, the school faced serious challenges, not only from the students' frame of mind, but also from the weather. 'The children's school work suffered from their discomfort due to lack of clothing in the cold weather. In the rainy season their school attendance suffered because many were without umbrellas and raincoats.'[8]

Many of the former child internees remember with great respect and affection the largely volunteer teachers who tried their very best to educate them. 'Most of the volunteer teachers had to instruct entirely from memory,' recalled one former pupil. 'Geography was taught by an ex-mountaineer, there weren't many places in the world he hadn't been. His lessons were embellished with stories of adventure that kept us enthralled. The same was true of Mr Willis who taught us maths. He was a surveyor and to impress us with the importance of trigonometry, he recounted stories of his surveying days in the wilds of Canada.'[9] Some of the religious personnel imprisoned alongside the adults and children were also impressive teachers. 'Father Thornton had a passion for English literature and seemed to be able to recite from memory ... How grateful I am to him for the rich memory of those words that have kept me company through seemingly endless nights.'[10] Such teachers generated results, and at Stanley two sets of matriculation examinations were held for submission to the London Matriculation Board. One child internee, Ruth Baker, later went on to an impressive academic career as a bio-chemist at Oxford University.

The provision of education was not only a boon to the children themselves, but also to their parents. As mentioned above, having a school in the camp allowed adults some time, space and privacy in their extremely overcrowded living spaces, usually overrun with noisy young children. The sense of normality and continuity even in captivity was a very significant aid to the mental well-being of the adult internees. 'The school day, week and term gave structure to the lives of all the internees,' wrote Bernice Archer. 'The education of the children offered employment to interned teachers, academics and other professionals who were able to imbue the next generation with Western education and culture which was being eroded by the camp environment.'[11]

The interned women organized Christmas and birthday parties for the children. There were musicals, plays, recitals and variety shows, and despite the severe lack of books, school lessons tried to make up some of the gaps in children's knowledge due to having

41

their schooling so violently interrupted by the war and internment. For adults too, education could offer a way to stay sane, with language courses among the most popular, along with lectures on subjects as diverse as photography, yachting, journalism, and poultry-keeping. Of course, the internees were still prisoners, and apart from the diseases and rampant malnutrition that might kill them, the Japanese remained a significant threat. Seven internees from Stanley were executed by firing squad in October 1943 after being discovered in possession of a radio – but not before they had all been publicly tortured before the assembled camp as a warning. The Japanese did not permit radios under any circumstances, and they were constantly vigilant concerning escape attempts, potential resistance activities and sabotage. A handful of adult men managed to escape from the camp and make it into Free China, but some others were recaptured and sentenced to hefty periods in solitary confinement under appallingly brutal circumstances.

Internment inevitably broke down some of the rigid class and race divisions of the time, as people were forced to rub along with others of different nationalities and skin colours. Some parents tried to enforce their colonial attitudes upon their children. Anneka Kekwick, a child internee at Stanley, recalled: 'Of course, my father was very strict about who I mixed with. He didn't want me to mix with people with mixed blood – the Eurasians.'[12] But children are generally colour-blind, and in the playgrounds of the internment camps, parents could not prevent cross-national and cross-cultural friendships from happening. Children had to play outside, unchaperoned for the first times in their lives, because the family rooms were too crowded.

'Outside', though surrounded by barbed wire, represented freedom from adult or parental control, constraints and structured time. It was the social and recreational area for the children, the space where relationships and friendships were made, both with other children and with adults. It was where mud, old ammunition, and stones replaced traditional toys, and where the imagination could run free as new play materials were discovered and games created. It was outside the school and family room that the children had the greatest

42

opportunity to shape their own internment world; it was also where the internment would shape them.[13]

'I had more freedom from my parents than I had before the war, because the children all seemed to get together,' recalled child internee Dorothy, who was in Stanley Camp. 'It was very much like them and us. We were like a colony of our own ... The grown-ups were quite removed, they were sort of busy trying to survive.'[14] Children naturally formed gangs, which roamed ceaselessly around the environs of the camp, and sometimes sneaked out beyond the wire. 'There were all sorts of friends,' recalled one former child prisoner, 'we could choose our own friends rather than have your parents choose your friends for you ... We had a lot of fun ...We were not supposed to talk to the guards but we did.'[15] Free for the first time in their lives from the constraints of a colonial lifestyle, child internees made the most of their time in the camps. 'The kids used to wander everywhere. They couldn't keep us in. Boys and girls together. Most of us were bilingual. We used to go and talk to the guards ... crawl under the wire and come back. I remember taking bullets to bits and we would string the cordite together and use a magnifying glass to set off an explosion ... The kids ran wild.'[16] Rosemary Murray recalled of Stanley: 'There were always gangs and going out ... We built a network of roads in the mud in the hills. Someone discovered that they could use a slimy gutter as a shute, it was thick with slime and you shot down bullet-like.'[17] The children were often busy with mud. 'We would spend a week making mud bombs and come the day we declared war on each other, we would go up to the hills and throw these mud bombs at each other ...'

The close proximity of male and female children and teenagers led to some of the older children experimenting with sexual activity. Children spied on adult couples, and, as Hilary Hamson recalled at Stanley, boys and girls 'investigated all the nice parts of each others' bodies.' They also frequently defied their parents, and even the Japanese guards, by climbing out on the roofs of their barracks at night to talk into the early hours. 'It was these sorts of things that we would never, never have done in normal life,' said Hamson.[18]

American citizens suffered equally cruel imprisonment at the hands of the Japanese, when the Philippines finally capitulated after the epic battles of Bataan and Corregidor Island. Many of the Allied civilians captured at the fall of the Philippines in spring 1942 were herded into the campus of the University of Santo Tomas, located on the outskirts of the capital, Manila. It was a venerable institution, established by the Spanish in 1611. About 4,000 American, British and other Allied men, women and children, along with a few Germans and Italians, were imprisoned in the makeshift internment camp, initially under Japanese Consular Service officials rather than the military. The inmates represented all of pre-war white society in the Philippines, and most of the internees were middle-class professionals or foreign expert workers who had been wrenched from well-paid pre-war jobs and cast into the camp.

[The internees] included bank presidents, missionaries, teachers, company vice presidents and their wives, teenagers from private schools, veterans from the Spanish-American War, newspaper editors and reporters, doctors, military nurses, housewives, children, musicians, writers, prostitutes, engineers, chemists, plumbers, electricians, administrators, society belles and Rotarians, college professors, clergymen, nuns and priests, and even professional entertainers.[19]

The diversity of the internees' working backgrounds at Santo Tomas was equalled at Baguio Camp, another major internment centre established in the Philippines. In January 1945, it was noted that there were among the prisoners four engineers, eight doctors, ten nurses, thirteen teachers, forty-three miners and at least one geologist, chemist, pharmacist, dentist, translator, and journalist.[20]

Jacqueline Honnor was a British child internee in Santo Tomas. The reason why so many British ended up incarcerated there was because of the government evacuation scheme in Hong Kong that had seen hundreds of women and children needlessly shipped to Manila before the Japanese invasion. Two ships, the SS *Anhui* and the SS *Harrison* had left Hong Kong each with over 300 British women and children on board and headed straight for the Philippines. The unfortunate evacuees subsequently found

44

themselves trapped by the Japanese assault on the Philippines and were then swept into the internment camps alongside the mainly American colonial population, when Manila fell to the Japanese on 2 January 1942. As in Hong Kong, the thousands of new internees were held in temporary accommodation while their captors tried to organize proper camps for them. It was a period of great uncertainty for the adults, and this stressful atmosphere was picked up by the children. 'The convent was already crowded with women and children and while our mothers waited in hushed anxiety we children uproariously trampled over the flower beds and gardens,' recalled child internee Robin Prising. 'The delirious rampages of Hide and Seek were not part of an ordinary game, for by our hysterical screams and laughter we were expressing the suppressed, nerve-taut shock of our terrified, whispering parents.'[21]

Jacqueline Honnor remembered her first view of Santo Tomas Camp: 'It was a large stone building with little towers and gargoyles and various outbuildings, surrounded by a cement wall, so it was an ideal place for us to be.' The Japanese initially segregated the prison accommodation. 'Women with children under ten ... were put into the annexe, women with children over ten in the main building; boys from the age of twelve and men went into another building.'[22] Robin Prising gives his first impressions of Santo Tomas, when he was herded into the men's section of the camp. 'The gym, the largest dormitory in Santo Tomas, resembled an emergency hospital thrown together in the midst of a typhoid epidemic. About three hundred men slept here, the stench in the cavernous gym was heavy and sickly sweet – I gagged when I first was ushered there. Even when I was out of the building the odour still clung to my body.'[23]

Conditions were quite spartan in the beginning, as both the Japanese and the internees needed time to organize the camp. 'We slept on the floor for quite a while,' recalled Honnor. 'Our cook was able in due time to push some mattresses over the wall for us, we already had our pillows, and we all slept on floors and tables.' The Japanese refused the prisoners many of the basics that they had taken for granted before the war, a situation that greatly exacerbated their suffering. 'We had no mosquito nets or anything like that, and very, very poor washing facilities. So, rather an unpleasant time ...' Not only the Japanese, but also Mother Nature, appeared to be conspiring against the internees at Santo Tomas. 'Almost immediately we had an earthquake – all we needed!' remembered Honnor. 'I remember the room sort of dancing around as I tried to hang on to the top of the table.'[24]

The Japanese authorities at Santo Tomas soon realized that keeping families separated within the grounds of the large campus was ludicrous, and also a huge waste of effort, and they soon permitted the men to rejoin their wives and children. It was a rare humanitarian gesture on the part of the Japanese that was not followed in many of the other internment camps, particularly those located in the Netherlands East Indies. 'We were suddenly allowed to live as a family,' recalled Honnor. 'So we started off under a mango tree.' Because of the overcrowding a sort of shanty settlement rapidly grew up on the campus, the main university buildings being already full to capacity. 'My parents made the mangoes into jam and sold it,' remembered Honnor, 'and we slowly got money together and my father built us a shack – literally a shack. It had to be on stilts because of the flooding, and the roof was a special kind of palm leaf. We were not allowed walls, as the Japanese had to see into the place, so we had an overhanging roof. Father made four bunks and he built a table with a bench either side of it. Then we had a *punka* – a sort of fan, which you pulled with bits of string and it brought air in. This sounds extraordinary, but seen from the angle of a child: here we were in this shack and life was very primitive – but it did not bother us one little bit. My brother and I were not a bit put out that one day we had a lot, and the next we had nothing. We were perfectly comfortable with it.'[25]

In all of the Japanese internment camps, parents realized that they must either make an effort to continue with their children's' education or let their children suffer the consequences in later life. This was successfully tackled, as we have seen, in Stanley Camp in Hong Kong and at Changi Camp in Singapore. Providing education at Santo Tomas soon involved the many teachers and professors who had been interned, though the Japanese did not make things easy. Education represented an attempt at some semblance of normality and of taking a stand against a Japanese policy that would rob the children of not just their health, but also their future should they survive the ordeal of the camps. 'They started up a school in the camp, with American-style education,' recalled Honnor. 'We had no books, no writing materials, but we had a lot of people who had been teachers before the camp; we had blackboards from the university, and we had some books, a library of English books. We had school every day from about nine until twelve and we had different grades, according to our ages.'[26] The education provided at Santo Tomas witnessed 85 children at 'High School', of whom 40 completed either the first, second or third year, and 20 finished the fourth year and graduated. 'I look back with awe and respect for those amazing teachers, so challenged, so inspired and so brilliant, who, with so little, taught us so much,' said former child internee Karen Lewis.[27]

As the British had discovered in Hong Kong and Singapore, getting organized was the key to survival in the camps, and would help in the maintenance of a basic standard of existence. The British were as enthusiastic in the American-dominated Santo Tomas Camp as in the camps where they predominated elsewhere in Asia, creating committees and taking responsibility alongside the Americans. 'My mother, being English, was given the class of twelve- to thirteen-year-old boys, who were running very wild,' recalled Honnor. 'We had a tremendous mix of nationalities, some well behaved, some not ... They really did their best at school, but of course everything had to be learnt by rote.'[28] It was a tribute to the dedicated teachers and parents who kept education classes running under such conditions that so many interned children did not miss out on too much of their elementary education during the war.

At Santo Tomas and the other internment camps outside of the Netherlands East Indies, older children were assigned work duties by the Japanese. The adults looked to the children to perform many of the menial tasks that had formerly been assigned to their servants – for example, washing clothes, tending vegetables in the small allotments, collecting food from the kitchens, and gathering fuel for heating. At Santo Tomas, the commandant ordered all children who were aged twelve and above to be assigned toilet duties, which in the main meant handing out carefully rationed sheets of toilet paper and cleaning the toilets and bathrooms.

Robin Prising, who entered Santo Tomas with his sick and elderly father, worked hard. 'I did all my father's duties for him, swept beneath our beds, cleaned the passage and corridors when our turn comes up and washed our clothes. He was too ill and old to do such things himself ... Before the war we both had pos under our bed which Alfred [the servant] used to empty each morning. Now my turn had come.'[29]

In the Netherlands East Indies, today's Indonesia, tens of thousands of white colonists fell into Japanese hands with the surrender of British and Dutch forces on Java in March 1942. The East Indies Dutch were treated with utter contempt by the Japanese and were subject to a particularly harsh regime inside the civilian intern-ment camps that were established on the numerous islands of the Indonesian archipelago. These camps ranked at the very bottom of the pile in terms of food, disease and brutality, when compared with those for British and American civilians. As to why the Japanese were more brutal towards Dutch civilians than British or American internees – one may speculate that this stemmed from pre-war Japanese views of the different white nationalities. Britain had a long history of cooperation with Japan and was responsible, along with the United States and France, for helping to bring the Japanese out of a feudal state and into the industrialized world after the Meiji Restoration in 1868. Japan had assiduously followed Britain's lead ever since, from creating a carbon-copy of the Royal Navy, to its empire building activities in Asia. Britain was the world's biggest imperial power at the start of the war and the United States the greatest economic power. Holland, on the other hand, was already a defeated nation under the control of Germany, and its colonists had been notorious for their harsh treatment of Indonesian natives. They were roundly detested by those they ruled and the East Indies were already a hot-bed of nationalist sentiment and outright rebellion, before a single Japanese soldier stepped off a landing barge. Perhaps in an effort to appease the Indonesians and engender collaboration with their new regime, the Japanese deliberately treated Dutch civilians with disdain and cruelty. If so they succeeded, for considerable collaboration did indeed occur in the Netherlands East Indies. The Japanese fostered anti-imperialist and nationalist parties and even raised armed forces as part of their great propagandist lie: that Japan had conquered Asia to free its oppressed peoples from white colonial rule. They even had a name for this state-sponsored fantasy – the Greater East Asia Co-prosperity Sphere.

One of the most deplorable episodes concerning the Japanese invasion and occupation of the Netherlands East Indies was the raping of Dutch women. It has been revealed that Dutch women and young girls were sexually assaulted at Tarakan, Menado, Bandoeng, Padang and Flores Island in during 1942. Sexual assaults on British and American females by Japanese troops were rare, but in the East Indies they appear to have adopted a different attitude. For example, at the town of Blora, close to Semarang in Java, twenty European women and girls were imprisoned in two houses beside a main road by Japanese troops. Over a period of three weeks, as Japanese units passed by these houses, the women and their daughters were brutally and repeatedly raped. The older women protested in vain to passing Japanese officers, who more often than not simply laughed in their faces, until one day a senior Japanese officer happened by the houses and witnessed what the Emperor's soldiers were doing. He immediately ordered the assaults to cease and the women were released and sent to the relative safety of an internment camp. However, the assaults were condoned by Japanese military authorities, and no soldiers were ever punished for these crimes. After all, over 80,000 Chinese women had been raped after the fall of Nanking in 1937 and no one was ever punished for that, so when a handful of whites suffered the same fate the Japanese authorities barely registered the fact. The Blora rapes highlighted the deplorable state of discipline that existed in the Japanese Army regarding the treatment of non-combatants, and the often casual sadism and brutality of the average soldier. The Blora assaults and the other rapes that occurred in the Netherlands East Indies during the invasion could be dismissed as excesses committed by young soldiers who had recently been in combat, but later efforts were made by the Japanese to recruit young women and girls from the internment camps for use as sex slaves in army brothels, and this clearly cannot be explained or excused as the 'spoils of war'. Clearly, for Dutch children, a period of darkness and suffering awaited them all as their ordered colonial world was suddenly split asunder.

Borneo, a large island lying at the eastern end of the Netherlands East Indies archipelago, was captured by Japanese forces in January 1942. The island had been divided between Britain and Holland, the British controlling the north and northeast, which was itself divided into the colonies of North Borneo, Brunei, Sarawak and the offshore Straits Settlements island of Labuan. The rest of the island was known as Dutch Borneo and formed part of the Netherlands East Indies. Unusually, the Japanese established a joint Prisoner-of-War and Civilian Internment Camp in the town of Kuching in Sarawak, in March 1942. A British Indian Army barracks consisting of long wooden barrack blocks and associated buildings covering fifty acres were surrounded by five miles of barbed wire fence and named Batu Lintang Camp. It held a maximum population of around 3,000 British, Dutch and Australian soldiers, as well as Dutch Catholic priests and nuns, British civilians, including several dozen children, and British nuns. The civilians were separated from the POWs by internal fences, the entire complex falling under the command of Lieutenant Colonel Tatsuji Suga.

The short and rotund Suga was overall commandant of not only Batu Lintang Camp, but also all the other military and civilian camps on Borneo. The Japanese created camps at Jesselton, Sandakan and, briefly, on Labuan Island. The commander at Batu Lintang during Suga's frequent absences was the deputy commandant, Captain Nagata. The guards were mainly Koreans, interspersed with some Formosans from Taiwan. Suga was an interesting study, a man somewhat different from the formal stereotype of the Japanese officer. For example, his beliefs placed him alongside the people that he ruled. 'During our time in the internment camp, Colonel Suga had often come into church services in the women's section and sat near the back,' recalled Hudson Southwell, an Australian missionary internee. 'Once he told Winsome [Southwell's wife] directly, "I'm a Christian." This was a startling admission for a Japanese officer to make to a prisoner during wartime.'[30] Suga had been heavily influenced in his belief by his brother, who was a devout Roman Catholic.

Suga was already retired from a long career in the army when the war started, and volunteered to work in the prison camp system, where he felt that his language skills would be of good use. A devoted father and husband, Suga appears to have had some sympathy for the people he was in charge of guarding, particularly the small children at Batu Lintang. 'I suppose the thing that really sticks in my mind is Colonel Suga coming through the gates in his car and we would sneak into it and hide,' recalled Rosemary Beatty, who was a young Australian child internee in the camp. 'Then he would drive off and find we were there. He'd take us up to his residence and serve us coffee, fruit and show us magazines ... He'd even give us lollies to bring back to camp.'[31] However benevolent Suga may have been to the child internees, he nevertheless held command responsibility for a network of camps in which thousands of people died through disease, starvation and outright murder. Some historians suspect that although Suga appeared to be a fundamentally decent man, he could do little to restrain officers under his command, such as Captain Nagata, from abusing and killing prisoners, nor could he improve conditions inside the camps because he himself came under the control of the *Kempeitai* military police, who continually interfered in camp administration from their lofty and untouchable position as the real power on Borneo.

For the purposes of this account, only the civilian areas of the camp will be referred to, but it should be noted that the military POWs had either formed part of the original British Indian Army garrison for Sarawak, or they were British and Australian soldiers who had been shipped in from Malaya, Java or elsewhere in Borneo. The civilian internees were primarily British and Dutch people who had been living and working in Borneo when the war began, including, as mentioned, large numbers of Roman Catholic religious personnel who had been ministering to the native population.

The male and female civilian internees' compounds were each headed by a 'camp master' or 'camp mistress' who was chosen from among the prisoners by the Japanese. Each barrack block housed between thirty and one hundred people and had its own 'barrack master' or 'barrack mistress', who was appointed personally by Lieutenant Colonel Suga and who was ultimately responsible for the conduct and behaviour of the prisoners. As elsewhere in the Japanese slave empire, a prisoner who agreed to take on a position of responsibility constantly ran the risk of being punished for the actions of those he/she represented. The camp and barrack masters and mistresses were extremely brave people who thought it their duty to try and set an example to their fellow inmates and to act as a kind of buffer between the Japanese camp administrators and the general prisoner population.

The Japanese policy of removing young boys from their mothers at around the age of ten years was rigorously enforced at Batu Lintang. The lads were shifted into the men's civilian compound where many were reunited with their fathers. Some fathers had managed to keep their young sons with them in the men's compound since their arrival at the camp. Don Tuxford, a Briton who had married a local girl, was in the men's civilian compound with his eight-year-old son in 1942. His daughter Julia was interned in the women's compound with Tuxford's mother and sister. Because Tuxford's wife was not British, she had remained free outside of the wire, but her Eurasian children had been forcibly interned as enemy aliens.

Most of the children at Batu Lintang were to be found inside the female camp, which was positioned slightly away from the male compounds that held British, Australian, Dutch and Indian POWs, male civilian internees, and religious personnel. Nearly all of the women internees were either British or Dutch. There were a handful of Eurasian and Chinese women, and four Americans, including the famous writer Agnes Keith, who later wrote a book about her experiences in Batu Lintang that was made into a Hollywood film.

One male internee described the accommodation inside the women's camp as 'new and fair', and commented that in his opinion the women 'had a reasonable area for cultivation'. The wooden barrack block was very small, and each prisoner was allotted a personal space for sleeping and storing property that measured just six feet by four feet (1.8 m × 1.2 m). The first camp mistress was a British nun called Mother Bernadine, but after she became ill another Briton, Mrs Dorie Adams, took over. Adams was the wife of the camp master in the civilian men's compound. The number of women and children in the camp fluctuated because of disease. In March 1944 the women's camp comprised 279 people, divided into 160 nuns, 85 secular women and 34 children.

By September 1944 the camp population had dropped to 271 and at liberation in September 1945, to 237.

Of the 34 children in the camp, the oldest had been only seven when Batu Lintang first opened in early 1942. Women often went without food to make sure that the children survived, and it is thanks to their willingness to sacrifice themselves for the sake of the little ones, that not one single child died in Batu Lintang during the war. As well as fighting against starvation, the women prisoners struggled with disease, forced labour, harsh treatment, and deplorable living quarters every day of their imprisonment. The Japanese later forced all the women to work for them, primarily repairing uniforms, for which they were paid some 'camp dollars', printed paper currency that was introduced by the administration. The prisoners jokingly referred to camp dollars as 'banana money' because of the banana trees that appeared on the ten dollar note.

Batu Lintang, in common with the other camps in the Netherlands East Indies, became a place where inmates were ground down through a combination of disease, starvation and vicious maltreatment by the guards. Harsher than camps in Shanghai, Hong Kong and elsewhere, at Batu Lintang women and children internees were forced to slave alongside Allied military prisoners under an unremittingly hostile regime and, by the end of the war, an average of two prisoners died there every day. As time went on, the women and children internees were so hungry that 'I can quite truthfully say that our mouths water, and that we "slaver" as dogs do before meals,' recalled Hilda Bates, a British prisoner. In this camp 60 per cent of the guards would later have one or more crime against the prisoners ascribed to them, when Australian investigators began to unravel the truth after the war.

5

City of Terror

Adults were beaten up all the time and we got quite blasé about seeing this and it ceased to mean anything.

Moira Chisholm, British child internee
Shanghai, 1943

The time it took for the Japanese to intern Allied civilians differed from place to place. Sometimes they moved incredibly quickly to gather up and throw into camps enemy aliens, but in other places the Japanese seemed content to allow Allied civilians limited freedom of movement for many months after assuming power. In Hong Kong, internment had occurred within a couple of weeks of General Malby's surrender on 25 December 1941, an event the local Chinese had christened 'Black Christmas'. Elsewhere, the process was convoluted. In October 1942, Allied nationals living in Shanghai were required to purchase red armbands from the Japanese, who were quick to realize that they could make some money out of the new regulations. Allied civilians had to wear the armbands whenever they left their houses, as degrading a symbol as the yellow Star of David that Jews were forced to display on their clothing throughout German-occupied Europe.

Allied civilians in Shanghai had been living under an increasingly invasive Japanese occupation authority since the takeover of the International Settlement on 8 December 1941, but they had still been theoretically 'free' in many aspects of their lives. People could still go out and meet friends, dine in restaurants and attend the cinema. Children had continued to attend school. Also, at this stage, most of the Allied civilians were still living in their own homes, though many were under constant surveillance by the *Kempeitai*, Japan's dreaded military police. They could be subject to arrest, interrogation and detention at one of a number of torture centres that had been set up throughout the city.

The new red armbands were each printed with a letter denoting the wearer's nationality ('B' for British, 'A' for American, 'N' for Netherlands and so on) and an individual identification number below the letter. Local Germans, allies of the Japanese, took to wearing Nazi swastika armbands so that they would not be interfered with by Japanese sentries, who were extremely suspicious and wary of all Westerners in the city. At the same time that Allied civilians were being forced to buy armbands, the *Kempeitai* also issued new rules concerning the behaviour of Westerners. The Japanese had been content to permit Allied civilians to run occupied Shanghai for them until they were in a position to replace the multitude of Western managers, technical personnel and foreign experts who kept the city functioning. The Shanghai Municipal Police officer corps still primarily consisted of British and American men, the public utilities were still run by foreign engineers, and the banking houses and great businesses of Shanghai like Jardine Matheson, the Hong Kong and Shanghai Banking Corporation, and British-American Tobacco continued to function under their pre-war managers.

However, although the Japanese decided they would have to tolerate whites running the city's utilities for a time, they did decide to ban Westerners from the social life of Shanghai. They gave orders that Allied nationals were forbidden from entering theatres, cinemas, dance halls, nightclubs, the Canidrome in the French Concession or the Race Course (which now forms People's Square in modern Shanghai). In addition, all Allied nationals were ordered to surrender their radios, cameras and telescopes to the *Kempeitai*. Failure to do so would lead to individuals being tortured as suspected spies. Such measures heightened the atmosphere of fear and insecurity that gripped the foreign population of occupied Shanghai. Fathers feared a knock on the door in the middle of the night, wives feared being separated from their husbands, and children were confused by the sudden changes to routine and much-diminished social standing. 'The honeymoon period was over,' wrote *North-China Daily News* reporter Ralph Shaw, who was himself later interned. 'The Japanese were showing their teeth and, from their record of cruelty on China, we knew that many of us were going to suffer indescribable ill-treatment.'[1]

One British boy decided at this stage to leave Shanghai and to embark on a hare-brained adventure through Japanese-occupied China. 'When I ran away from home, I was a child of eleven, and had the silly notion to go to the next large city, which was Nanking, some 300 miles away,' recalled Norman Shaw. 'I just followed the railway tracks far out into the countryside, where there was nothing for miles and miles.'[2] After Shaw had walked for several hours through the night he was stopped by a Japanese railway worker who was manning some signalling equipment. 'He searched me, found my identity card with the red band on it – the sign of an enemy national. He then made me take off my woollen sweater, which he kept, and told me to go on my way.' Shaw trekked on until he came to a small village. 'It was a cluster of bungalows built on stilts, about twelve in all, which housed Japanese troops!' Undeterred, Shaw approached the dwellings in the darkness. 'As I got up to one ... I saw a man on the porch, so I dived under the bungalow but he saw me, shone a torch and fished me out. I was terrified as it was a Japanese officer with his huge samurai sword.'[3] Encounters between Allied children and the Japanese were often very different from the experiences of their internee parents with the occupiers, and very often rather surreal. 'He searched me, got my identity card out and saw I was British, so he practised his English on me, with a few questions. He took me inside and gave me something to eat and a cup of tea. Then he got some English children's books out and got me to teach him to read. He was quite kind to me and told me to go back home.'[4]

The following morning the kindly Japanese officer placed Shaw on a train back to Shanghai, not realizing that the English schoolboy was not yet done with his hair-brained scheme. 'I got off at the next stop and carried on my adventure on foot,' said Shaw. 'I kept walking and it was soon dark again and you had to watch your footing otherwise you would be in the paddy fields. As I kept going I heard voices in the distance where there was a convoy of

Chinese farmers all carrying sacks of rice and grain – men, women and children. I joined them on their journey to Shanghai city, they were smuggling goods to the black market.' This was incredibly dangerous work as the Japanese normally bayoneted smugglers to death on the spot if they were apprehended by army patrols. On his return to Shanghai, Shaw stayed with a friend's family. 'As a runaway from home and school, the school informed everybody to notify them or my parents of my whereabouts if seen or contacted. Later I found out that my father was in deep trouble with the Japanese for not producing his family for internment. He told them he could not find me so they thought he was stalling confinement.'[5] Shaw was eventually reunited with his parents and spent the rest of the war in internment camps in Shanghai.

Many British and American fathers and husbands did suddenly disappear from their families in Shanghai on the night of 5/6 November 1942, when the Japanese launched a huge raid on addresses across the city. The aim was to arrest all Allied men that they considered a threat to security, or who were seen as potential troublemakers. A total of 243 Britons, with 65 Americans, 20 Dutchmen and an assortment of Greeks, Canadians and other Allied nationals making in all 350 men, were taken into custody by the Japanese. Labelled by the Japanese as 'Prominent Citizens', they were bundled into army trucks and driven to a rudimentary internment camp set up at Haiphong Road in former US Marine Corps accommodation. Shortly after these arrests, the final internment of an estimated 7,600 Allied men, women and children living in Shanghai was put into effect by the Japanese. In achieving the internment of all of these people the Japanese forced the British Residents' Association to collaborate with them in drawing up lists and deciding who went into which camp. It was probably better for everyone that the British organized this themselves, and the Japanese in Shanghai and Hong Kong recognized the organizational abilities of the British and by and large let them get on with it.

Between January and July 1943, Allied civilians were rounded up and told that they could bring into the camps whatever they could carry. Their homes and the remainder of their possessions now belonged to the Emperor. Entire lives carefully constructed in the Far East were wiped out at a stroke. Schools were closed, education for white children was now officially at an end and the process of segregation enforced. The whites were force-marched through downtown Shanghai by Japanese soldiers toting long rifles and fixed bayonets, the new masters of the city trying hard to humble the Caucasians by parading them before huge crowds of mostly silent Chinese onlookers. Moira Chisholm was nine years old in 1943 and recalled the round-up: 'The Japanese came and collected us in trucks and took us to a football pitch to sort everyone out in alphabetical order.'[6] Single men were sent over the Huangpu River to Pudong (then called Pootung) and interned in a dilapidated old three-storey godown, or warehouse, belonging to British-American Tobacco (the site today occupied by the Pearl Oriental TV Tower, the symbol of 'New Shanghai'), while the rest went into six other camps in the city or at Lunghwa (immortalized in J.G. Ballard's book and Steven Spielberg's film *Empire of the Sun*) just south of the metropolis (today's Longhua district). Fortunately for the internees, only the Haiphong Road Camp was run by the Japanese Army, and the other seven camps came under the jurisdiction of the Japanese Consul-General and his Consular Police. Food was always short, there was severe congestion, minimal washing facilities and sporadic bouts of brutality, but on the whole disease claimed a greater number of lives than Japanese beatings or firing squads. 'Almost everyone who had diabetes died,' recalled Ronald Calder, who as a child was imprisoned in Lunghwa Camp, 'because of the poor quality of insulin.'[7] Dysentery was also rife among the internees. 'Every time you got an illness it spread and there was never a chance to get well again.'[8]

Child internee Moira Chisholm later recalled that in her camp there were numerous beatings handed out to adult internees by the Japanese guards. 'Adults were beaten up all the time and we got quite blasé about seeing this and it ceased to mean anything.'[9] Children were quickly desensitized by the cruelty and meanness of their everyday lives inside the camps. At least, unlike in the Netherlands East Indies, in the China camps families remained together for the duration of the war. Chisholm's father had been a prison officer in Shanghai before internment. 'We got a family room for my Mum and Dad and sister, who was four at the time', remembered Chisholm.[10] The Chisholm family was probably sent initially to Chapei Camp in Shanghai, in today's Zhabei district. The camp was the former Great China University Campus, and the accommodation consisted of two three-storey blocks and a chemical factory on a fifteen-acre site that had been badly damaged by fighting during the Japanese invasion of China in 1937 – the remaining buildings were in a state of disrepair. The camp housed 1,536 internees at its height.

Conditions in the Shanghai internment camps were generally good when compared to the hell-holes run for civilians in the Netherlands East Indies, such as the infamous Tijdeng Ghetto discussed in the following chapter. Everyone mucked-in, families lived together, and the prisoners took to organizing the camps themselves. 'The camp-dwellers were at least able to obtain basic levels of food and shelter and, with notable exceptions, were not subjected to the kind of barbaric cruelty routinely inflicted on Allied servicemen in Japanese prisoner-of-war camps.'[11]

The internment camps in Shanghai make an interesting study of how the Japanese dispersed the large Allied civilian population after initially concentrating them for sorting and recording. The Japanese method of creating internment camps was brutally simple and economic – requisition some buildings, throw a barbed wire cordon around the area and establish a small guard detachment. None of the camps in Shanghai were purpose built. Children went with their parents into one of several 'family camps' located in and around the city. Chapei Camp has already been mentioned, but others of comparable size were Ash Camp on Great Western Road, Columbia Country Club Camp, Lunghwa Camp and Yu Yuan Road Camp.

Ash Camp was a former British Army barracks complex that gained its name because of the ash that had been used during the construction of the foundations for the buildings and pathways. Before the withdrawal of the British North China Command in 1940, it had served as barracks for a famous Scottish regiment, the Argyll and Sutherland Highlanders. The eastern half of the former barracks complex was still in use as a military base in March 1943, when the internment camp opened. These blocks housed Chinese troops loyal to the Wang Ching-wei puppet regime that was created by the Japanese to try to give the impression that the

Chinese had some say in governing the city. The western half of the camp was used to house Allied nationals, a majority of whom were former employees of the Shanghai Municipal Council, along with their families. The wooden barrack blocks were partitioned into family rooms. Older teens and unmarried inmates lived in six- or seven-bed dormitories. Just over 500 internees were held in the camp, which suffered from frequent flooding when it rained heavily in Shanghai.

The former Columbia Country Club, once an American expatriate social centre with tennis courts and beautifully manicured lawns, was also turned into a family camp by the Japanese. From the autumn of 1942 until the end of the winter it was used to house enemy nationals from the so-called 'Outports', who were awaiting repatriation. The Outports were smaller foreign concessions that had been established in Chinese towns and cities, particularly along the Yangtze River. In May 1943, the Columbia Country Club became a standard internment camp. It consisted of just the two-storey clubhouse building that was set in five acres of grounds. Fewer than 400 internees were held at the camp during the war.

The Lunghwa Camp was opened in March 1943 and held almost 2,000 internees. Its commandant was the pre-war Japanese Consul-General in Shanghai, Mr Hayashi, though later in its history a far stricter commander was appointed. '[Hayashi] was considered quite civilised,' recalled teenaged internee Heather Burch. 'He had been to London before the war.'[12] The buildings were formerly the Kiansu Middle School. The complex had been badly damaged during fighting in 1937 and consisted of 7 large concrete buildings as well as wooden barracks and numerous outbuildings and ruins. There were 59 dormitories, and a total of 127 family rooms.

Rachel Bosebury remembered when the Japanese arrived at her family's apartment building to intern the British civilians living there. 'We went in April of 1943,' recalled Bosebury, who was nine at the time. 'A big, old truck came for us. We were allowed to take one box of stuff for all of us and we weren't allowed any knives. You had to have tin plates and cups.' The journey to Lunghwa Camp was not memorable to Bosebury. 'I don't really remember that much about the truck. When you're a kid, anything like that is a bit exciting. I was always wondering where we were going and what the Japanese were going to do to us.'[13] Ten-year-old James Maas also recalled the moment of internment: 'We were allowed to take our clothes and took as much as we could. I took some toys and books.'[14]

On arrival at Lunghwa Camp, the Boseburys were assigned a family room in D Block. Also interned alongside them were the Tullochs, a Scottish family working in Shanghai. Valerie Tulloch, who was eight years old at the time, recalled how her family was soon split up because her mother was ill and was sent away by the Japanese to a hospital in the city. 'We were allowed to visit her only three or four times. I think whenever the Japanese guards thought she might be going to die. We missed her terribly, not only on an emotional, but also a practical level. She was good at knitting and sewing. Life would have been much easier if she had been in there with us.'[15] The Tullochs were assigned a room in the block nearest the Japanese guardhouse, and next door to another Scottish family, the Calders. Valerie Tulloch would become close friends with the Calders' eight-year-old son Ronald. James Maas recalled the spartan accommodation at Lunghwa: 'We used a heavy trunk to sit on and had a folding table and three folding canvas chairs, which had our numbers on the back ... It was a change, true, but we were with the same people, our friends, all together. So a boy of my age adapts pretty quickly and I took it in my stride.'[16]

The other camps in Shanghai were soon filled up with internees as the city was systematically cleared by the Japanese of enemy aliens. Yu Yuen Road Camp in the centre of the city incorporated the former Western District Public School and the Shanghai Girls Public School. Most of the inmates, who numbered just under 1,000, were former Shanghai Municipal Council employees and their families. The remaining internment camps were either 'men-only' or for religious personnel such as priests and nuns.

Not all of Shanghai's foreigners were incarcerated in or near to the city. The Japanese shipped out over 1,400 internees on barges and river steamers up the Grand Canal to Yangchow (now Yangzhou), where the canal bisects the Yangtze River. In and around the small city of Yangchow the Japanese established three camps: Yangchow A, B, and C. Camp A held 377 British civilians in the former Southern Baptist Mission hospital, the internees living in the wards, corridors and even the bathrooms, as there was no running water in the camp. Yangchow B was the former Baptist Mission Julia Mackenzie Memorial School, and 382 internees were herded inside. Finally, Yangchow C was three miles northwest of Camps A and B, in the former American Episcopalian Boys' School. It consisted of a walled compound, numerous houses and a church, and accommodated 673 internees in harsh and spartan conditions. At all three Yangchow camps, the internees faced water shortages to add to their misery. Camps A and B were shut by the Japanese in September 1943 and the internees transported by train back to Shanghai, where they were sent to the camps established within the city. Yangchow C remained in operation as an internment camp until October 1945, the inmates having been overlooked following the Japanese surrender and the arrival of American and Nationalist Chinese forces in the region. In Shanghai in April 1945 the Japanese closed Yu Yuen Road and Columbia Country Club Camps and transferred their prisoners to a new centre called Yangtzepoo Camp, located inside the Sacred Heart Hospital in Shanghai. Over 1,300 internees were crammed into the hospital buildings.

The regime at Lunghwa Camp has been recalled by several former internees as dreadful, but not nearly as bad as Japanese prisoner-of-war camps. 'We did learn right away to behave, not to say a word if the Japanese were talking, you shut up,' recalled child internee Rachel Bosebury. The daily *tenko* roll-calls were taken very seriously by the Japanese, the camp being administered and guarded by the Consular Police and not by the Imperial Army. 'You had to learn to stand up at roll call every morning and not make a sound until they went through the buildings and told them you were all clear to go back in your rooms.'[17] The Consular Police were reputed to be more humane in their treatment of prisoners than the regular army, though they wore military uniforms, while the ordinary soldiers carried rifles and the officers were armed with *samurai* swords and automatic pistols. Many of the camp guards were press-ganged Koreans, and several did abuse the prisoners on occasion. 'If you moved or went in your room or had to go to the bathroom or anything, it didn't matter if you were a little baby or a grown-up, you didn't dare do that because you could get slapped around or beaten for moving,' recalled Bosebury of *tenko* time. 'You learned very much to be afraid of the Japanese guards and not to dare do a thing you weren't supposed to.' Bosebury remembered two Japanese guards in particular, whom the children had nicknamed 'Snake Eyes' and 'Never Smile Again', and who were deemed to be quite malicious. 'One would do the roll call and you'd think they were down and out of the building, another would come up the other stairway and try and catch anybody who moved before the all clear for our building was sounded,' said Bosebury. 'They caught a woman; she was the Belgian Consul's wife ... we heard her getting slapped because she was ill and turned to go back to bed before the all-clear sounded. The other guard came around and I remember everybody had to stand and watch and listen.'[18] James Maas also recalled *tenko* and the assault on the Belgian Consul's wife:

> We had inspection twice a day – roll-call. We all had to stand to attention outside the door and a very small Japanese with a very big sword would come clattering along and check off the list. If you weren't standing up, it was *very* serious. One lady, the wife of the Belgian consul, was feeling a bit rotten one day and sat down. Another guard spotted her and came up and gave her a *tremendous* slap. Her son had to be restrained ... All the while, that violence was under the surface.[19]

For young white children from respectable homes to suddenly be exposed to the worst kinds of brutality and violence was a steep learning curve for most of them. 'If you want to know what it was like, it was pretty awful,' said Bosebury, though she and other former internees have made the point that Japanese brutality at Lunghwa was constrained because the Swiss Consul continued to oversee the prisoners' welfare from his office in Shanghai. 'The Japanese didn't dare go too far because there was a Red Cross presence – other nations observing.'[20]

Fear of the guards was the one constant for the internees inside Lunghwa Camp. 'I don't recall anything but total fear of the Japanese guards,' said Bosebury. 'We kept away from them as much as possible, any guards. You didn't go anywhere near the guardhouse, you knew not to even walk anywhere close to the no-man's land [by the perimeter wire] ... I never got to know them,' admitted Bosebury. 'They didn't speak English anyway. They roamed camp and they could walk in on you or anything anytime they wanted to.' The guards were always on the look-out for contraband, and perhaps an opportunity to steal from the prisoners. 'They did periodic searches if they thought you might have a knife or something. They could come in in the middle of the night, wake us all up and go through our rooms.' Everyone, including young children, witnessed acts of Japanese brutality in the camp and they all knew what the Japanese were capable of if anyone stepped out of line. 'They were people to be feared,' said Bosebury, 'because they had the guns, and they were cruel. You had this constant fear that you might have been shot, picked up, tortured, anytime. That was a fear, and it's terrible.'[21]

Fortunately for the internees at Lunghwa, the Japanese authorities administered the camp in a similar fashion to Stanley Camp in Hong Kong, leaving the mostly British internee population to organize themselves, with minimal interference from the Japanese commandant or his men. Guards 'roamed camp', occasionally terrorizing the inmates, and they conducted the twice-daily *tenko* roll-call, but the day-to-day running of the camp was the responsibility of the prisoners.

The Swiss Consul-General made sure that Red Cross parcels were delivered to Lunghwa Camp regularly, which was an almost unheard-of luxury within the Japanese prison and internment camp system. As with Stanley Camp in Hong Kong, food was a major preoccupation for the internees, as the Japanese simply did not provide enough of it. However, because the British were left to create a camp organization, an efficient system of committees and work details meant that nobody actually starved to death. 'Lunghwa Camp was mostly British. We did have Americans and Dutch and a few other nationalities, but it was mostly a British camp, and they organized, and they had different people doing various duties,' recalled Bosebury. 'My mother had to take turns in the kitchen, and my dad had to work in the kitchen.' A small farm was established, 'so that the little children got milk. They had goats.'[22] 'We had a camp council which we voted in and a labour exchange to distribute jobs, which everyone had to have,' recalled Heather Burch. 'People were allowed to choose and we worked normal working hours.'[23]

The few American citizens in the camp made a big impression on the British children. 'It was a family camp, there were not too many young men,' recalled James Maas. 'We got the crew of an American ship, which had been seized at the beginning of the war. They were transferred to the camp to do some work. The Americans weren't too cooperative, but they produced a little bit of colour and excitement when they played softball and would get angry and noisy, which amazed us kids. To us, this was un-British behaviour!'[24]

Bosebury recalled the maggots present in the food issued by the Japanese, which some prisoners nevertheless ate, claiming that it was at least 'fresh meat'. Bosebury had a hard time accepting the poor quality of the rations. 'I couldn't eat it. It was really ghastly awful. They say when you're really starving you'll eat anything; it's not necessarily true because I just about starved. The gosh awful, rotten smell that permeated our building when they brought that stuff in two or three times a day,' recalled Bosebury. From the central kitchens 'huge cauldrons of stew and rice were toured in on carts by camp service and we all queued,' remembered Heather Burch.

Money still played an important part in the lives of the internees in Shanghai, and Burch's family was fortunate to have been wealthy before they were interned. 'We had left money with some Portuguese or Norwegian friends in Shanghai and once a month we were allowed a food parcel, but they had trouble finding this in the city for themselves let alone us.'[25] Eight-year-old Ronald Calder ate all the weevils and maggots that he could find in his food, understanding the value of the protein in a diet largely devoid of meat. 'My father made my mother take them out. I would shout "Can I have those, please?" Since then I have eaten whatever is put in front of me.'[26]

As at Stanley and many of the other camps, education for the children was seen as very important. The Japanese provided no dedicated teaching facilities, so it was left to a committee of prisoners to scrounge for books and writing paper and to find teachers from among the many professionals who had been interned. The head of the Lunghwa Camp School was the former headmistress of the British School in Shanghai. 'At first the Japanese allowed us to have a school in the buildings that we used for kitchens and stuff,' recalled Bosebury, 'and then they moved us to another building.' For paper, she remembered they used cigarette packets, which were opened up to provide a rudimentary writing surface. Some internees had brought books with them into the camp. 'People loaned whatever they had so that you could borrow books to read,' said Bosebury. Bosebury described one elderly gentleman by the distinctive name of Mr Riddler, who became one of the few sources of entertainment for the children. 'Mr. Riddler had some books, and because he didn't want to loan them to the kids in our camp, he would sit and as long as the light held in the evening, we'd sit out on the lawn and he'd read to us from some of the great books ... He would read in such a way that it was like storytelling time, but that was our only entertainment.'[27] Valerie Tulloch enrolled in the camp's Brownie Pack, begun by an industrious woman who had been a Brown Owl before the war started. 'She embroidered little badges for us to earn,' recalled Tulloch. 'We did things like gardening and hostessing and I really enjoyed it.'[28]

James Maas stressed how important educating the children became to the internees. 'There were a lot of ex-missionary teachers. My mother was also a teacher, and we kept up quite a good standard. They kept to the normal curriculum and everything was quite well taught – maths, English, French, history, geography, all the usual subjects, science and biology ... It was fairly relaxed, but I began to work quite hard for the exams when I was about twelve, I began to realize I worked for *myself*, not for my parents or the teacher. They did give exams. Whether they counted I don't know.'[29] Like Rachel Bosebury, Maas recalled the poor facilities and equipment that the students had to contend with because of Japanese indifference to educating interned children. 'There was a building set aside for the school, and we had desks; we didn't have much paper to write on. We had to open cigarette packets and bind them together for paper ...'[30]

Children soon adapt to new environments, and the youngsters imprisoned inside Lunghwa Camp did so very quickly indeed. 'We children just played our games together – we were always outside shooting or exchanging marbles,' remembered Maas. 'We had a strict code or rank of marbles and that took up a lot of our time. And then there was football and softball – the American influence. We were always kicking a ball around because there was a big playing-field right outside the block. The camp would have covered forty-three acres, so plenty of space to wander but not too close to the boundary. Certain parts would have been out of bounds ... We didn't mind being restricted to camp. We kept busy all the time and we just accepted it, up to my age anyway. I adjusted.'[31]

Adding any more children to the camp population was not seen as desirable by the internees, though with many married couples and single adults in the camp it was inevitable that women fell pregnant and children were born under Japanese rule. 'Malaria was a big problem and we all took quinine,' recalled Burch. 'It was also supposed to act as a contraceptive, so the married women used it for this as well. They wanted to avoid getting pregnant, because if you did then you had to go to a hospital in Shanghai and then to a different camp for mothers and babies.'[32] Married women were better off than in the Netherlands East Indies, having been permitted to remain with their husbands, and no one wanted their family unit to be broken up during such uncertain and stressful times.

Even though becoming pregnant was actively avoided, in the early months of internment many women had entered the camps shortly after having conceived. Although in most cases they had subsequently been separated from their husbands, their babies were carried the full term and born into the straitened circumstances created by Japanese rule. Unsurprisingly, the Japanese made absolutely no allowance for pregnant women or nursing mothers inside the camps, but the prisoners themselves banded together to create a hospital and maternity facilities with the limited equipment and drugs at their disposal. Fortunately for all, there was an abundance of doctors, surgeons, nurses and midwives among the camp populations, so at least medical professionals were available in most cases to assist with births, and to help the babies and mothers afterwards.

Nel Halberstadt was a young Dutch woman who was pregnant when she entered Camp Kares-e in Bandoeng. The camp was located in West Java in the Netherlands East Indies. Her husband was in the Army Air Force and he was taken as a military prisoner and sent away to slave for the Japanese. 'I was growing enormous,' said Halberstadt, describing what it was like as the months passed. 'The baby started to assert itself and one evening, when my pregnancy was in its seventh and a half month, I was scared to death by a Jap, who suddenly appeared in front of my nose, just when I went outside.' A calamity ensued. 'I slipped down the few steps and ended up lying in a puddle of amniotic fluid. At my shrieks people flew towards me to help. My father almost attacked the Jap, but managed to chase him from the yard. I think the man was shocked by all the chaos.' Fortunately Halberstadt's parents were with her in the camp and they would prove invaluable. 'Supported by papa and mama I walked to the small hospital, which had been set up by a midwife. There, the midwife, Sister Martha, welcomed me and a Salvation Army nurse dressed me in an old gown and took me to the delivery room. It already contained three women with legs up high in various stages of labour.'[33]

Halberstadt's labour was very short, but memorable. 'I strained a few times . . . and out slipped a small parcel. The baby was lying, completely wrapped in the membrane, in the bedpan. Sister Martha and the other nurse threw themselves on me and the bedpan, removed the child and took it out of its membrane. 'Aduh, born with the caul,' Sister Martha exclaimed. Apparently this is supposed to be a sign that the child will have second sight,' recalled Halberstadt. 'I was totally confused. I have born a child without very much pain and no shriek had passed my lips. "It has been born too early," Sister Martha said. "She will need to go into the incubator."'[34] Both mother and daughter were to face three more years of grim internment camps before eventual liberation, and providing sufficient nutrition for a growing baby was to prove nearly impossible in most of the internment camps. Many children suffered the effects into adulthood, including being small in stature, or still carrying the residue of infectious tropical diseases or deficiency disorders.

The famous British writer J.G. Ballard, who was imprisoned with his parents inside Lunghwa Camp for the duration of the war, provided an analysis of the internee population that he had carefully observed as a young boy, and that later influenced his writing of the internment camp novel *Empire of the Sun*: 'Some of the prisoners behaved with great steadfastness. Most were withdrawn and listless. A few were scrimshankers, petty thieves, or open collaborators with the Japanese. But you'd expect that. I was happy there. It was like having a huge slum family.'[35] Ballard particularly recalled how parents sacrificed themselves to protect their children: 'Our parents starved themselves for us.'[36] The point has often been repeated by other child survivors of the camps. 'My mother once told me that I said, "Oh, Mummy, I'm *so* hungry!" I don't remember saying that, but I remember being hungry,' recalled James Maas. 'But on the whole it wasn't too bad because parents were very sacrificing, and we did get Red Cross parcels, which were a godsend, and I got most of the contents of those, and there were a few treats in them. I have a photograph, which was taken in August or September '45, of Mother looking very cheerful, although very thin, and I look entirely normal.'[37]

Cleanliness was a major issue and concerned the internees in Shanghai greatly. 'The camp had previously been a Chinese dormitory and after being disused for so many years after the bombing [in 1937], there was nothing but lice and bedbugs, and filth that you had to learn to live with or fight,' recalled Bosebury. The internees did what they could to eradicate the filth, but the Japanese did not issue disinfectant, which made the job of cleaning the camp extremely difficult. 'I can remember my mother staying up most of the evenings with a match trying to go around the seams of our mattresses to make sure there weren't any bed bugs there at night.'[38] Fresh water was a problem in Shanghai and clean water sources were very important to prevent any outbreak of cholera. 'Everyday a drinking water truck arrived,' recalled Heather Burch. 'My father was one of the people responsible for dishing water out. We called it the Dewdrop Inn. We had to boil it to make it safe.'[39] Another water collection shack was christened 'Waterloo' by the prisoners, complete with a mocked-up London Underground sign.

The death rates for civilian internees in the Shanghai camps were low compared with the huge numbers of Allied prisoners-of-war who died in Japanese slave labour camps, and compared with civilian deaths elsewhere in Occupied Asia. Figures derived from incomplete records for the Shanghai camps list a total of 26 deaths in 1943, rising to 39 in 1944, and 49 in 1945.[40] Most victims were the middle aged or the elderly, though at least 10 children also died. All along the China coast and in the interior ports British and other Allied nationals were interned. They were business people and missionaries, language teachers and university professors, engineers and administrators, and many had lived in China for decades, some had even been born there. It was a terrible wrench for most of them to be plucked from jobs and professions that they loved and to be parted from their Chinese friends and colleagues. The psychology of internees was as important a factor for survival as their ability to combat disease and starvation. For many of the older people, the shock of being plunged into a camp in old age was simply too great to bear. Perhaps the most famous British person to die in an internment camp in China was Eric Liddell of *Chariots of Fire* fame. He had been Olympic 400 metres gold medalist at the 1924 summer games. Liddell had been born in China, where his father was a missionary and after retiring from athletics he had returned to the land of his birth to assist with his father's mission in Shandong Province. Liddell and fellow Allied nationals were interned at Weihsien Camp in the city of Weifang, and he died there from a brain tumour in February 1945, at the age of only forty-three.

6

Hell's Waiting Room

Much sickness was caused by poor sewerage and the women had to ladle the overflow of the cesspits into open drains which became a source of constant infection. Many women and children had open sores on their ankles and legs from infected cuts and the bacteria caused skin ulcers. I was one of them and had to have my sores washed out and bandaged regularly.

Hetty, Dutch child internee
Tjideng Ghetto, Batavia, Java

By 1943, after a year of internment in Japanese camps, Allied civilians started to notice that their living conditions were beginning to seriously deteriorate as events elsewhere began to conspire against their survival. The war was now going badly for the Japanese, following the defeat of the Imperial Navy by the Americans at the Battle of Midway in June 1942. After Midway, the Empire was forced onto the defensive, as the Americans began a two-pronged assault against Japan, and British and Commonwealth forces readied themselves to strike back from India. General Douglas MacArthur led the thrust by the US Army across the central Pacific towards the island of New Guinea, with the eventual liberation of the Philippines as his ultimate goal. In the northern Pacific, Admiral Chester W. Nimitz and the US Pacific Fleet 'island-hopped' towards the Japanese Home Islands, by-passing many of the more serious enemy garrisons that would be left, in Nimitz's immortal words, to 'wither on the vine'. Britain was slower to begin the fight-back, but Admiral Lord Louis

Mountbatten's South-East Asia Command had begun making plans to insert special army units known as Chindits behind the Japanese lines in occupied Burma, to disrupt the Japanese position, and Mountbatten and his generals were formulating concrete plans to invade the colony in the near future. The eventual goal of the British was to recapture Malaya and Singapore.

The effect upon the Japanese of suddenly finding themselves thrown onto the defensive was dramatic and unpleasant. With each defeat suffered by the Imperial Army or Navy, the Japanese directed their fury at the Western prisoners that they held. Although military prisoners-of-war were appallingly badly treated by the Japanese, civilian internees, including women and children, also suffered conditions of incredible hardship, brutality and bureaucratic indifference far in excess of those experienced by Allied military prisoners who fell into German hands during the Second World War. The civilian internment camps slid inexorably into squalor, disease and starvation, often overlaid by stupendous acts of barbarity by the vindictive Japanese. Starvation conditions were exacerbated by every Allied success, as Japanese supply ships were sunk in unprecedented numbers by Allied submarines and the Japanese diverted most of the available food, especially in the Empire's outlying regions, to their military garrisons. Allied military POWs were forced to act as slave labour, in mines in Japan and Manchuria, in factories, on the Burma-Thailand Railway, and a multitude of other projects that cost thousands of lives. Civilian internees were generally left to rot inside their camps, labelled 'useless mouths' by their Japanese masters. Combined with the institutional racism of the Japanese military towards Western and Eurasian peoples, the last phases of the war were the most dangerous for internees and their survival was by no means certain. Japanese resistance was fierce, suicidal and quite effective in slowing down the Allied assault on the Home Islands and in 1943 it looked as though the war would drag on for a very long time.

I have previously mentioned that civilians unfortunate enough to be interned in the Netherlands East Indies endured great hardships and privations in a string of camps set up by the Japanese throughout the archipelago. Tijdeng Ghetto in the city of Batavia was one of the worst. Established in present-day Jakarta, on the island of Java, the camp was for women and children only. In March 1942, when the Japanese took control of Batavia, all Allied men and boys over the age of twelve were removed from their families and placed in male-only camps. The Japanese reasoned that as so many men and teenage boys had been members of the reserve *Stadswacht* Home Guard, they could be deemed military POWs, and they were treated accordingly. The thousands of women and the 33,700 children who remained were put into several camps that were initially under the control of the Japanese Consular Police.

The Tijdeng Ghetto consisted of a closed-off section of one of the poorer suburbs of Batavia. There were dozens of small houses, all badly constructed and each standing on a small plot of land. The Japanese then shut the internees off from the rest of the city with a barbed wire fence and, later, a wall made of matted bamboo. The physical size of the Ghetto was progressively reduced by the Japanese, even as the population of the camp was dramatically increased. Dutch internee Michel was seven years old when he was herded into the Ghetto with his mother and three siblings. 'Our new house was not in a very nice part of the town,' he remembered. 'The houses were made of sugarcane matting and plastered with cement. The roofs were baked clay tiles and the floors were cement. They were all of the same design.'[1]

Initially, the Ghetto held only about 2,000 women and children, but by June 1945 this figure had increased to 10,300, as the Japanese gradually shipped in thousands more people into the compressed area. In 1942, under a more considerate Consular Police administration, the women internees were able to cook in the kitchens of the houses, visit shops within the Ghetto area, and attend church services. One internee, a 21-year-old Dutch woman called Riet, recalled that the regime was fairly relaxed. 'The first year was not too bad as we were under an Economic administration and the camp commandant was a kind man – even interceding and defending us against bad rulings.'[2] The contrast between this and what was to come later, under Imperial Army control, was stark. 'The commandant loved music and even encouraged musical entertainment choirs and even Church services. We were also allowed visitors at this time,' wrote Riet. 'The Commandant was also lenient with regard to attending roll-call twice daily –

one could miss roll-call if not well.'[3] This liberal regime came to an abrupt end when control of the Tijdeng Ghetto was transferred to the Imperial Japanese Army in April 1944, and a new commandant, Lieutenant Kenichi Sonei, was appointed.

Under Sonei's command, the Tijdeng Ghetto became one of the foulest camps in the Japanese Empire and the thousands of mainly Dutch women and children interned there were systematically starved far more severely than at many of the other ghettos and camps. The conditions at Tijdeng were comparable to those in the Jewish ghettos set up by the Germans in occupied Poland. The youngest children worked in the small allotments that the commandant permitted, growing vegetables to supplement the meagre rations distributed to them by the Japanese. 'Twice a day we got "bread" which was hard and transparent. Each person got 5cms. The mothers made soups out of tea with spices in it,' recalled a young Dutch child internee named Hetty. 'I had to knit socks for the Japanese soldiers for which we were rewarded with a piece of sugar. It was the only sweet I ever tasted in the 3½ years. This put me off knitting for the rest of my life.'[4] Hetty had entered the Tjideng Ghetto as a seven-year-old child with her mother and brother. Her father had been a member of the *Stadswacht*, and this meant that the Japanese considered him to be a military prisoner-of-war. Hetty's father was sent to Struiswijk Prison on the outskirts of Batavia while the rest of the family was initially held under house arrest. Hetty, like thousands of other children, was never to see her father again – he drowned off the coast of Sumatra when the rusting and unmarked transport ship he was on, the *Junyo Maru*, was sunk by an Allied submarine – just one of thousands of Allied soldiers who perished at sea as the Japanese shipped prisoners around their vast empire to act as slave labour. Hetty and her family were sent to Camp Kramat, an internment camp in Java, in November 1942, and in August 1943 the whole family was sent to the Tjideng Ghetto. They were forced to leave behind all their possessions except for some clothing and bedding. 'At the thought I became physically ill and had a temperature,' recalled Hetty.[5] They were transported in tricycle taxis to Tjideng.

Hetty's first house in the Ghetto was on two storeys, but packed with nearly forty people. 'We had our own little pad curtained off by some material (maybe sheets hung up from a cupboard to the wall). I remember the cupboard had a hole in the back panel and every time my mother or I changed I saw the eye of a peeping tom, a boy who later left the camp when he was 12,' wrote Hetty. Privacy was almost impossible for internees in any of the camps across Asia, and was to have a deep impact upon their morale and mental well-being.

In the Tijdeng Ghetto, *tenko* was a gruelling ordeal for the internees. 'This meant standing to attention any time of the day in the hot sun or at night for long periods of time while counts were made of those present,' recalled Hetty. 'The soldiers often made a mess of this and hence we had to endure lengthy periods of waiting till they got it right. The camp commander used these occasions to carry out house inspections and to search for illegal goods or anything they fancied for themselves.'[6] Hetty's mother only had a few valuables left, and she was determined that the Japanese would not get their thieving hands on them. 'I had a teddy bear in camp and my mother hid a few pieces of jewellery and some money in its tummy,' said Hetty. 'I had to carry that teddy bear with me whenever we had "tenkos" or house inspections. I do remember often being afraid.'[7] Another Dutch child, Hardy, recalled: 'Radio and photo-equipment was gathered by the Japanese in big trucks. Several times the people were driven out of the houses to a square or out of the camp. The Japanese were looking for hidden money, jewels, radios, flags, etc. Once we spent the night in a room with 20 other people, some suffering from diarrhoea. I can still remember the dark and the smell.'[8] The children were also forced to witness the most appalling acts of violence and brutality carried out by their guards on fellow internees.

Once the Imperial Army took over control of the Ghetto in April 1944, camp discipline became very severe. The level of brutality in Japanese prison camps depended largely upon the personality of the camp commandant. The new commandant, Lieutenant Kenichi Sonei, was ruthless and sadistic, perhaps even psychologically unbalanced. 'If women refused to bow to the Japanese they were hit to the ground and often had their hair shaved off,' recalled Hetty. 'The worst punishment was to be bound to a chair outside the camp entrance gate and have to sit for 48 hours in the sun and through the night without food and drink. At full moon Sonei would order the whole camp – including the sick – to attend roll call or tenko where he made everyone stand at attention for him. He would then make the women and children bow down to him time upon time again. If he was not satisfied he would cut the food rations.'[9] Many prisoners later considered that Sonei's worst excesses occurred when the moon was full, as if he underwent a psychological change. Sonei instilled great fear through the Ghetto population every day, but with a full moon the internees believed that this officer's sadistic mania was aggravated.

Sonei had formerly been an officer at the infamous Bicycle Camp for military prisoners-of-war, which was also located on Java. Bicycle Camp was a hell-hole, pure and simple, with no redeeming features whatsoever. In April 1942, one month after the Dutch and British surrender on Java, 2,600 British, Australian and American military prisoners were marched to the town of Bandoeng, and thence into a former Dutch barracks complex that had originally been built to house Indonesian colonial troops. The camp soon gained the nickname 'Bicycle Camp', as the original colonial occupants had been military cyclists. The POWs were joined shortly afterwards by bedraggled Australian and American survivors from the cruisers HMAS *Perth* and USS *Houston*, sunk during the Battle of the Sunda Strait, who numbered around 500 officers and ratings, all in an appalling state of neglect. The naval prisoners marched slowly and painfully into Bicycle Camp, covered by Japanese guards toting their long rifles and fixed bayonets, as the military POWs silently watched the tragic procession, pressed up against the perimeter wire. Most of the shipwrecked sailors had lost nearly all of their clothing and many could only walk with the assistance of their comrades.

Since being taken prisoner by the Japanese, the seamen had been denied medical attention with the result that over 80 per cent of the men who shuffled into the camp were ridden with either malaria or dysentery, some unfortunates had both. Immediately after being captured the sailors had been herded by Japanese sentries into the town of Serang, accompanied by some Australian troops who had surrendered on Java, some Australian and British soldiers who had managed to escape from Singapore before the end of resistance there, and many Dutch civilians with young children in tow. The Japanese had placed them all inside a cinema, their guards refusing any medical aid for those who were injured or ill. 'At night they had to lie on top of each other in the stink of festering wounds. The latrine was an open pit outside, with flies rising off it in huge clouds, making a blaring noise like a brass band.'[10] The Allied senior officers among the prisoners were taken away and then the rest of them were herded into the town jail, packed tightly into cells by the *Kempeitai* military police. The sailors were still denied medical care, systemically starved and given little water until, in April, they were transported as pitiable, diseased wrecks to Bicycle Camp. The civilians fared little better and were shipped off to the Tjideng Ghetto, or to a series of other physically challenging camps across Java.

When Lieutenant Sonei took over as commandant of Tjideng in April 1944, the Ghetto population stood at 5,286 women and children, roughly double what it had been when the camp first opened. By the time he relinquished command in June 1945, Sonei had managed to increase the Ghetto population to 10,300, whilst simultaneously considerably reducing the physical size of the prison. Sonei's regime marked the end of any freedoms that the internees may have enjoyed under the humane Consular Police commandant. Church services were immediately banned; shopping was stopped as no more trading was permitted with the Indonesian population who lived beyond the Ghetto wall, and even cooking was forbidden inside the houses where the internees lived. All meals were forthwith cooked in a central kitchen and then distributed to the internees daily. However, Sonei's rules did not stop people from trying to trade with those outside the walls. 'In Tjideng the houses of the camp were isolated from the rest of the world by means of a high fence of barbed wire and platted bamboo – "gedek" – to keep us from looking out and making contact with the outside world,' recalled Hetty, who was only seven at the time. 'This did not stop us children from sliding somehow under the gedek and getting out of the camp to do some trading. An old blouse or pair of shoes for bananas, papaya, and sometimes a few eggs, even a chicken now and then. The penalties for discovery were very severe!'[11] Another child prisoner, Hardy, recalled a similar black market for food. 'People exchanged bottles for little fish with the "inlanders" outside the camp. It was thrown over the gedek and the canal.'[12]

Procuring sufficient food to maintain body and soul was an obsession for all of the Ghetto internees. The Japanese did not provide enough to actually keep people alive, so everyone had to resort to bartering or even stealing in order to survive, and by doing so they were breaking camp rules and could be heavily punished. Child internee Michel recalled how even children's toys became currency: 'In camp I kept myself busy playing and collecting toys by swapping and bartering and soon I had lots of toys. My mother persuaded me to exchange them for food as every time a kid had a birthday his mother wanted a toy so she exchanged it for food. The only set back was that the food was eaten and my supply of toys was dwindling so the bartering was even harder for me.' Michel hit on a novel way to keep the supply of food coming. 'I made my own lead soldiers. I had a mould and pinched lead from the roofs which leaked terribly in the rainy season afterwards. Soldiers were toys and food so bad luck for the roof.'[13]

The Japanese officially banned education for the children under their control in the Netherlands East Indies – a very different situation from Hong Kong or Shanghai where education was treated as a 'right' for the children and properly organized by internee committees – but lessons could nonetheless be 'bought' in Tjideng. 'There were many teachers in the camp who gave lessons in return for bread,' remembered Hetty. 'This had to be done in secret and someone had to stand guard and whistle when a Japanese guard came near the place where we had "school". We learned the three "Rs" and used slate or tiles with little pieces of lead from the roofs of houses as pencils.'[14]

As elsewhere in their Empire, the Japanese authorities at Tjideng expected the prisoners to organize themselves. A system was instituted whereby each house had an appointed leader from among the women prisoners and each street, or block, had a 'block leader'. As usual this responsibility brought great risks, since the Japanese tended to punish the leaders for the infractions of the led. 'In our second house my mother was chosen as the head of the house, the "kapala",' recalled Hetty. 'This meant being in charge of delegating all the jobs that had to be done as well as being responsible for the behaviour of the women and children towards the Japanese officers. She also had to sort out strife between the women, she was good at that. She also had to organise the work shifts. I felt very proud of her, I remember.'[15]

Tenko was called twice a day. As the overcrowding in the Ghetto became progressively worse, with every room in every house literally wall-to-wall with mattresses, including the corridors and kitchens, some people had to live in garages or sleep on patios. Washing facilities almost ceased to exist as Lieutenant Sonei ordered the water supply shut off to the houses, and the toilets could no longer be used because the septic tanks were never emptied. Doors were removed and burned for firewood, and even some windows and walls were removed from the houses. It was not unusual to find eighty women and children living in one small suburban house designed originally for a single family. 'The women in the house, realising they had to live together in very cramped quarters with the children, immediately made up a set of rules regarding the washing of clothes, general cleanliness and behaviour towards each other,' recalled child prisoner Hetty. 'Cooking was done in the central kitchen and food was fetched in turn by two women for the whole house. No cooking was allowed in the houses.'[16] As a young boy, Hardy experienced the over-crowding: 'The second place we lived was in the middle of the Tjitaroemweg along a canal. This house was not so big although there were 64 people "living" in it. We were housed in the half of a garage with a friend of my mother and her two children. We slept under each other.'[17]

The grim conditions in the Tjideng Ghetto were certainly exacerbated by the attitude and behaviour of Lieutenant Sonei. Undoubtedly a man of psychopathic tendencies, Sonei constantly attacked and victimized his charges and clearly enjoyed doing so. Former internees recalled many examples of Sonei's brutality. His *tenkos* lasted for hours, recalled Hardy: 'Sometimes we had to join a "kumpulan" (roll-call) and stay for hours in ranks. When it was done too slow the guards beat the women who were in charge of a (street) block. Once we stood a full night long and those who fainted were beaten up.' Fear of the guards and particularly of Lieutenant Sonei was constant, but was especially in evidence during the *tenko*. 'On one of the kumpulans I was sick and fell on the road, but my mother picked me up and helped me to bow,' recalled Hardy. 'She told me afterwards she was terrified. We had to make endless bows.'[18] Michel recalled a dangerous game he played with the Japanese. 'The most daring thing to do was to skip compulsory line up which was twice a day and try to knock some green mangoes off the tree in camp with a flat stone,' he recalled. 'If there was line up all the people were at the assembly so you had a clear go to steal mangoes. The point was if the Japanese found out that you were not at kumpul you were history.'[19] The length of the *kumpulan*, an Indonesian word used by the Dutch in place of the Japanese '*tenko*', was a good enough reason for young boys to risk disappearing on foraging expeditions. 'Kumpul … could last until late in the afternoon if we had to be punished. Everyone had to stand in rows of ten for hours; all the women and children in the afternoon sun.'[20] Sonei ordered the sick to attend *tenko*, adding to their distress, and *tenko* could be called at any time, day or night, depending on the whim of the commandant.

The commandant constantly reduced the food rations to punish various infractions of his own insane rules. 'The regime of the Japanese became more and more severe and cruel,' said Hardy. 'The food rations became smaller and smaller. There was a little bit of bread, rice, and "starch-paste". Instead of meat the cook-shop made milled intestine.'[21] The prisoners tried other ways to obtain food. 'We tried to grow fish in the water well in front of the garden,' recalled Hardy. 'It was a hopeless task because most of the time there was no water in it.'[22] Little boys took to thieving like Victorian street urchins. 'One day I stole a piece of bread from a truck in the market-place. A guard saw what I did and came after me. I ran away and I hid myself. He did not find me.'[23]

Michel's mother managed to obtain a much sought after job in the camp kitchens. She noticed that there was an open drain for the water on the floor to run outside, and this gave her a novel idea. 'She quickly told me, one day, that I had to go to the back of the kitchen and watch the drain,' recalled Michel. 'I did what I was told and soon there were potatoes rolling down the drain which I picked up and put in my pockets. This was ok for a short time till my mother got found out and was reported. She got a severe beating and lost her job in the kitchen.'[24] The kitchen was somewhere Michel had already taken to hanging around before his mother was punished. 'I had to do a lot of jobs for my mother like catching water or standing in queues till she came to take over. Also if we were lucky I had to boil eggs at the kitchen steam overflow pipe. There was at the back of the kitchen a pipe where the excess steam was expelled and we found this a very good way of boiling eggs or other things. I found this out but soon everybody was doing it so you had to queue again.'[25] Michel was busy in the back garden of the shared house where he lived an overcrowded life. 'I made a veggie garden and planted a sort of spinach that grew very fast. It was not very nice, a bit slimy but it was food. I also managed to get some corn seeds.'[26]

The experiences of young children in the Japanese internment camps were necessarily different from those of their parents and other adults. Children view the world in a different way. 'It is funny but as a kid you adapt a lot better than if you are a grown up,' wrote Michel. 'I never seemed to have a dull time because I was always doing or making things out of nothing. There were lots of other kids in camp so we just played.'[27] 'My mother loved a cigarette now and then,' recalled Hetty, 'but since there were no matches to be had she would send me to find a light somewhere. In order to keep the cigarette burning I used to take a draw on the way back. Sometimes I came back with half a cigarette, the rest I had smoked myself.'[28]

As mentioned, Sonei ordered many women to have their heads shaved for breaches of his rules, usually after first receiving a severe beating from the guards. He encouraged his men to beat women and children, often very severely, and even ordered older internee boys to beat to death the pet dogs brought into the camp by families. In a rage he was known to upend pots of food in the communal kitchen and once ordered his men to bury bread desperately needed by the starving internees. This last episode was witnessed by a 21-year-old Riet. 'On one occasion when a woman did not bow, the commandant made us dig a hole and bury the bread and he kicked over the food in the kitchen and made us go without food for 3 days.'[29]

Prisoners were responsible for new arrivals in the Ghetto. 'When new internees arrived we had to search their belongings,' recalled Riet, 'and if we had missed anything and it was found by the soldiers in their search, we would be beaten – not just one searcher, but all.'[30] As in the POW camps, civilian internees had to bow incessantly to the Japanese. The Japanese were obsessed with this form of obeisance and any internee who forgot, or refused, to bend at the waist very soon discovered the Japanese propensity for painful retribution. 'We had to bow to the soldiers and even to the trucks if they passed us,' wrote Riet, 'not doing so resulted in a savage beating and kicking.'[31]

Riet, who was imprisoned along with her mother and a younger brother, recalled the inferior bill of fare offered by Lieutenant Sonei. 'Breakfast was gluey, had sago in it with very little nutritional value. Lunch and dinner was a handful of rice and vegetables that were leftovers from the markets and were often more water than vegetables. When there were no leftovers, we were given water lilies, sometimes with the flowers still on the stalks, which the women in the kitchen made edible with the use of herbs.'[32] A novel source of food was soon discovered. 'We used to search for snails to give to the sick in place of egg whites.' Sonei was rewarded for his regime of terror by his superiors, who promoted him to captain. The death rate under his command was between six and ten women and children *every* day.

Disease stalked civilian internees every minute of their existence and even in the best run internment camps nearly everyone became sick at some point during their confinement. Because the Japanese authorities did not ordinarily issue medicines to the prisoners, many readily treatable diseases became death sentences. Child internee Hetty recalled the situation at the Tijdeng Ghetto: 'Much sickness was caused by poor sewerage and the women had to ladle the overflow of the cesspits into open drains which became a source of constant infection. Many women and children had open sores on their ankles and legs from infected cuts and the bacteria caused skin ulcers. I was one of them and had to have my sores washed out and bandaged regularly.'[33] 'Most of the time we played in the street,' recalled another young child internee, Hardy. 'I got a severe ulcer on one of my toes. They put me in a hospital at Laan Trivelli. It became a very big ulcer and at last they had to remove the nail. I was lucky because of the good food there.'[34] Hardy's next experience of hospital was far less sanguine. He was struck down with dysentery, caused by the appalling state of sewerage in the camp. 'One day my mother and her friend carried me on a stretcher to the dysentery-house. I screamed very much because we all knew that you would never come back from there.

I stayed there for a month and went through the dying of a little girl (two years old?) in a baby-bed. The atmosphere was horrible. I heard screaming and crying in the opposite houses under big trees. I was told there were mad people housed there. In spite of everything I recovered.'[35]

Hygiene levels dropped to new lows as Captain Sonei's regime became ever more depraved. The toilets had already ceased to work because of the overcrowding and ' "chamber pots" (old tins) had to be emptied daily. Water was no longer available from household taps, and instead it had to be fetched daily from a central point.'[36] Child prisoner Hardy also noticed the state of the sewerage. 'The garden behind the house was a mess. The sewerage had broken down and the dirt and shit was canalized in open gutters throughout the garden.'[37]

Even going to the dentist became, because of an almost total lack of proper medication and instruments, another torture to be endured by even the smallest children. 'My teeth would be drilled without anesthetic with blunt drills and then filled – with what? When we were back in Holland I had to go on endless trips to the dentist to get the proper fillings for my teeth.'[38]

The prisoners, including the very young, were required to perform some labour for the Japanese. 'Sometimes we had to work in a field, I think to grow crops,' recalled Hardy. 'My physical condition was very bad. On the hottest moment of the day I sat shivering in the sun. It was not malaria, but because of weakness and severe loss of weight I was very cold.'[39]

Elsewhere in the Netherlands East Indies, Dutch children and their mothers were shunted from camp to camp by the Japanese, and each new location was usually more miserable than the last. Seventeen-year-old Elizabeth van Kampen was one of a group of Dutch colonists loaded aboard trucks that bumped along a rough road, clouds of choking dust thrown up by their wheels. In the back sat white women and children, their faces full of apprehension and confusion. Japanese guards sat either side of the tailgates at the back of the trucks, their rifles propped between their knees, their expressions bored and listless under the hot sun. The convoy was making its way across the island of Java in February 1944. 'All along the road were many very young Indonesians laughing and were calling us names,' wrote van Kampen. 'Of course the white masters were now nothing more but slaves to the Japanese Army. I bent my head, my eyes were full of tears.'[40]

Elizabeth van Kampen's personal story was typical of the experiences of thousands of Dutch civilians whose lives were devastated by the twin experiences of invasion and internment. Van Kampen's father had taken a job in the Netherlands East Indies in 1920, when he was twenty-two years old, working as an engineer for a Dutch shipping firm. He met his wife while on a long leave in Holland in 1926, and Elizabeth was born there in 1927. Van Kampen's father had then moved the whole family east to the huge island of Sumatra, and later to neighbouring Java, in 1928.

Johan Rijkee was only a young child when the Japanese invaded. His father worked for Royal Dutch Shell at the Palembang oilfields. The family was soon cast to the winds, as Johan's father remained behind to assist the Dutch Army with blowing up the oilfields before the Japanese arrived, while Johan and his mother and sister travelled by train and then ship to Java in an attempt to escape the invaders. Their journey ended at the town of Malang, where, after three weeks, Johan's father had managed to join them. However, they could not find passage off the island and when the Japanese arrived Johan's father was arrested and sent to an all-male internment camp. Later on in 1942, the rest of the family was forced into a makeshift camp created by the cordoning off with barbed wire of a housing estate in Malang to create a ghetto known as District Malang, a similar arrangement to the Tijdeng Ghetto in Batavia.

In November 1943, Johan and his family were transferred to Karangpanas Camp in Semarang on the north coast of Java, and then Karangpanas Semarang Camp in the centre of the island. The 500-mile (805 km) journey was so exhausting for civilians who had been on starvation rations for years, and exposed to a myriad of tropical diseases, that on arrival at the new camp Johan was one of several who were immediately admitted to the makeshift hospital. 'This "hospital" was just an empty room without any furniture,' remembered Johan. 'Since our luggage never arrived, I and many others, had to lay on the cement floor.'[41] After three weeks Johan left the hospital and joined his mother and sister in a barrack block. 'In the barrack there was a long continuous plank bed alongside both walls. Each person was allocated 20 inches (50 cm) of space. No more space or privacy. This was a real concentration camp ... In this camp a lot of the men were already very old and since they were dying like flies my mother managed to obtain mattresses for us.' Death came to the barrack blocks daily. 'The dead were carried to the make-shift morgue on a stretcher covered with a white sheet and when I asked what was happening I was told that the person was asleep.'[42]

At her Javanese internment camp, Elizabeth van Kampen had also fallen ill. 'Every two weeks I had a malaria attack,' she recalled. 'I had tropical abscesses underneath my feet and in the end I also suffered from oedema. My mother too had malaria and another type of oedema, my younger sister had jaundice and the youngest one also had malaria and she became completely apathetic.' Children perished under these conditions. 'I have seen it daily how little children died of hunger and mothers who stood there with no tears left in their eyes when their dead children were carried out of the camp.'[43]

Once boys were old enough they would be forcibly removed from their mothers and sent to men's internment camps. Heart-rending scenes were played out. 'I have seen little boys ... taken away from their mothers and ... sent to a camp for men only. They stood there on a truck, 10 years old leaving their mothers while their fathers were somewhere else, maybe Burma or maybe dead,'[44] wrote van Kampen. The attitude of the Japanese commandant and his men to the suffering of the women and children was confusing to the internees. '[The] whole situation was so inhuman,' recalled van Kampen, 'we were all completely lost in a sadistic and very racial discriminating world. We couldn't understand Japanese, so they screamed louder and louder.'[45]

As in the rest of the Occupied Territories, child and teenaged internees were almost daily forced to bear witness to horrific bouts of physical abuse and torture perpetrated by their guards against anyone deemed to have broken the camp rules. The 'punishments' that were meted out to internees would today be classified as torture. 'I have seen how women have been beaten up so badly that almost all their bones were broken,' recalled Elizabeth van Kampen. 'I can still hear the screaming in my head, we all had to stand there to watch.' Lengthier punishments were often perpetrated by the guards, the rationale being to serve as a warning to the other prisoners to obey with a capital 'O'. 'I have seen three women be hanged for twelve hours long under the burning tropical sun, with their hands tied up on their backs. We had to watch all the time with tears in our eyes.'[46]

At Bangkinang Camp on Sumatra, a small contingent of British internees formed a distinctive section of the mainly Dutch prisoner population. Being such a tiny minority affected British children significantly. 'The part that I remember most vividly in Bankinang is how I lost the command of English, my native tongue, because we were with so many Dutch,' recalled child internee Paget Eames. 'There were also some Eurasians, some Indians, and a lot of Tamils, Chinese and Malays.' Eames described the regime: 'The Japanese even made the children work – we had to go and tend their gardens and collect buckets of water for them. We had to bow every time we saw a Japanese soldier and my friend and I would bow but we swore in Dutch under our breath as we did so, and we always had to say, "*Nippon banzai! Nippon banzai!* [Japan ten thousands years!]"' Punishment occurred regularly. 'If anyone committed an offence, they were made to stand out in the sun for a very long period.' Eames's mother was a pillar of strength under very trying circumstances. 'Every day my mother said to me, 'Look, we're going to make it.' She also told me to keep the idea of my father with me, because we didn't know what had happened to him.'[47]

In June 1944, internee Johan Rijkee and his family were transferred again. They were taken out of Karangpanas Semarang Camp in Java, where they had been imprisoned for many months, and driven by bus to Camp 6 Ambarawa in the central part of the island. Predictably, conditions at the new camp were not much of an improvement and in many ways the family's situation was deteriorating – the case for all prisoners of the Japanese. The Japanese continued to concentrate civilian internees into bigger camps, whilst concurrently reducing the sizes of camps.

> This camp was better organized than the previous one. However it was a very crowded camp. Space per person was now 18 inches (45 cm). The food situation was still very bad but at

least they gave you something twice a day. Many times we were chased out of the barracks, when the Japanese wanted to search for forbidden articles such as money, pencils, paper, diaries, gold items etc. I managed to hide my father's signet ring by putting it on one of my toes and covering it with dirt or mud.[48]

The cruelty of the Japanese guards was as evident at the new camp as before, and Rijkee, still only a very young child, witnessed several harrowing incidents that were to stay with him into adulthood. 'One day while I was sweeping, two Japanese were beating an Indonesian gentleman with bamboo sticks. When the blood was pouring out of his mouth one Japanese got an old food tin to collect the blood. They then forced the man to drink his own blood.'[49] The emotional roller-coaster of civilian internment damaged children permanently, and in effect the violence that they were exposed to, and sometimes received, was a form of mass child abuse perpetrated by a nation state.

The Japanese hated idleness, and any work, no matter how demeaning or pointless, was made compulsory, largely to increase punishment. Children were forced to labour alongside their parents. 'The hardest job was cutting grass between the barracks which was done by using a kitchen knife,' recalled Rijkee. 'Somebody then stole my knife, which was a major disaster because my mother had now only one knife left. The lightest but most frightening job was sweeping the Japanese quarters near the gate. Not only were the Dutch inmates punished there, but also Indonesians from outside the camp.'[50] It was whilst sweeping this area that Rijkee had witnessed the torture of a local by two Japanese guards recounted above. Such sights were part of the normal, everyday rhythm of Japanese internment camps. Yet the usual sadistic cruelty could be suddenly punctuated by unexpected kindnesses from the Japanese towards the children. 'Another time when I was sweeping the Japanese Commander's bedroom, he came rushing in and ushered me outside pointing to a high flying British or U.S. war plane,' recalled Rijkee. 'He then forced me to hide under his bed. I suppose he wanted to convince me that the plane was the real enemy. When I finished cleaning his bedroom he gave me a biscuit.'[51]

7

Hard Times

My brother told me that he remembers me sitting with this bowl of ghustly porridge stuff, which was just packed with weevils, and I was delicately picking out each weevil and putting it on the side of my plate, whereas he was eating it all and saying, 'It's more protein.'

Jacqueline Honnor, British child internee
Santo Tomas Camp, Manila

There was a difference between the experiences of those children who were interned in the single-sex camps and those who lived in the mixed camps. The single-sex camps were mainly located in the Netherlands East Indies and, as we have seen from descriptions of the Tjideng Ghetto in Batavia, they were extremely grim places compared with the mixed camps in Shanghai, Manila, Hong Kong and Singapore. In the former the Japanese forced everyone except the very smallest children to perform manual labour and they actively banned education. The mothers and other women in these camps leaned very heavily on the older children to take up some of the duties of absent husbands and fathers, including work and childcare. Inevitably, many of the youngest children were left unsupervised for hours at a time, and their lives lacked the structure afforded to British and American interned children in the mixed camps. An astounding 33,700 out of a total of 41,260 Western children interned by the Japanese during the war were Dutch, and they suffered the majority of the ill-treatment given out by the Japanese.

HARD TIMES

Ernest Hillen was eight years old when he entered Bloemenkamp internment centre. His mother was immediately sent to work. 'My mother was a mover, handing furniture out of houses and, after sorting ... loading it on to huge wooden carts that had been pulled by buffalo before the war. These she and other "furniture ladies" then pushed to already empty houses for storage for the Japanese: to be used in their quarters or shipped to Japan. She did this all day long in the sun, growing brown and thin.' Hillen's elder brother also worked. 'Jerry was put to work in the kitchens where boys of his age [12] lifted drums of boiling water or soup or rice from wood fires and toted them around on bamboo poles. I was left alone.'[1]

Some of the mothers in the Dutch camps tried to begin education classes for the youngest children, but the pressures of work interfered with this. At one camp, the Japanese tolerated a school for three months before shutting it down, also outlawing a whole host of other activities important to the internees. 'No more shows, no more school, no more gym, no more church, no more meetings unless with guards, no more nothing,' recalled one former internee, 'instead we had to work harder.'[2] 'Education was not allowed,' recalled another internee, 'so if there was a bit of education we had to do it in secret. I had the Old Testament with me ... I feared that I would forget how to read so every day I read for half-an-hour. I taught my sister to reckon [add-up] and a bit of reading and writing but we had to do it with some wood in the sand. I taught them to sing several songs. I told them fairy stories.' In this case, an older child was effectively a mother to her younger siblings, and a teacher. 'It was difficult. My little sister would ask "What is a horse?", "What is a sofa?", "What is a father?" This was so difficult ... That was the only education we had.'[3]

Connie was ten when the Japanese sent her to work. 'The Japanese insisted I did one-and-a-half hours every day cleaning the streets with other girls of my age ... Some had to clean the toilets, the drains and the floors. After the morning parade I had to clean and wash the vegetables, clean the big pots they used to cook rice. I would then go to my sisters where my next duty was to catch flies. Everyday we each had to hand in ten dead flies. The Japanese ordered this.'[4]

Eleven-year-old Eurasian British internee Eileen Harris was imprisoned in Sime Road Camp in Singapore. The Japanese had suddenly moved her, her British father, Malay mother, and six siblings from the infamous Changi Prison after eighteen months of tough internment. At Sime Road, the internees were segregated according to gender and herded into wooden huts, ninety persons to each hut. Although Harris was in the same camp as her father, who ironically had been a prison warder before the war, she had little opportunity to see him during the duration of their imprisonment.

At Sime Road, working closely to Prime Minister Tojo's orders, the Japanese used the entire camp as a giant pool of slave labour, including the very youngest children. In some spurious and convoluted way, the Japanese believed that this illegal action was somehow helping their war effort. 'Every morning we were all put to work, cutting grass, cleaning drains and knitting socks for the Jap soldiers,' said Harris, describing the experiences of young children inside the camp. At Sime Road, some of the organization present in the other British camps, such as Changi, appears to have been lacking – probably due to malnutrition and, in some cases, outright starvation amongst the prisoners. 'We had no schooling, so played amongst ourselves most of the time.'[5] Starvation was, it appears from the available evidence, deliberately engineered by the camp authorities. 'The food was awful,' wrote Harris, 'rice boiled until it looked like wallpaper paste, a bit of salt, fish and plants were added to make it interesting.' Children actively foraged for food just to survive. 'Hiding and exploring one day, a friend and I realised that a nearby underground sewer ran past the Japanese quarters and right beside their food store. At great risk, while she kept guard, I crawled along the sewer tunnel, out of a drain cover and into the food store. There, I stuffed what I could into my flimsy clothes and crawled back again ... Most of the food I managed to get back was given to those who were really very ill.'[6] Her father, alongside all of the other male prisoners, was sent out to labour in the fields, where he was regularly brutalized by sadistic guards. 'My father was very badly beaten and he never forgave them.'[7]

In the Netherlands East Indies, Ernest Hillen's mother coped with the horrors of internment through sheer determination. She was

...erated Dutch and British children stand in the open gate to the infamous Tjideng Ghetto in ...tavia (now Jakarta), Java, September 1945. In total, 33,700 Dutch children were interned by the ...anese during the Second World War, often in appalling circumstances.

...uses on Laan Trivelli, a road inside the Tjideng Ghetto, indicating the overcrowding from which ... internees suffered. Designed to accommodate 2,000 internees, by June 1945 the Ghetto held ...300 women and children.

Young children play beside their accommodation huts at Kampong Makassar Camp in Java. The 3,500 internees did not learn that the war was over for several days after the Japanese surrender in August 1945.

e female washhouse at Kampong Makassar Camp.

tram Road Jail, Singapore. This former British prison ended up holding captive hundreds of tish families, including many young children.

Ash Camp, Shanghai. Located in a former British Army barracks, the prisoners marked the roofs of huts and the central square with large 'PW' letters to indicate their location to Allied aircraft around the time of the Japanese surrender. Food and medical supplies were parachuted to them.

Japanese guards at Tjideng Ghetto sit sullenly outside of the guard house. The Japanese remained under arms after their surrender to protect the camp from Indonesian nationalists.

Liberated American and British women and children pose with GIs at Santo Tomas Camp in the Philippine capital Manila. US Army forces literally broke into the camp and fought with the Japanese guards in early 1945 as General MacArthur's forces overran Luzon Island.

Many of the families imprisoned at Santo Tomas had been forced by overcrowding to live in shanties on the university grounds. Conditions were rough and ready and added greatly to the hardships many American and British families suffered.

An American soldier poses with liberated internees in the Philippines, 1945.

Living conditions for Dutch women and children inside the Tjideng Ghetto were overcrowded and very basic.

Two Dutch boys inside the
Tjideng Ghetto.

Royal Navy ratings from HMS *Cumberland*
pictured with liberated Dutch children at
Tandjong Priok Camp, Java, September
1945.

General Hideki Tojo, Japanese Prime Minister and Minister of War, who was directly responsible for the appalling conditions that existed inside civilian internment camps across Asia.

Japanese soldiers at Santo Tomas Camp during negotiations with the US Army to obtain the release of 200 white hostages being held inside the Education Building.

'stubborn about routine', and she focused her children's minds on the ideals of family and national and Western cultural rituals in an effort to civilize her sons and survive. 'Always say "good morning" at the start of the day,' recalled Hillen, 'drinking tea in the afternoon (or hot water if there was no tea): talking in the evening; and celebrating – our birthdays, those of friends in the camp, my father's, those of family members in Canada and Holland and of the royals of both countries and all feast days of both. "It's fun," she told us, "this is how we'll survive." '[8]

Many mothers severely disciplined their children in the Dutch camps. The mothers 'were hyper-nervous, underfed, overworked, and were cooped up in the heat in such appalling condition for so long that they were often at the end of their tether. As a result, some disciplined their children harshly and then were racked with guilt.'[9] As we have seen, some of the boys over ten or eleven years of age were taken away from their mothers and placed in the men's camps, where they also faced serious challenges. 'It was lousy-bad,' recalled one boy prisoner at Ambarawa 8 Camp. 'Looking after the old sick men. We had to do the dirty work ... Emptying pots because they were not able to get to the toilets, cleaning them, taking them to a special place when they were dead and putting them in a coffin – sometimes twenty and thirty a day ... We were cutting wood, unloading trains ... At the end they put two camps together. Obviously things got worse.' Large numbers of young boys eked out an existence completely separated from their families. 'We were eight hundred boys in one barracks close together, all night people always going to the toilet ... It was always dirty, other people didn't manage to get to the toilet in time ... It was terrible, you were never alone ...'[10]

Ten-year-old Olga Henderson was at Changi Camp along with her parents and two brothers. This was a mixed-gender camp. They were forced to tend allotments and then to hand over all the vegetables that they managed to grow to the Japanese, who, due to the very successful Allied submarine campaign against Japanese supply lines, were also starting to feel the pinch. Inadequate rations forced even young children to risk their lives scavenging around the camps. 'We used to go out at night on raiding parties,' recalled Henderson. 'You had to be quick to get in between the searchlights. If you were seen, the guards would open fire.' Being captured on any of these illicit operations would result in physical punishment, children included. 'If you were caught, they'd make you kneel on the tarmac road all day in the sun. If you fell over, the guards would whip you until you got on your knees again.'[11]

Henderson was a member of the Girl Guides and she, along with seventeen other young girls, decided to make a patch-work quilt as a birthday present for their leader. This seemingly innocuous activity was fraught with very real danger, for the Japanese had forbidden practically every leisure activity enjoyed by prisoners on pain of a beating or even death. The Japanese commandant was determined to make prisoners' lives absolutely devoid of diversions and interests. Their humanity was being carefully and deliberately stripped from them by the Japanese regime. Henderson and her friends determined to make the quilt regardless of the rules, determined perhaps to retain something of their old lives amid the horror of the camp, by engaging in an activity that young and free girls enjoy all over the world – needlecraft. Every scrap of material required for the quilt, which eventually measured six feet long and three feet wide (1.8 × .9 m), had to be scrounged, and putting the quilt together had to be done in the strictest secrecy. 'To get what we wanted, we had to steal or scrounge,' recalled Henderson. 'The fabric came from bedcases, pillowcases, anything. If someone dropped a handkerchief, you kept it. If you saw a bit of rag hanging on a line, we'd steal it.' The secret sewing circle met once a week 'in a hut with two little windows with grilles on. We used to show each other what we had managed to scrounge. Pickings were so thin that the quilt took over two years to make. To get thread, we'd unpick worn-out clothes. The back of the quilt was made of calico flour bags.' The girls worked in constant fear of discovery by roving Japanese guards. 'The Japanese couldn't know about it – they'd beat you if they found you doing something you shouldn't. If you heard their boots on the concrete floors, you'd have no time to hide. You'd just have to shove the bit you were working on down your knickers, needle and all.'[12] The quilt now resides in the collection of the Imperial War Museum in London, one of the more unusual objects to have emerged from the Japanese internment camps.

At Santo Tomas Internment Camp in Manila, food had become the main topic of conversation among the American and British internees, for there was never enough to feed the almost 4,000 men, women and children. The camp was desperately overcrowded, and the living conditions of many of the internees were terrible as insufficient accommodation space had meant that hundreds of families were living in destitution inside a shanty town on the campus. 'The really vital part of our day was getting food any way we could,' recalled British child internee Jacqueline Honnor. 'My brother had a spinach garden, and we grew ginger, which seemed to do well. The Japanese kept pigs and they would put out their pig swill and I'm afraid the kids would go and get it if they possibly could.'[13]

For the first two years of the war, the commandant had allowed the internees to barter for extra rations with local Filipinos, who had been permitted to enter to camp to trade. Allotments had also been laid out to grow vegetables, though some of the campus grounds were taken up by shanties, which limited how much food the internees could grow. Fraternizing with the local population was stopped when the Imperial Army took over the running of the camp in 1943. The new commandant, Lieutenant Colonel Toshio Hayashi, instituted controls over the rice issued to the prisoners in order to make more available to Japanese troops, who were running low on supplies as General MacArthur's army prepared to invade the Philippines any day, and this caused terrible suffering among the internee population. The Japanese cut the rice ration from three servings a day to only two. 'My brother told me that he remembers me sitting with this bowl of ghastly porridge stuff, which was just packed with weevils, and I was delicately picking out each weevil and putting it on the side of my plate,' remembered Honnor, 'whereas he was eating it all and saying, 'It's more protein.' '

Hunger drove some internees to extreme lengths to feed themselves and their families. Stealing among the prisoners increased dramatically, leading the camp committee to take steps to punish those who were caught, not only to enforce a sense of community upon the prisoners but also to prevent the Japanese from taking over the punishing of the internees themselves. Extra-curricular activities dropped off sharply as vitamin deficiency diseases like beriberi and scurvy increased, and one of the first things to go was the education classes for the children. 'Some people became panic-stricken and ate boiled hibiscus leaves or cats but the doctors soon put a stop to this for those people became very sick. However, the large flock of pigeons that had nested in the eaves gradually disappeared,'[14] recalled American internee Ada Hayes. A few of the elderly internees at Santo Tomas actually died of starvation, but fortunately the children fared a little better. Parents made sacrifices for their children, and even the Japanese occasionally showed a glimmer of humanity towards them. 'During the periods when the Japs were dining, the children would hang around the table. When they could not stand it any more, they would toss scraps of food from the table to the wide-eyed hungry children.'[15]

'A typical day would be getting up in the morning, having ginger tea and anything we might have to eat – part of a banana, if we were lucky,' recalled Jacqueline Honnor. 'Then we had to go on roll-call, and that would consist of us all standing in a line in the sun where we would be counted. The officer would go up and down with his long sword, and we would bow. They were never cruel or nasty to us, to my knowledge. But I do know that people who tried to escape had a bad time.'[16] The internees were indeed fortunate that at Santo Tomas the commandant, although strict, was not actually a psychopath like Captain Sonei at the Tjideng Ghetto in Java. Children amused themselves as best they could. 'We used to play skipping-rope games: two children turning the rope and somebody jumping in. Sometimes one of the guards would jump in and we would deliberately tighten the rope to trip him up and he would go down with a splendid clatter, but he would laugh.'

The poor provision of food by the Japanese authorities was the single most pressing issue concerning all internees throughout the Occupied Territories, not least at Santo Tomas. 'A lot of the time the food was very, very tiny salt fish, some sort of protein, and rice.'[17] In December 1943, the Japanese commandant issued a single shipment of Red Cross parcels to the prisoners, the only time that this was ever done. Usually the Japanese simply illegally stockpiled Red Cross supplies and pilfered them themselves, or cynically left them to gather dust in warehouses where thousands were discovered after the war. These parcels could have saved countless lives. 'There was a food kit, medical supplies, clothes and badly needed shoes,' recalled Lieutenant Rita Palmer, a US Army nurse interned alongside the civilians at Santo Tomas. 'The next day there were 15 "kit" casualties, as the doctors termed it, from eating the chocolate bars.'[18] Jacqueline Honnor also recalled the Red Cross shipment: 'We had about four food parcels from the Red Cross in total, and that saved our lives. They contained powdered milk, corned beef and stuff like that, all good protein.'[19] The internees had made efforts to create a store of canned goods in case the Japanese severely cut the rations, but this proved impossible to maintain because of the very large numbers of prisoners crammed into Santo Tomas. The stored food was all eaten.

Increased American air activity over Manila, including several air raids, caused the Japanese to close the main gate to the camp permanently in January 1944. No more bartering with the locals was permitted and no more supplies of fresh food could be brought into the camp legally. Thereafter, the prisoners would have to survive on a steadily decreasing ration of rice twice a day. 'The rice became more and more watery as time went by until it was a teacupful of rice a day, and that was it. We all became obsessed with food, rather like anorexics,'[20] said Honnor. The only way to obtain fresh food was through contacts in the Philippine Underground movement or by growing it in the allotments. '[When] it seemed as if conditions could be no worse the Japs would take more food from them [the internees] and each one dipped into his supply of stored goods,' recalled Palmer. 'Thus when the real emergency arrived nothing was left to eat.'[21] Obsession with food affected the camp children as much as the adults. 'There were a few recipe books in the library and, even at the age of ten, I could copy out recipes,' recalled Honnor. 'You were sort of mentally eating.'[22]

In the single-sex camps in the Netherlands East Indies, many young children could barely recall having seen a Western man. Young boys were bereft of male role-models, and instead hero-worshipped any of the women in the camp who demonstrated grit, determination and bravery before the Japanese. Ernest Hillen recalled Mrs Crone, who was 'built like a tree', standing up to a fearsome beating from a Japanese guard. 'I'd seen worse,' said Hillen. 'I felt no pity, just pride.' On the rare occasions when Western men entered his camp, Hillen was very disappointed. Once, a group of male prisoners arrived to help the women repair fences. They looked cowed and beaten. 'Mrs Crone called them the bruised ones. I thought they just looked sorry for themselves, not the way men should. After the second day I didn't bother going to watch them again.' Hillen was later transferred to Kampong Makassar Camp. By this time, even though still a young boy, he was as inured to pain and suffering as any battle-hardened soldier. 'I could walk down our barrack past women and children with broken teeth and bleeding gums, hair growing in tufts and faces and stomachs bloated with hunger oedema and beriberi, boils as big as ping pong balls and oozing tropical ulcers and not let myself *see* them: pain was pain.'[23] Violence had also become so commonplace that Hillen hardly took any notice. 'I saw many women and older children slapped and kicked sometimes until they fell down, that after a while I didn't bother telling my mother about it any more.'[24] The boys at Ambarawa 8 were similarly becoming emotionally remote from pain, suffering and death. 'We carried twenty or thirty bodies of the old men a day ... It was very hot so you could not leave them more than twelve hours. We carried these dead bodies outside the camp, we didn't mind that. So many things were happening. You were so, how do you call it ... numb.'[25] The piles of corpses represented only work for the young boys detailed to dispose of them. 'Dozens of corpses were carried out the gate daily. The men died of exhaustion, dysentery, hunger and oedema. The dead were placed on big straw baskets attached to bamboo sticks left and right. Friends or strangers picked up the baskets and carried them out of camp ... It was a horrible sight especially those who died from hunger oedema, water burst through the baskets.' But, no matter how unpleasant the task may have been, the boys soon became hardened. 'Every day we saw the same sight. We got used to it.'[26]

Much younger children were also affected by what they witnessed. At Los Banos Camp in the Philippines, one young mother noted that her 'two children Robin and Larry, no longer played soldier. Now their game was funeral – imitating what their childish eyes saw every day.'[27] Elizabeth Gale, who kept a secret diary, observed the play of her young daughter and friend at Pootung Camp in Shanghai. 'The little girls spend hours playing happily with their dolls house. Today they pile all the furniture into one room because it is bomb day, they say. Last week they took the dolls' beds and the bath tubs out and shook them vigorously because it was de-bugging day.'[28]

At Batu Lintang Camp in Kuching in Sarawak, the joint POW and civilian internment centre, conditions for the prisoners deteriorated at an alarming rate. The Japanese, short of fresh food themselves, ordered that all of the women internees should work as agricultural labourers and grow vegetables for the guards' consumption. The male POWs and civilians in the camp also laboured, and collectively they named themselves 'white coolies'. Such was the severity of the regime at Batu Lintang that out of 395 male civilian internees in the camp in August 1945, only 30 were fit enough to report for work. The rest were too ill or had already died. In the women's camp, where 37 young children also lived, the women their sacrificed their own health in order to save these young lives. The biggest threats remained starvation and disease, the hand-maidens of Japanese prison camp policy.

Women and children internees at Batu Lintang received the same rations as the male prisoners. At the beginning of the camp's operation, that consisted of rice and local vegetables. Every ten days or so, the Japanese provided a little meat to the prisoners. Usually this was pork, and it was normally found to be of very poor quality. Typically, the prisoners' meat ration would consist of a pig's head or some offal. The daily rice ration in late 1943 was 11 ounces per person, including children. By 1945 this ration, already inadequate to sustain life, had been reduced by the Japanese to only 4 ounces a day. The children also received 1.5 ounces of milk each day. People were reduced to using the black market to obtain fresh food, and even resorting to eating the kinds of animals not normally seen on a European menu, such as snakes, snails, frogs, dogs and cats. On special occasions the Japanese would show some largesse to their prisoners – though their generosity was extremely limited. Christmas was an important time for the internees, and the women would go out of their way to provide the children with presents and a little yuletide cheer.

The presents were normally small stuffed toys made from old clothes and rags – the stuffing very often sand. The Japanese contribution to the prisoners' Christmas was practically an insult. At Christmas 1943, the commandant gave the women's camp a single turkey – for 271 women and children. The 1,000 British soldiers held in one of the POW compounds received only 58 chickens for their Christmas dinner in 1942. At Christmas 1944, no chickens or turkeys were forthcoming from the Japanese, but each woman and child did get a single egg. The precarious nature of the food situation at Batu Lintang could have been alleviated to some extent if the Japanese had seen fit to issue the Red Cross parcels, which continued to arrive from the day the camp opened until its liberation by Australian troops in September 1945. In cynical fashion the Japanese simply hoarded the life-saving parcels and, as at Santo Tomas, only once during the entire war did they make an issue of parcels, in March 1944. On that occasion, each of the prisoners ended up with one-sixth of a Red Cross parcel, equating to a single tin of food. The story was similar in most of the other camps, with the noted exception of the internment centres in Shanghai, which did receive a constant stream of Red Cross parcels and visits from the local Swiss Consul-General.

A camp hospital had been created at Batu Lintang Camp by the Japanese medical officer, Lieutenant Yamamoto. Prisoners tried to avoid this building as much as possible, for it was filthy and resembled more a morgue than a treatment centre. Yamamoto was a strange sort of doctor, inclined to beat any patients who boldly and unwisely asked for medicines. Indeed he was so slovenly and incompetent that apart from issuing orders that stated that sick prisoners would receive no rations, Yamamoto left the actual medical duties to several prisoner doctors, including Dr Gibson, who ministered to the needs of the women and children. Yamamoto's attitude to sick prisoners was summed up by one prisoner doctor as 'live and let die.' The prisoners clubbed together and tried to produce a stock of food and drugs with which to help those who were sick, but the death rate was such that special re-useable hinged coffins were required due to shortage of wood – burials occurred virtually every single day of the war. The death rate among the British POWs and male internees was appalling, with two thirds, around 600, of these men dead by the time of liberation. But tropical diseases and disorders stalked all the prisoners, regardless of their gender or age. Tropical ulcers would turn septic without treatment and could kill, dysentery was rife due to the poor sanitation in the camp, and malaria, beriberi, dengue fever, scabies, and septic bites and sores killed hundreds of others.

Malnutrition remained the chief cause of death at Batu Lintang. The basic diet distributed by the Japanese, and deemed by them suitable for all the prisoners, contained only a daily allowance of one and a half ounces of protein, equating to only 1,600 calories. This diet was a slow death by starvation, and even when supplemented with a little meat or vegetables, it was still completely inadequate. The women and children prisoners were so emaciated after a few months of this, that even moving around had become challenging. 'Some of us find it advisable to rise slowly after laying down,' recalled Hilda Bates, who had formerly been a civilian nurse in Jesselton, 'as due to malnutrition, any rapid movement is apt to cause dizziness or even a black-out.'

The Japanese policy of segregating married couples in the East Indies was especially keenly felt at Batu Lintang, as families were here separated by only a few dozen yards of dusty ground and barbed wire. Unlike in so many Japanese internment camps, where husbands had been sent away to outlying camps or even on ships to different countries, at Batu Lintang the husbands were often in the adjoining compound. In Shanghai, where a similar situation existed, the Japanese had initially attempted to segregate married couples, but had realized that this was ridiculous, and in Shanghai, Hong Kong and at Santo Tomas Camp in Manila, families had been reunited for the duration. Not so at Batu Lintang. Here, the Japanese permitted very irregular meetings between married couples, and they also displayed unnecessary mental cruelty to add to the physical cruelties inflicted daily upon the internees. At the first Christmas that the prisoners spent in Batu Lintang in 1942, the Japanese even refused to allow the men to see their wives and children for a few hours on the 25 December.

8

Comfort Girls

We were given flower names and they were pinned to our doors. They started to drag us away one by one. And I could hear all the screaming coming from the bedrooms, you know, and you just wait for your turn.

Jan O'Herne, Dutch teenaged internee
Ambarawa 8 Camp, Java

One aspect of the internment of Allied civilians has not often been addressed, and that was the enforced sexual slavery of teenaged girls. Not only were the girls in the camps subjected to starvation and disease and witnesses to bestial acts, they increasingly had to fear sexual abuse as well. On many occasions the Japanese came looking for sex slaves from among their female internees and teenaged girls were especially prized. The fact of white women being forced to become 'Comfort Women' as the Japanese called them, was not really spoken about until many decades after the war. A high degree of shame was attached to the experience, but now in old age many of the women who suffered this final indignity under Japanese rule have started to come forward to tell their stories. It makes for sober and disturbing reading.

Japanese soldiers treated the native women of the Occupied Territories with a contempt that is difficult to comprehend over sixty years later. In the Japanese military mind women appeared to serve one purpose – to provide entertainment for their soldiers, and whether they provided that entertainment freely or through duress did not matter, both were equally acceptable. Japanese soldiers were able to obtain sex whilst on campaign in two ways. Firstly, through rape. Wherever Japanese soldiers went, women could expect to be raped. They famously raped British Army nurses at the fall of Hong Kong and female Dutch colonists in the Netherlands East Indies. The taking of sex by force was often not an individual pursuit, but a group exercise encouraged by senior officers. The second way was to visit prostitutes, or 'Comfort Women'. Entire battalions of young native girls and women were attached to Japanese divisions in the field and the supply was regularly replenished. Most of these women were not prostitutes, for the term implies some form of financial reward in return for sexual favours; they are better described as sex slaves – young women forced to give their bodies, often on pain of death.

The Japanese set about the procurement of women for their brothels with a remarkable degree of organization. The abuse of women was institutionalized and condoned at the highest levels of command. The women came from a variety of different nationalities and found themselves involved in this sex trade through a variety of different paths. One of the responsibilities of the *Kempeitai* military police was to procure the 'prostitutes' for Japanese units, to establish and run brothels in the occupied territories, and to control the unfortunate women who were imprisoned within them. Between 1941 and 1945 anywhere between 60,000 and 200,000 young women of many creeds, colours and nationalities were forced into military brothels by the *Kempeitai*, including at least 300 white women and teenage girls. Initially, the Japanese relied on recruiting real prostitutes from Japan and Korea, but once this supply of bodies dried up they turned with alacrity to deceiving women into becoming sex slaves or simply coercing them into cooperation by various despicable methods. The *Kempeitai* used all of its nefarious talents for intimidation and violence. What occurred in the occupied Netherlands East Indies went even further, with the *Kempeitai* targeting white women for the first time.

'One day the Japanese came into our camp to choose comfort girls to take away with them. We had some very pretty girls,'[1] remembered Paget Eames, who was a child internee at Bangkinang Camp in Sumatra. On the neighbouring island of Java the Japanese were particularly industrious in trying to recruit young white women. Java was under occupation by the Japanese 16th Army, itself under command of 7th Army Headquarters in Singapore. The organization of army brothels was not centralized. Instead, local 16th Army officers ordered the local field *Kempeitai* to begin establishing 'Comfort Houses' for the garrison. The commissariat officer of the 16th Army was ordered by the chief-of-staff to issue licences to brothels. A licence would only be issued if the 'prostitutes' had signed a document that stated they were working voluntarily for the army as sex workers. The Japanese always had a weather eye on any future criminal proceedings that could have arisen from evidence of coercion. The *Kempeitai* did use coercion and sometimes violence to obtain the necessary signatures on their forms, and then these were then forwarded to 16th Army Headquarters in Batavia (now Jakarta).

The women who staffed the comfort houses were from several national groups. Some were Japanese or Koreans who had been legitimately recruited and shipped in to service the troops and were actually being paid. Others were Indonesian women recruited locally, who had often been deceived into becoming sex workers by Japanese procurers. A smaller number were European women who had been in the internment camps and some were European women who, because of their nationality, had remained at liberty outside the camps when the Japanese occupation began. Up to mid-1943 native and non-interned European women were mainly recruited to act as housekeepers for individual Japanese officers or civilians. When Japanese troops wanted sex they usually went to local brothels or to individual European or native prostitutes.

The *Kempeitai* instructed local hotel owners to convert their establishments into brothels in mid-1943. Prostitution was to be expanded. The Japanese decided to create brothels 'themed' along the lines of race or nationality. European women and girls were targeted for recruitment from the internment camps to offer one such 'theme'. Brothels employing European women were established at Batavia, Bandoeng, Pekalongan, Magelang, Semarang and Bondowoso. 'This change of policy was probably due to the increasing incidence of venereal disease and the inability of the privately-run brothels to remedy this problem. In addition, fewer European women were available for work in the brothels, as most of them [living outside the internment camps] preferred to establish a relationship as mistress to one Japanese man.'[2] The *Kempeitai* viewed female internment camps as a source of largely untapped potential. 'They believed that among the twenty thousand women interned in these camps enough volunteers could be found to solve their recruitment problems.'[3]

How white women and girls ended up as comfort women in the Netherlands East Indies was complex. The women fell into one of three general categories. Firstly, there were those women who had been working as prostitutes before the war and who had continued in that profession after the Japanese occupation. Secondly, some women from internment camps volunteered for work as barmaids or waitresses to escape from the terrible conditions in which they found themselves living and many of these were subsequently coerced into prostitution by unsavory Japanese and Korean pimps. For example, in June 1943 the Japanese owner of the Akebono restaurant in Batavia was instructed by the *Kempeitai* to open a brothel. He set up an establishment called the Sakura (Cherry Blossom) Club. Of the twenty European women working at the club, eleven had volunteered for the job to escape Cideng Internment Camp in the city. In late 1943 the *Kempeitai* ordered the establishment of a second military brothel in Batavia for army officers. Called the Theresia or Shoko Club, it was run by a Japanese pimp. He used European women as procurers, and in December 1943 the *Kempeitai* ordered him to obtain more white women. Using his European procurers, the pimp went to Cihapit Internment Camp in Bandoeng and successfully recruited eleven white women to work as prostitutes. The third group consisted of European women who were simply taken by force from the internment camps in groups and used as sex slaves by Japanese troops.

Recruitment drives did meet with considerable resistance from women inside the camps. Paget Eames recorded that when the Japanese tried to take girls from Bangkinang Camp in Sumatra, 'a small group of women in the camp intervened and they hid the young ones. The Japanese only wanted virgins so Mother was quite safe, and when they saw there weren't any young women there, they got very angry and demanded volunteers.'[4] On 25 January 1944, *Kempeitai* troops arrived at Muntilan Camp in Java in a bus, bringing with them a copy of a list they had previously forced the women camp leaders to draw up recording suitable young women and girls. A *tenko* was immediately called and the women on the list were ordered to go to the church (the camp being situated inside a monastery) for an inspection. The camp leaders and the camp doctor followed behind, protesting loudly to the Japanese officers that this was illegal and against the Geneva Convention. Their protestations were pointedly ignored until the Japanese tried to remove a group that they had selected from the camp. Resistance was strong. A large crowd of women and teenaged boys had gathered outside the church while the Japanese were inspecting the women. When the church door was flung open and the *Kempeitai* tried to escort the women to their bus violence broke out. The furious internees, their patience already exhausted by the inhuman treatment that they had all suffered from the Japanese, hurled clumps of dirt and stones at the Japanese soldiers. In turn, the Japanese reacted violently, *Kempeitai* officers even slashing at the unarmed women and children with their swords. By these methods, the Japanese managed to force their way through the crowd and the young girls were roughly bundled aboard the bus and driven out of the camp, many of the mothers left behind screaming and tearing at their clothes in anguish as their daughters disappeared to an unknown fate.

Three days later the *Kempeitai* came back to Camp Muntilan. Another *tenko* was called and the remaining prisoners were offered a deal. The Japanese would accept volunteers to replace the women they had taken by force before. A handful of women, mostly respectably married, but a few of whom had been working as prostitutes before the war, raised their hands and volunteered in order to spare the younger girls from multiple rape. On 28 January 1944, thirteen young women from the camp were taken to Magelang.

At Bangkinang Camp the 'volunteers' demanded by the *Kempeitai* were slow in coming forward, after the older Dutch women had hidden the young women from the Japanese. 'There was a group of Indonesian and Malay prostitutes,' recalled Paget Eames, 'who finally got up and said, "Look, this is just another job to us, let us go." But the Japanese weren't satisfied as there weren't enough of them, so some strapping Dutch ladies volunteered.' This time, the Japanese were brought up short by the attitude of the Dutch women, and a rather amazing thing happened. The truck, aboard which the Dutch women and the native prostitutes had been loaded, turned back up at the camp. 'We heard that these big Dutch ladies had stopped the truck, beaten up the drivers and had driven the truck back to the camp. We all waited, wondering what was going to happen to us ... but the Japanese were embarrassed about being beaten up by the women and we didn't hear any more about it.'[5] This incident did not prevent some Dutch women and girls from voluntarily going with the Japanese. 'No one made any judgement about that. The important factor was staying alive,' recalled Eames.

The treatment handed out to the young women who were taken as comfort women was horrible. Jan O'Herne was an attractive teenaged Dutch girl who had been born in Bandoeng in Java. O'Herne, along with her mother and two sisters, had been imprisoned in a condemned army barracks at Ambarawa, which had been hastily turned into a civilian internment camp. 'I'd been in the camp two years,' recalled O'Herne. 'The Japanese gave an order that all young girls from 17 years and up had to line up in the compound. These high military officers walked towards us and started to eye us up and down, looking at our figures, looking at our legs, and it was obviously a selection process that was going to take place.'[6] The girls were herded aboard an open army truck and 'driven away ... as if we were cattle. And I remember we were so scared and clinging to our little suitcases and clinging to each other.' Driven to a large colonial house about twenty-five miles from the camp outside the town of Selarang, the abuse began soon after arrival. 'When we got to the house, we were told we were there for the sexual pleasure of the Japanese military ... you know, our whole world just collapsed from under our feet. And we started protesting straightaway. We said that we were forced into this, that they couldn't do this to us, they had no right to do this, it was against the Geneva Convention, and that we would never do this. But they just laughed at us, you know, just laughed. They said they could do with us what they liked.'[7] The *Kempeitai* had named the brothel 'The House of the Seven Seas'. 'We were given flower names and they were pinned to our doors,' recalled O'Herne. 'They started to drag us away one by one. And I could hear all the screaming coming from the bedrooms, you know, and you just wait for your turn.' O'Herne did not have long to wait. There stood this large, fat, bald Japanese officer looking at me, grinning at me, and I put up an enormous fight, but he just dragged me to the bedroom.' O'Herne and the other girls were all virgins when they were assaulted. 'I said, "I'm not going to do this." And he said, "Well, I will kill you. If you don't give yourself to me, I will kill you." And he actually got out his sword. I went on my knees to say my prayers and I felt God very close. I wasn't afraid to die.' O'Herne was then raped. 'He just threw me on the bed – got hold of me, threw me on the bed and just tore off all my clothes and most brutally raped me. And, I thought he would never stop. It was the most ... the most horrendous ... I never thought suffering could be that terrible.' After the Japanese left, 'I thought, "I want to go to the bathroom. I want to wash this all away. I want to wash away all the shame, all the dirt. Just wash it away, wash it away."'[8] The bathroom was already filled with sobbing girls. 'We were all there in the bathroom, you know, all totally hysterical and crying and just trying to wash away the dirt, you know, the shame. Within one night, we lost our youth. We were just such a ... such a pitiful little group of girls, and we were just embracing each other. And how many times was each one raped that night? You know, I shall never forget that first night. And we felt so helpless. This was going to happen from now on, night after night.'[9]

O'Herne and her companions endured four months of being raped every day and every night before they were suddenly released and sent back to their camp. During her time in the brothel, O'Herne had tried to appeal to a Japanese Army doctor who inspected the girls regularly for disease, but to no avail. 'When the doctor came, I went to him and I said, "Look, I want you to know we're here against our will. Use your influence. Go to the highest authority, report this, that we are forced into this."' The response of the doctor was extraordinary: 'He just laughed and he ended up raping me himself. And from that time onwards, every time the doctor came for his regular visit, he used to rape me first.'[10] When O'Herne was reunited with her mother at Muntilan Camp, finding the words to explain her ordeal proved impossible. 'That first night back at the camp, I couldn't even talk or say anything to her. I just ... I can feel it now, laying in my mother's arms, you know, in the hollow of her arms ... her arms around me ... And then the next day, I told her what had happened to me and so did the other girls,' remembered O'Herne. 'We had all these girls with all these mothers ... And the mothers just couldn't cope with this story, this happened to their daughters, you know. It was too much for them – they couldn't cope with it. And we were only to ever tell our mothers just once. And it was never talked of again – it was just too much for them.'[11]

9

God Save the King

The guards stopped the beating and the internees dragged the man inside for his protection. The whole camp came out and then the Japanese got scared of so many people – they called it the Lunghwa Rebellion. Soon after that truckloads of armed soldiers came in, and they were on all the roofs of the buildings with guns.

Rachel Bosebury, British child internee
Lunghwa Camp, Shanghai

Not every internee was prepared to accept the overlordship of the Japanese and many did resist to one degree or another. Any kind of resistance, however mild, could bring down horrific punishments upon the transgressor, so adults were particularly careful not to discuss their illicit activities around the children. The adults feared that the information would be quickly leaked around the camp by the children and would eventually reach the ears of the Japanese, with dire consequences. 'Children just say things,' recalled Rachel Bosebury, a prisoner at Lunghwa Camp in Shanghai, 'and we found out after the war that there was a radio on the third floor of the D Block men's bathroom. I always used to wonder why the men went to the bathroom so much … I never knew that till after the war … but you could have been killed for having it.'[1] The Japanese had everywhere confiscated radios, telescopes, binoculars, cash and a host of other paraphernalia from internees that they considered a security threat or contraband. In many prisoner-of-war and internment camps throughout

Asia radios were secretly constructed from parts smuggled into the camps, allowing prisoners some link to the outside world and the progress of the war, especially by following BBC reports, or reports from Radio Chungking in Free China. Many POWs and internees unfortunately paid for these illicit machines with their lives when they were discovered by the periodic Japanese searches, and the *Kempeitai* military police brutally tortured everyone who was found in possession of an illegal radio or even remotely connected with it. It was all part and parcel of the climate of fear deliberately engendered in the camps, and it was extremely successful in preventing serious escape attempts or rebellions from occurring.

Escape was a form of resistance that the Japanese punished with extreme severity, and by most prisoners it was not even considered. The problems of being on the run hundreds of miles behind enemy lines were almost insurmountable. Westerners stuck out among the native populace and unless contact could quickly be made with an underground organization it was unlikely that locals would risk massive retribution from the Japanese to aid escapees. In the Netherlands East Indies the white colonists were roundly hated by the Indonesians, who often killed escaped prisoners-of-war or internees, though a slightly better opportunity existed in occupied China, the Chinese having no love of the Japanese. The odds were still stacked in the favour of the Japanese, but a few internees did manage to escape into Free China, risking all to do so.

Rachel Bosebury recalled what happened after a group of four internee men escaped from Lunghwa Camp in 1944. American internee Kay Pait made it as far as the Nationalist capital at Chungking, and freedom. When the Japanese discovered the men missing from their block at *tenko* the next morning they interrogated a young man from the same barrack who had unwisely elected to remain behind when his comrades had broken out. 'Whenever anybody did anything wrong the Japanese shut the whole camp down,' remembered Bosebury. 'If people escaped ... we'd be confined to our room and down to one meal a day,'[2] said James Maas. The young man was grabbed by the guards. 'They started beating this man, terribly, and he ran out to this football field between D Block and H Block. They tried to catch him in the field.

It was so terrible the way the Japanese guards held onto and tried to beat him with bamboo that people poured out of my building.' Incredibly, the internees came out in force and physically stopped the guards from assaulting the prisoner any further. It was an extraordinary moment of collective defiance by the internees to Japanese authority. 'The guards stopped the beating and the internees dragged the man inside for his protection. The whole camp came out and then the Japanese got scared of so many people – they called it the Lunghwa Rebellion.'[3] The 'Rebellion' did not last for very long. 'Soon after that truckloads of armed soldiers came in, and they were on all the roofs of the buildings with guns,' recalled Bosebury, who added: 'We behaved, or else!' The unfortunate internee the guards had assaulted was taken away by the *Kempeitai* military police to one of their detention centres in Shanghai, and he was not seen alive again.

The camp commandant punished the internees for having stood up to the Japanese authorities during the so-called 'Lunghwa Rebellion'. The prisoners were no longer permitted to eat together in the mess hall, and instead 'you had to eat in your own room; if you broke any rule, the guards were allowed to beat you,' recalled Bosebury. Barricades of barbed wire were erected between the accommodation blocks at night to prevent any fraternizing between the prisoners. 'If you got anywhere close to the barbed wire, you could be hit, beaten, or killed – take your pick.'[4]

Some of the young boys in the camp were quite brave and deliberately challenged the camp rules. 'We would dare each other to run out of the front gate of the camp, cross the road and run back in again,' remembered Ronald Calder. 'I became a very good thief, too. I got caught stealing food from the home of one of the guards and was shooed away by his wife.'[5] Generally, although the Japanese guards were not averse to hitting children, they realized that such pranks were just a case of 'boys being boys', youthful high spirits, and let it go.

Taking action was always difficult for civilian internees. The draconian punishments that the Japanese handed out for even the slightest deviation from the rules effectively prevented real resistance to their regime. Most internees were cowed and frightened. Even the act of refusing to bow to the Japanese sentries, as we have seen in several accounts, would result in an immediate, and often severe, beating. Not bowing low enough could also garner the same reaction from the hyper-sensitive guards. Not turning up for *tenko* could result in a visit to the hospital once the guards had finished. However, we have also seen that some adults risked death by constructing and concealing radio receivers, while others attempted to escape. A seventeen-year-old British girl witnessed an extraordinary act of defiance which was carried out at Weihsien Camp in northern China one blazing hot summer's day.

At Weihsien, *tenko* occurred once a day, the entire camp population being divided into six groups, with a separate roll-call for each. Once a month, the whole camp of 1,500 Allied civilians was gathered together on a dusty field and carefully counted. One day when the mass *tenko* was being held, the internees stood in the usual bored, listless ranks as Japanese soldiers marched up and down the wilting lines counting and recounting for hours on end. 'Between counts – it invariably took several before they reached the correct total – the internees sat or lay down, some reading or chatting, school children playing, parents trying to amuse fractious toddlers … anything to relieve the boredom,' recalled the British teenaged prisoner who witnessed the parade. Among the huge crowd were several members of the Salvation Army, who had brought with them their instruments. They played a constant stream of band music in an attempt to entertain the internees and help the time pass more quickly. 'So it went on for a couple of hours in the intense heat, and still the numbers were not right. At last the guards realised they had not counted the internee official who was accompanying them around! So, to the great relief of all, the order to dismiss was finally given.'[6] What happened next was something on a par with the so-called 'Lunghwa Rebellion' recounted above.

> Everyone stood up, turned, and carrying their varied belong-ings, or children, surged forward, eager to leave the field and the sun. All, that is, except the Salvation Army bandsmen, who stayed to play their fellows off with cheerful music. Suddenly, with great daring, they played the National Anthem – the fifteen hundred moving internees stopped as one man, dead in their tracks. Gone was boredom, forgotten the heat and

the guards, backs were straightened, heads held high, not a muscle moved as they remembered King and Country. Standing to attention they affirmed their loyalty to all that was dear, although hundreds of miles away.[7]

The reaction of the guards was almost farcical. 'The Japanese were furious; this was something completely unexpected. They shouted orders to move, no-one even noticed. They jumped up and down with rage – everyone else stayed immobile until the last note of "God Save the King" had died away. The internees then dispersed, but with far lighter hearts and jauntier steps than before.'[8]

At Santo Tomas camp in Manila, a mutinous sense of humour was maintained by many of the inmates. Jacqueline Honnor, a British child internee, recalled one incident. 'We had a loudspeaker system for our instructions, and an American circus troupe had managed to keep a radio receiver hidden and would give us the news from this in a way that sounded perfectly innocent.' The circus folk secretly listened to their radio for any news of the progress of the fighting. 'When the island of Leyte fell [October 1944], for instance, we were told that we had to do something that day and it was "Better Leyte than never". But when the Japanese looked at the transcript, it said, "Better late than never". This roar went up through the camp'[9] Morale was maintained until close to the end of the war, through music and song. 'In the evenings, we would have singalongs and little amateur theatre groups.'[10] But no matter what the internees did to try and raise their battered spirits, hunger and disease, exacerbated by the Japanese Army's refusal to allow them to trade with the locals, meant that the final few months at Santo Tomas would prove to be extremely difficult for all concerned. 'Daily life, it was a question of *surviving* and of the children trying to learn,' said Honnor. The same could be said of any of the internment camps. As their empire imploded, the Japanese became ever more brutal in their treatment of the captives, venting their frustrations at losing the war on the helpless and the sick.

10

The Final Stretch

The trying conditions of life under internment at Batu Lintang camp tested to the limits of the human struggle for survival. Food shortages, diseases and sickness, death, forced labor, harsh treatment, and deplorable living quarters were daily occurrences in camp.

Keat Gin Ooi, 1998[1]

'Mother became very ill during the final year, suffering from dysentery and beriberi,' wrote Dutch child internee Hetty at the Tijdeng Ghetto in Java.

> Her legs were so swollen from oedema that she could no longer walk. She lay on her bed and every few hours I had to turn her over by holding her by her hip bone – there was only bone to hold like a hand grip – and pull her over to lie on the other side to prevent bed sores. Many mothers died in the camps because they gave much of their rations to their children who were always hungry. My mother did not go along with this saying that she needed to stay alive for her children so my brother and I gave part of our rations to our mother. However she weighed a mere 41 kilograms when liberated![2]

The tragedy that befell Hetty's family was repeated thousands of times throughout the Occupied Territories during the last year of the war. The military situation had radically altered for the Japanese since the heady days of victory in early 1942. The

Japanese were fighting a purely defensive war by late 1944, their supply situation was fast becoming extremely perilous in some areas and the anger and shame of being on the losing side was contributing to Japanese indifference to the sufferings of Allied civilians in their charge. Japan's attempt to invade India had been roundly defeated by British and Empire forces at the twin battles of Imphal and Kohima. The British would, in turn, invade Burma themselves in December 1944 on the back of their overwhelming victories. The Americans continued to dismantle Japan's Pacific empire, island by bloody island, edging ever closer to the ultimate prize, the Japanese Home Islands. The Allied submarine campaign had totally devastated the Japanese Merchant Marine, vastly complicating the nation's ability to supply its outlying garrisons and causing shortages of food and raw materials on the home front that seriously limited Japan's ability to continue the war. About the only aspect of the war that was still in their favour was the continued willingness of Japanese soldiers to lay down their lives for their Emperor. Fanatical and suicidal defence was slowing down the Allied advance, and also seriously worrying Allied commanders, who knew that the capture of every tiny Pacific island would result in huge casualties among the invaders as well. The prospect of taking the war all the way to the beaches of Kyushu in Japan horrified the Allied leaders, as the resultant bloodbath would have dwarfed all of the other campaigns put together. In the West, the war appeared to be entering its final stages. The British, Americans and Canadians had successfully broken out of their Normandy beachheads and recaptured France. The Battle of Monte Casino in Italy raged on, but the U-boat menace was well on the way to being defeated by superior Allied technology and weapons in the Atlantic. Nazi Germany could not last much longer, especially with the Red Army gearing up for another huge offensive on the Eastern Front that would bring its forces within striking distance of Berlin before long.

All the good news of Allied advances and victories meant little to the families that were being systematically starved and abused inside the Japanese internment camps. The piles of corpses grew ever larger as month followed month and no liberation arrived. During the last six months of the war 'about six or seven people a day died in our camp,'[3] recalled one survivor, and this was not an unusual figure. In some camps the figures topped twenty people a day. Parents struggled on simply to protect their children, for if the parents died of illness or starvation, their children would have been doomed as well. The potential fate of children ignited a grim spark of determination in parents to endure what was yet to come with fortitude. All were determined to survive the war and to keep their families intact.

In Shanghai, Rachel Bosebury, a child prisoner in Lunghwa Camp, recalled how her parents' health deteriorated as they sought to protect their children. 'My mother was quite ill with something glandular, and there was a doctor in Shanghai that could have operated on her. He wasn't part of the nations that were interned, but the Japanese wouldn't let her get that operation.' Bosebury recalled the bitterness of internment, and how it affected her parents. 'I'm sure my parents were a lot more angry, a lot more unforgiving, a lot more hating of the Japanese, even long after the war.'[4]

In the Netherlands East Indies, Paget Eames, a British child internee at Bangkinang Camp in Sumatra, recalled the deteriorating food situation in the last year of the conflict. 'Hunger was the main thing. We didn't get any Red Cross parcels. During the day we had a can of cooked rice for the adults, half for the children and virtually anything that you could grab hold of.' Formerly honest children were soon being encouraged by their parents to become thieves. 'Towards the end you were picking grass,' recalled Eames. 'When I went to work for the Japanese, tending their gardens, Mum would say, "Okay, you can steal." So I used to take back in my knickers anything that was green.' Mrs Eames worked hard to keep her children fed. 'By this time Mum was quite resourceful: she would take eggshells from the Japanese dustbins and put them on the coal fires and powder them down to make calcium for me and make me swallow it, whether I liked it or not.'[5]

The behaviour of the Japanese, Korean and Formosan guards remained fairly unpredictable, but sometimes they were kind towards the internees, particularly the little children. 'They could give you the odd sweetmeat and sometimes show you pictures of their families,' recalled Eames. 'They were especially understanding to children. Sometimes we got the impression that they were, in the main, not happy with what they were doing but had to do what they did.'[6] Kindness was not the sole preserve of the occasional guard, for the entire experience would have been utterly intolerable without the kindnesses of fellow internees. 'There was a great deal of kindness among the prisoners there,' recalled Eames of Bangkinang. 'There was very little ratting on people. You needed each other and therefore you stayed with each other. We just kept very busy. I can remember – this is very vivid – running across the camp yard just before sunset and looking at this whole camp, so much space, and very few people around. It was at that moment, in complete isolation, that I wondered, What am I doing here? What's happening? You grew up very quickly. You learnt to fight your battles very quickly. You learnt to steal and lie. You had to. You *had* to.'[7]

Another Dutch child, Rose, had been imprisoned at a camp in Bandoeng on Java for two years before she and her family were transferred to the infinitely worse surroundings of Kampong Makassar Camp for the last few months of hostilities. Her enduring memory is of the journey to the camp. 'I got a seat on the train because I could hardly walk any more,' she recalled, her health was wrecked after two years of subsisting on starvation rations at Bandoeng. 'You could not look out of the windows, but I managed to find a chink and watched violent storms accompanying the train, a whirlwind black and threatening, coming closer and closer.'[8] The storm was almost an omen for what was to follow. 'When we arrived at the camp, we had to leave our suitcases on a large field. That night a tropical storm drenched the field and the cases. In the morning the sun twinkled in the broken pieces of a red goblet. All the suitcases lay open, the contents all but destroyed.' Herded into rows of wooden huts with grass roofs, constructed upon dark red earth, the children had nothing to play with because the Japanese had ordered them to leave all of their toys behind at the other camp. But being industrious and monumentally bored, the children soon began to make toys, including 'stilts', built out of old cans with string to hold them to one's feet, and castanets made from bits of wood. The Japanese shortly after banned these harmless activities as well. At the previous camp the girls had amused themselves indoors. 'While we still had paper and crayons, we made paper dolls which were cut out and then dressed in paper clothes,' recalled Rose. 'We even made board-games, using shells or pebbles to mark our positions.'[9] All this stopped at Kampong Makassar, where the Japanese instead put the children to work catching flies. The camp was filthy, the inmates largely diseased wrecks of human beings, and legions of flies were multiplying at a prodigious rate. Fly catching would come back to haunt Rose in her later life, as well as memories of the camp's appalling sanitary arrangements. 'Going to the latrines took all your energy, especially since the whole camp seemed to be down with dysentery.' The Japanese enforced their will at Kampong Makassar as severely with the children as with the adults. 'The object-lesson of the girl who was hanged by her wrists between two trees because she had forgotten to wear her number taught us once and for all that the Japs were to be obeyed.'[10]

Nel Halberstadt, who had given birth to a daughter whilst interned at Camp Kares-e in West Java in 1942, was another Dutch civilian transferred to Kampong Makassar, which was under the command of a Japanese lieutenant named Tanaka. In total, 3,500 women and children ended up inside the camp, where conditions were actually considered to be slightly better than at the infamous Tjideng Ghetto in Batavia. The prisoners occupied 19 wooden barracks, and each adult was allotted 60 centimetres of space, and each child only 45 centimetres. At the conclusion of the morning and evening *tenko* parades, all of the women and children were required to face in the direction of Tokyo and bow deeply to the Emperor, known as performing a *keirei*. 'If you did not bow correctly, even a centimeter too high or too low, you would be beaten,' remembered Halberstadt. On one occasion, she failed to perform a *keirei* correctly. A Japanese guard immediately attacked the young woman. 'I fell to the ground when he hit me and he started to kick me in the stomach with his big, heavy boots.'[11] This assault resulted in Halberstadt being hospitalized with internal bleeding and left her with permanent damage to her stomach muscles. Kampong Makassar was a work camp. 'Everybody had to work,' recalled Halberstadt, 'outside in the fields, inside in the pigsties, kitchens, hospital or was put to work in the building group who maintained and built the barracks.'[12] Older women, such as Halberstadt's mother, were given the task of looking after the young children, while all the young women and the teenaged children were assessed for work by the Japanese. Most were declared to be fit and sent to work.

The food supplies at Kampong Makassar were as inadequate as most of the other internment camps in the Netherlands East Indies. Halberstadt, and a group of other women from her barrack, decided to ask for more food from the commandant, Lieutenant Tanaka, many of them having to feed young children as well as themselves. The reaction of Tanaka was predictably unpleasant, for he believed that his regime was essentially correct and that he was therefore infallible. 'When sixteen of us from our hut rebelled and asked for more and better quality rations,' recalled Halberstadt, 'we had our heads shaved as a humiliation and were thrown into a very small, windowless punishment hut. The following day all the food for that day was gathered up and taken to the big *tenko* field. We had to dig a large pit and throw our food in and cover it with earth.' Not satisfied with just punishing this particular barrack block, Tanaka then punished the entire camp, including all the young children and babies. 'The whole camp then was denied food for two days. The Japs also switched off the water supply where they could, 'recalled Halberstadt.[13]

Dutch child prisoner Hetty and her mother were prisoners at the Tjideng Ghetto in Batavia, ruled for the final year of the war by its lunatic commandant, Captain Kenichi Sonei. 'There was much more overcrowding and maltreatment during the last year of the war when the camp was under the brutal regime of Sonei,' remembered Hetty. 'If women refused to bow to the Japanese they were hit to the ground and often had their hair shaved off.'[14] Many of the internees who survived Tjideng recalled that Sonei's behaviour became steadily worse as the months passed, and that the moon continued to affect his mood. 'At full moon Sonei would order the whole camp – including the sick – to attend roll call where he made everyone stand at attention for him. He would then make the women and children bow down to him time upon time again. If he was not satisfied he would cut the food rations. He was a sadist . . .' But, under such circumstances, even a mentally deranged commandant had to be obeyed. There was no recourse for frightened and disgruntled prisoners to complain;

the Japanese granted full authority to prison camp commanders. The only interference in this command would be by the local field *Kempeitai* military police, and their behaviour was even more sinister than the camp guards.

At Muntok Camp on Banka Island, located south of Singapore, men, women and children from several different nationalities had been starved and cruelly treated since March 1942, when most of them had washed ashore on the island's beautiful palm-fringed beaches, shipwrecked victims of the huge exodus from Singapore during the final desperate days of British resistance. The camp was segregated by gender, and the men were mainly military prisoners-of-war. The Japanese often deliberately blurred the legal boundaries between military camps and those intended only for civilians, another good example being Batu Lintang Camp in Sarawak discussed earlier. The internees at Muntok were mainly British, Dutch, Chinese and Eurasians, and they had been joined by a party of Australian Army nursing sisters, who, like the many British civilians, were captured after their evacuation ships had been sunk. The death rate for this camp was extremely high, even by Japanese standards. A total of 33 per cent of women and children interned at Muntok perished, with the death rate for men an alarmingly high 55 per cent.

Drina Boswell had entered Muntok as a sixteen-year-old survivor of the sinking of HMS *Giang Bee*, a British evacuation ship from Singapore that had been blown out of the water by Japanese destroyers off Banka Island in February 1942. Boswell's mother was ill for most of the internment period and, as she was the eldest surviving child in the family, Drina took over responsibility for her two younger sisters and little brother. The Japanese forced her to work, so she dug and helped to fill graves, dug and helped to clean out latrines, chopped wood, tended vegetable allotments, and worked in the camp 'kitchen'. Providing food was an especially difficult and disheartening job, for as in every Japanese camp, the raw materials supplied at Muntok were almost a joke. Rice commonly contained sand and even fragments of glass, while meat, if it was distributed at all, was normally rotten. On one occasion, when the prisoners had asked the Japanese for some fresh meat, the guards had responded by throwing a live monkey into the kitchen. What vegetables that the prisoners

119

managed to grow were for the Japanese guards only and any internee who was caught taking a few green leaves was severely punished. Drina, and her younger sister Joan, did little jobs for some of the Dutch internees who wanted to avoid work and they used the small sums of money they made to buy extra food on the thriving black market. The youngest Boswell child, Maisie, attended a rudimentary school run by Dutch nuns in the camp, but at other times she just sat by her mother's bed, too frightened to leave. Drina's younger brother Kenny was forcibly removed from the women's section when he reached the age of eleven, and was sent to the men's camp. As in so many of the camps, the Japanese authorities in Muntok appeared to take a sick delight in forcing the prisoners to endure extremely long *tenko* roll-call parades twice a day, where the emaciated and ill women and children were forced to stand for hours under a blazing tropical sun. If anyone passed out, they were revived and then beaten by the guards. Drina Boswell recalled two occasions when she herself was physically assaulted by Japanese guards, once for defying one, and on another occasion for failing to bow to a guard.[15]

On 2 March 1944, the women, children and all of the civilian men were suddenly ordered to leave Muntok and travel to Palembang Internment Camp. Palembang Camp was located across the Banka Strait from Muntok on the huge island of Sumatra. It housed 250 women and children from Muntok and conditions were just as grim as those they had left behind on Banka Island. 'The small bungalow where we were to live had been stripped of almost all furniture and there was a barbed wire boundary,' wrote British Army nurse, Phyllis Briggs. One of the other nurses, Mary Jenkin, had adopted an orphaned three-year-old Russian boy named Mischa, whose parents had perished during the Singapore exodus. 'Mary, Mischa, and I were ordered to share a bedroom in house number 9 – the bedroom was already occupied by three Missionaries, two British Army wives and a fat Dutch woman with a large smelly dog which she refused to part with,' recalled Briggs. Conditions were spartan. 'The only furniture in the room was a cupboard, so we all slept on the floor. The others insisted on the door and windows being shut at night to keep out the mosquitos [sic].'[16]

Briggs spent most of her time with a group of fellow Britons in the garage of a nearby house, and only slept in no. 9 at night. Mary Jenkin took special care of Mischa, treating him like her own son. 'She made clothes for him and a little mattress out of sacking.'[17] Briggs' group constructed a fireplace out of stones and mud. 'The wood for the fire was often damp and we spent hours "fire flapping" using a piece of cardboard to try and bring up a flame.' The usual twice-daily *tenko* parades continued at Palembang. The prisoners had to line up beside the road outside their houses and be counted off by the guards. 'We had to bow to the guards as they came by. If we did not bow low enough we would get a face slap.'[18] The starvation diet was occasionally supplemented with a little meat or some duck eggs. The vegetables that the Japanese provided were usually rotten, and the rice was full of grit and weevils, a familiar story throughout the internment camps. 'The people I felt sorry for were the mothers,' recalled an Australian Army nurse, Pat Gunther, 'how do you explain to a three-year-old that there is no food? When we had a sale, a certain amount was skimmed off for the children and, although half the people in our camp died, we only lost one of the children.'[19]

In October 1944, the Japanese suddenly decided to transfer all the internees at Palembang back again to Muntok Camp on Banka Island. Transfers were terrible ordeals that often led to many unnecessary deaths, as the exhausted and sick were sent on gruelling journeys. Another group of prisoners was also transferred in from a camp at the malarial port of Bencoolen. By this stage of the war all of the internees were suffering badly from malnutrition and tropical diseases. Shortly after their arrival back at Muntok, an illness broke out and swept through the internee ranks. They named it 'Muntok fever'. With several hundred women and children crammed into a small camp and with many people also seriously ill with dysentery, the latrines were soon overflowing, open sewers that posed a serious health risk to everyone. 'There was no drainage,' recalled Briggs, 'just a large tank that rapidly filled up to almost overflowing, with huge maggots crawling about. One had to crouch on bamboo slats, a foot on each side with the foul tank below. Some of the women volunteered to clean out the tank, using buckets and emptying them outside the camp.'[20]

Fuel for cooking was a problem at Muntok and eventually the Japanese permitted small groups to forage for logs outside the camp, still under guard. The Japanese also forced the internees to dig graves for those who had died in the camp. 'Some of the stronger women and young boys became the regular grave diggers.'[21] The prisoners' bodies were literally wasting away, the camp death rate was climbing, and the prisoners' mental state was also close to collapse as the hopelessness of their situation scratched away daily at their morale.

'Whatever role people had in civilian life they took it there,' remembered British child internee Jacqueline Honnor of Santo Tomas Camp in Manila. 'We had doctors, nurses, but very little medicine, and as the war progressed, the doctors were being required to sign death certificates for people who had clearly died of malnutrition, but [they] were not allowed to put that on.'[22] By early 1945 the thousands of men, women and children being held at Santo Tomas were suffering very badly from disease and lack of food. The chance of surviving the war seemed to be slipping further out of their reach with each passing day. Unbeknown to the inmates at Santo Tomas, their camp would actually be among the first Japanese internment centres to be liberated by the advancing Allies. But Honnor's health appeared to be fading. 'Eventually I started to faint all the time, and it was discovered I had a heart murmur caused by malnutrition.' For parents, the agony of watching their children wither away was matched by the fear of dying themselves and leaving their children as orphans. 'A lot of people got beri-beri, and my parents got desperately, desperately thin, but you can be sure they gave us more food than *they* had,' said Honnor. Several diseases periodically went through the camp population. 'There was a lot of dengue fever,' recalled Honnor. 'We all got it, you just ache *screamingly* all over and get a very high fever. The desperate worry was any sort of infection. People also got TB, and there was a lot of dysentery because the conditions were really so primitive.'[23] Many people died, and it seemed to the survivors that most of the deaths were from a demographic most would assume would actually have had the best chance to survive. 'There were a lot of single people in the camp, most of them under thirty-five or forty. They died because they had nothing to live for. Not a single parent died in the camp because they *couldn't*. Their big worry was "What if we die? How do the children get back to their homeland and families?" [24]

Members of an American circus troupe imprisoned at Santo Tomas Camp had built a radio receiver earlier in the war, and then carefully concealed it from the periodic Japanese searches for contraband. It was through this illicit source that the internees first heard the news everyone had been waiting since May 1942 to hear, that American forces under the command of General Douglas MacArthur had invaded the Philippines. MacArthur, true to his promise of 'I shall return' made during the dark days of American defeat at Bataan and Corregidor had returned, in overwhelming force. Lieutenant General Walter Krueger's US 6th Army had come ashore at Lingayen Gulf on 9 January 1945 with unprecedented firepower and determination. The capital city of Manila was MacArthur's priority target, and if Manila fell, Santo Tomas would be liberated. Fortunately for MacArthur's troops, the Japanese had done very little to erect proper defences, and this allowed American forces to advance rapidly upon the city. The American columns fanned out from the beachheads and found only intact bridges and shallow rivers that proved easy to ford. Japanese resistance in the countryside was sporadic and light, but the Japanese were prepared to make the Americans fight for every inch of Manila. Manila would become the Stalingrad of the war in Asia, and the desperate fighting would threaten the lives of all of the internees at Santo Tomas who had waited so long for liberation. The hour of release from bondage could also spell their deaths, for as well as the fighting to contend with, no one knew what orders the Japanese commandant might have received from the *Kempeitai* concerning what to do with his prisoners in the event that their liberation appeared imminent.

On 3 February, elements of the US 1st Cavalry Division, under the command of Major General Verne D. Mudge, entered the northern suburbs of Manila. The 1st Cavalry rapidly seized a vital bridge across the Tuliahan River, the main water feature that separated American forces from Manila city proper. Japanese defences had been laid out to cover both sectors of the city, a demarcation line established along the Pasig River that runs through the heart of Manila. The Imperial Japanese Navy had been ordered to defend the city to the last man and the last bullet, while Lieutenant General Tomoyuki Yamashita had withdrawn most of the Imperial Army troops from the city and retreated into the mountains, where he hoped to make a strong defence from prepared positions and high ground. Under the command of Rear Admiral Sanji Iwabuchi, 20,000 Japanese sailors and some army men dug in around the city and prepared to contest every street and building with the Americans. Iwabuchi deployed 4,500 of his men north of the Pasig River and 5,000 south of it, with a further 5,000 in place to defend Fort McKinley and Nichols Field Airfield. A few thousand more naval troops were deployed on partially sunken ships in Manila Bay, and east of the city towards the main army troops under General Yamashita, maintaining a link with those Japanese dug-in in the mountains.

The Battle of Manila was one of the great street-fighting epics of the Second World War, rivalling Berlin in its ferocity and destruction. Manila, a city so beautiful that it was described as the 'Pearl of the Orient', was three hundred years old. At its centre stood the Intramuros, a collection of churches and religious build-ings forming a mini-Vatican City. By the time the fighting was over, Manila was a burning ruin. Although much of the city was reconstructed after the war, many of the original buildings are gone forever. It is no longer a beautiful city. The American drive to liberate Manila and the fierce Japanese resistance also resulted in a human tragedy on an appallingly massive scale, marked by wholesale brutality. As they began to lose the battle, the Japanese defenders took out their frustrations on the local civilian population, in an orgy of rape and murder as monstrous as that perpetrated in Nanking in 1937. Japanese troops deliberately tortured and murdered as many innocent Filipinos as they could lay their hands on. It was Manila's *Gotterdammerung* and the Japanese Navy's darkest hour of the war.

With a bridge secured over the Tuliahan River, the first American unit into the city of Manila was a squadron of Brigadier General William Chase's 8th Cavalry Brigade and they drove straight into the Santo Tomas internment camp. An American P-38 Lightning fighter-bomber had overflown the camp only a few hours before and the pilot had dropped a message to the inmates which read: 'Roll out the barrel. There'll be a hot time in the old town tonight.' For the internees, who had been living on the edge of their nerves for three years, the sounds of fighting rapidly approaching the camp would have been almost unbearable.

General Chase's men broke into the camp at 9.00 pm having fought the guards at the main gate, a Sherman tank pushing the wrought-iron gates aside as it nosed into the main courtyard with its searchlight blazing. Rapid automatic fire had cut down those Japanese who were foolish enough to try to resist the Americans. The commandant, Lieutenant Colonel Toshio Hayashi, retreated with forty-six surviving guards and a large contingent of internees, to the Education Building, where they holed up. Some Japanese were separated from Hayashi's group. The prisoners began streaming out of the buildings and shanties as American infantrymen fanned out inside the perimeter, their weapons at the ready. 'We all walked out,' recalled Lieutenant Madeleine Ullom, a US Army nurse who had been captured on Corregidor in 1942. 'The captain of the Japanese guards came out, too. He reached in his shirt pocket for a grenade. He was going to kill us all. They shot him right in the neck.'[25] Ullom may be referring to a Japanese officer who rushed out in front of the American tank brandishing a drawn sword and a pistol. He had been shot down immediately and wounded in the stomach. 'Groaning and writhing on the ground, he was seized by the legs and dragged to the main building clinic, internees kicking and spitting at him, one or two men even slashing at him with knives, and some of the women burning him with cigarettes as he was pulled past them.'[26] The Japanese officer died later in the camp infirmary, but not before receiving medical treatment from American soldiers.

And then the worst possible thing happened. With thousands of men, women and children milling around the compound, shaking American soldiers' hands, crying with thanks, or asking for food, local Japanese forces turned their guns on the camp. It was an distinctive target. Artillery fire rained down for several minutes, huge detonations scattering prisoners and liberators alike as shrapnel and debris scythed through the air. The Japanese barrage tragically killed 22 unfortunate internees at the point of their liberation, and wounded a further 39. When the firing ceased the Americans soon realized that Lieutenant Colonel Hayashi and his remaining guards still retained control of the Education Building and that they were holding hostages. Demanding that he and his men be allowed safe passage to join Japanese troops in the south of the city, to die in the defence of the city, Hayashi threatened to slaughter his hostages unless the Americans agreed to his terms. Left with no alternative, on 5 February the American commander very reluctantly agreed to Hayashi's terms and the hostages were freed. After exchanging salutes, the Japanese troops were escorted out of the main gate and through a phalanx of stony-faced American soldiers. Hayashi and his men did not last long. They went to the area around the Malacanang Palace in central Manila, which was already largely occupied by American forces, and in the resultant fighting Hayashi and many of his men were killed. The rest ended up back at Santo Tomas as prisoners-of-war themselves.

As for the freed internees at Santo Tomas, they could begin to rebuild their lives now that the worst was over. Since the camp had opened in mid-1942, a little over 10 per cent of the internee population had died, mostly from tropical diseases and mal-nutrition, both deliberately exacerbated by the indifferent Japanese. Total deaths were 466 men, women and children out of 4,255 prisoners. Although conditions for the prisoners were considerably better than the horrific conditions suffered by military prisoners-of-war taken by the Japanese, it must be remembered that the internees in Santo Tomas and in the hundreds of other camps across Asia were civilians, whose only crime was to have been living in the Far East when the Japanese invaded, and to have been citizens of nations that were at war with Japan or Nazi Germany. The Japanese treated all of them, even the smallest children, as if they were military prisoners-of-war, and ran their internment camps according to military law and military discipline that resulted in such high death rates.

Liberation may have come to the internees held in Santo Tomas Camp in Manila, but for the vast majority of Allied civilians held prisoner by the Japanese liberation was still many months away, as Japan continued to resist and their camps remained deep behind enemy lines. Only the complete capitulation of Japan would bring about the release of most civilian internees, and no one could predict how long that might take. The Allied leaders were even planning for the eventual invasion of Japan itself, and many predicted that the war in Asia would probably drag on well into 1946 before the fanatical Japanese were finally forced to submit. If the war lasted that long not many of the civilian internees would still be alive, as their food rations continued to be cut by the increasingly desperate Japanese, and disease thinned their ranks day by day. Parents continued to sacrifice themselves for the sake of their children, but how long that situation could last was anyone's guess.

In occupied China, the internees were very far behind the front-lines, deep in Japanese-controlled territory. They would be among the last to be freed. In February or March 1945, the Chisholm family was moved to Yu Yuen Road Camp in Shanghai. 'There were no toilets and trenches were dug in the ground,' recalled Moira Chisholm, who was eleven at that time and had been a prisoner since early 1942. 'We were fed on rice and cracked wheat. One time we got pork and I remember being very ill.'[27] Chisholm's father had been a prison officer before internment and he stood out among the camp's inmates. 'My father showed he was a good leader and was given the position by the other internees as a leader and had to make decisions about food distribution and other things.'[28] As with all camps throughout the Japanese system, education was not compulsory and indeed was often actively suppressed by the authorities. 'There was no schooling organized at first but later we had lessons in the morning and afternoon,' recalled Chisholm. 'The teaching was all oral as there were no books and we had to just remember things.'[29]

The internees in Shanghai were, however, much better off than their compatriots at Muntok Camp on Banka Island. In April 1945, the Japanese decided to move the prisoners yet again. By this stage, nearly all of the internees were literally on their last legs. They were to be shipped back across the Banka Strait to a camp in Sumatra, located at Loebok Linggan. The Japanese herded the emaciated prisoners on to a small cargo ship. 'We were so crowded that we could hardly move, all packed close to one another on the open deck,' recalled one internee. 'Fortunately it did not rain and we remained like this all night. We sailed at dawn and sat on the hard deck in the blazing sun with aching backs. Once more across the sea and up that wretched river.'[30] A twenty-six hour journey by ship and train proved the undoing of many of the internees.

The journey killed eight people and many others died at the new camp soon afterwards, their health finally destroyed by the constant moves.

It was not only the internees at Muntok who were moved so close to the end of hostilities. The Japanese continued to herd internees around their crumbling empire virtually to the end of the war. Johan Rijkee, along with his mother and sister, had been interned at various camps on Java since March 1942. In May 1945, they were forced to walk to a new camp, Ambarawa 8, located in central Java. There they were put to work making rope. 'However the situation became so bad food wise that not many people were able to work,' wrote Johan. 'My mother became seriously ill and had given up. My sister and I had to fend for ourselves.' In the camps on Java, the food situation became so desperate as the end of the war approached that the internees had to break camp rules just to survive. The Japanese tolerated the prisoners' illicit trading with local people, and often took part in it themselves, on an individual basis. At Macassar Kampong Camp, most of the prisoners and some of the guards were eking out an existence from the *gedek* trade, as the illicit black market was called, where fresh rations such as eggs and fat were traded through holes in the camp's perimeter fence. However, if a newcomer arrived, or if one of the Japanese wanted to cross another guard, a 'discovery' would be made and the unfortunate prisoners who were caught at the fence immediately arrested. On the night of 25 June 1945, two Dutch women were caught trading. The punishment was extensive. Firstly, the women were placed in a detention cell that measured only 2 square metres. The Japanese beat the women severely with bamboo canes and then shaved off their hair. They were forced to sleep on the bare earth without a cover or a mosquito net, even though the camp was cold at night and in the early morning hours. During *tenko* the women were paraded past the assembled prisoners, dressed only in their underwear. The Japanese then forced the women to stand next to the Indonesian guards at the entrance to the vegetable gardens where the prisoners laboured each day, wearing signs around their necks that proclaimed their 'crime'. Their rations were stopped and the women were not allowed to wash. This extraordinary 'punishment' would perhaps better be described as sadistic cruelty and it lasted for an astounding seven days. After being returned to the prisoner population, they and their families were forbidden to work on any of the extra duties, thereby preventing them from obtaining more food with which to survive.

'One morning recently I awoke and discovered to my horror that my sight had become very dim,' said nurse Hilda Bates, a civilian internee at Batu Lintang Camp in Sarawak, Borneo. 'Later I realised this was due to vitamin deficiency in our poor diet.'[31] Thirty-seven small children were housed inside the women's camp at Batu Lintang and some of the women were literally starving themselves to death in order that the children might eat and survive. In the men's camp, the mixture of army POWs and civilian men, segregated by nationality in several compounds, were suffering horrific treatment at the hands of the Japanese. Over 600 men perished before the war ended, many of them from assaults perpetrated by the mostly Korean and Formosan guards. Some of the aforementioned children's fathers were housed close by their wives and families, but they were routinely denied access to them. Hilda Bates recalled how the guards would 'punish' male prisoners for infractions of camp rules, or more usually for their own pleasure. 'Their favourite methods of punishment are either kicking below the waist with their heavy army boots, face slapping or striking the head with a rifle butt.'[32]

It is interesting to note that the commandant at Batu Lintang, and overall commander of all prison camps on the island of Borneo, Lieutenant Colonel Suga, was recalled by many of the child internees as a kind and jovial figure who distributed sweets and played with the youngsters. In contrast, he permitted his guards to continually assault prisoners, his medical officer, Lieutenant Yamamoto, to withhold life-saving drugs from the hospital, and overall allowed hundreds of men and women to die of starvation and disease. Some have explained this contradiction in the commandant's behaviour by pointing out that Suga was often absent, touring other camps, and that in his place the second-in-command, Captain Nagata, was the *de facto* commandant. Be that as it may, Suga was fully aware of what was going on in all the camps under his jurisdiction and must bear command responsibility for the appalling conditions discovered by liberating Australian forces in September 1945. Another prisoner at Batu Lintang recalled how guards would torture internees who had failed to bow to them. 'A favourite punishment was to make the offender stand in the blazing sun with his arms above his head holding a log of wood,' said E. R. Pegler. Children regularly witnessed the guards assaulting people. 'If the prisoner or his arms sagged, he was punched or kicked. This treatment usually lasted until the prisoner completely collapsed.'

The only bright spot for the tortured souls of Batu Lintang was the obviously close proximity of the Allies by early 1945. The first Allied planes that overflew the camp were American Lightnings, on the morning of 25 March 1945. They were on their way to bomb a nearby airfield. Over the following weeks there were several such raids and a lone B-17 Flying Fortress would regularly bomb targets in the nearby city of Kuching. But the initial euphoria of seeing Allied aircraft above the camp soon wore off when no liberation followed in their wake. 'As the weeks dragged by, the lone planes of the Allies were a daily occurrence and as we had realised very early that they could do nothing to help us, we hardly took any notice of them,' recalled one internee. The types of aircraft that wheeled over the camp on their way to dealing death and destruction to the local Japanese garrison only had a limited range, so at least the internees could take heart that Allied forces were at most a few hundred miles away. For many, however, a nagging suspicion lurked in their minds that the Japanese would not permit their liberation – that the Japanese would kill them all before the first Allied soldier set foot in the camp. The internees and POWs were quite correct to fear such a thing, for Suga had indeed received clear orders to institute a massacre in the event of the camp's imminent liberation.

11

The Last *Tenko*

A Farewell to Stanley! It's over.
Of Internees there isn't a sign.
They've left for Newhaven & Dover
For Hull and Newcastle-on-Tyne.

No tales where the rumours once started.
The kitchen's devoid of its queues.
The strategists all have departed
With the lies which they peddled as 'news'.

No more of the lectures on Drama
On Beavers & Badgers & Boats,
On 'Backwards through Kent on a Llama',
And 'How to raise pedigree goats'.

No more do we carry sea water
And rations are things of the past,
Farewell to the Indian Quarter
For internment is over at last.

A Farewell to Stanley
by C.J. Norman, 1945*

The flash of the atomic explosion over Hiroshima was seen by many Allied prisoners-of-war and civilian internees who were held in Japan. Most did not think much about it and soon returned

* C.J. Norman was Commissioner of Prisons in Hong Kong in the 1950s, and had spent the war in Stanley Internment Camp.

to the grim business of personal survival. But warfare had changed forever on 6 August 1945: the age of nuclear Armageddon had arrived. The decision to unleash such terrible weapons on the Japanese had not been taken lightly by President Harry S. Truman, and his military advisors. Already, massive fleets of American B-29 bombers had reduced most Japanese cities to smouldering piles of rubble and ash, but the Japanese fought on. Allied submarines had sunk virtually the entire Japanese merchant shipping fleet, causing starvation in Japan and crippling the munitions industry, but still the Japanese fought on. American forces had captured Iwo Jima and Okinawa, virtually on Japan's doorstep, and threatened to invade Kyushu in the near future, but the Japanese resolutely refused to surrender and continued to fight. Emperor Hirohito and the Imperial Family spent days on end trapped in stuffy air-raid bunkers beneath the burned-out Imperial Palace in Tokyo, like their ally Adolf Hitler in his Berlin bunker, who three months before had faced total defeat and Allied retribution. Hirohito seemingly lacked the courage or the will to surrender and spare the Japanese people any further suffering. Another A-bomb was dropped on the port city of Nagasaki on 9 August and another 40,000 civilians died, but still there was no movement from the Japanese leadership to make peace. Peace feelers had been extended, secretly, through the Soviet Union, but the talks had always stumbled when America and Britain had demanded the unconditional surrender of Japan. Incredibly, it appears from available evidence that the only thing that really concerned the Japanese government was the future status of the Emperor in a post-war Japan, certainly not the millions of soldiers and civilians who had already been killed, or the millions who might have yet perished protecting the Imperial system.

The one event that galvanized the Emperor and his government into seeking surrender terms had nothing to do with America or Britain. As far as most Japanese generals were concerned, they were happy to let the Allies try to land on the beaches of Kyushu. The resultant bloodbath, with the Americans predicting their own casualties to be in the region of one million men killed and wounded, would mean that the Allies would soon lose their stomach for the fight and would come to some sort of negotiated settlement with the Japanese government. In the end, the event that made the Japanese leaders sit up and take real notice was the sudden Soviet invasion of Manchuria and Korea that began on 8 August 1945. The weakened Japanese Kwantung Army garrisoning China was incapable of fending off the massive armoured thrusts of the Soviets, with thousands of T-34 tanks sweeping across the Manchurian steppe. Only three months before those self-same Red Army soldiers and tanks had battled their way towards the ruined Reichstag building in Berlin. The Japanese High Command had kept a weather eye on the Soviets since 1939, but the Soviet-Japanese Neutrality Pact that they had signed with Stalin in 1941 appeared to have bought the Japanese peace and security to pursue their war with America and Britain unhindered by the Russian Bear. But now Stalin, ever the gambler, saw an opportunity to snatch huge swathes of the Far East for the Soviet Union, just as his forces now controlled half of Europe following Germany's defeat. The appropriately named Operation 'Autumn Storm' allowed the Soviet leader to claim an equal share in the spoils of Far Eastern victory by steaming in at the very end of the last act with overwhelming force and brutality. Stalin's intention was to invade Japan from the north and the Japanese had nearly all of their defences facing the Americans in the south. The outcome would have been the Soviet occupation of the Japanese Home Islands and the imposition of a communist government on the country. The Emperor and the governing class would be destroyed. Autumn Storm galvanized Hirohito and the peace faction of the Japanese government into accepting Truman and Churchill's terms, and they somewhat hastily ended hostilities on 15 August 1945, just as Soviet troops were preparing to launch amphibious assaults on the northernmost Japanese Home Island of Hokkaido. The Americans at least had assured Japan that they could keep their Emperor. Japanese troops, expecting the promised fight to the death with American soldiers, were confused, shocked and demoralized by Hirohito's exhortation to them to 'bear the unbearable' and lay down their arms. Most had expected a glorious death in battle, not the ignominy of defeat. For their prisoners, military and civilian, the most dangerous time was the few days either side of the surrender, when the Japanese were at their most unpredictable.

The incredible, and to many unbelievable, news that the Japanese had surrendered on 15 August filtered slowly through to the many civilian internment camps throughout Asia. In Shanghai, Rachel Bosebury and her family could plainly see that the war was almost over in the days between the bombing of Nagasaki on 9 August and the final capitulation six days later. Silver P-51 Mustang fighter aircraft wheeled over Lunghwa Internment Camp, their engines shrieking and the sun glinting off their sleek fuselages as they shot over the buildings. 'American planes came over and did a wiggle, over our camp,' recalled Bosebury. 'It was really funny because the Japanese kept us inside our building and we weren't supposed to look out but we did.'[1] The Japanese and Korean guards ran around the camp's compound, impotently loosing off potshots at the American fighters with their rifles. Bosebury remembered how Japanese fighter aircraft vainly tried to take on the Mustangs. 'We saw some dogfights. There was some fighting that we watched over Lunghwa Airport. That was towards the last few days of the war.'[2]

On 14 August, during the daily *tenko*, the Japanese camp commandant had stood before the assembled prisoners and in a loud harangue had announced that Japan would fight on and would never surrender. He had then ordered that the internees should remain in their rooms, and not socialize between the different blocks. On the following morning, the prisoners obediently stood outside their rooms ready for counting, as they had nearly a thousand times before. The internees were by now so thoroughly institutionalized that assembling for *tenko* no longer required any orders from the Japanese. But on this morning, the guards did not appear. Some took it as an ominous sign, because for several days previously, some of the adults in the camp had been heard discussing what the Japanese planned to do with them if the war ended. The consensus was that the Japanese might very well kill all of the internees before laying down their arms. This fear was not groundless, for the Japanese had formulated plans to murder Allied prisoners-of-war and civilian internees and in some instances actually did so.

One document discovered after the Japanese surrender that pertains to plans to murder POWs and internees has provided written proof that there were elements within the Japanese government and military establishment who were prepared to commit such crimes. The document was discovered among papers inside the journal of the Taiwan prison camps' headquarters in Taipei. It was a reply from the War Ministry in Tokyo, dated 1 August 1944, to an earlier question sent by an army officer in Taiwan concerning disposing of prisoners-of-war and the reply was addressed to the general officer commanding the *Kempeitai* military police on the island. Ultimate responsibility for this illegal order lay with the Army Minister of State in August 1944, Field Marshal Hajime Sugiyama. The document is chilling proof of a diabolical plan hatched in the highest echelons of the military in Tokyo to murder tens of thousands of helpless soldiers and civilians. It sets out in plain language both the circumstances under which camp commandants could kill their prisoners, and, alarmingly, even suggested methods that could have been used to achieve the desired results. 'Although the basic aim is to act under superior orders,' reads the document, 'individual disposition [disposal of prisoners] may be made in the following circumstances: (a) When an uprising of large numbers cannot be suppressed without the use of firearms. (b) When escapees from the camp may turn to a hostile Fighting force.'[3] Both of these scenarios were very remote by August 1945, as the prisoners literally lacked the physical strength to resist the Japanese. The 'circumstances' listed in the order were merely an excuse to murder. A commandant could claim that his prisoners were trying to escape and then kill them all under the terms of this order. The order also states that although Tokyo would prefer commandants to 'act under superior orders', a huge degree of latitude has been granted, and 'individual disposition may be made ...' In other words, if an officer ordered a massacre, he was unlikely to face any disciplinary hearings based on his decision, because he was acting on authority granted to him by higher command. As to the methods to be employed, the War Ministry order was emphatic about the results required: '(a) Whether they are destroyed individually or in groups, or however it is done, with mass bombing, poisonous smoke, poisons, drowning, decapitation, or what, dispose of them as the situation dictates. (b) *In any case it is the aim not to allow the escape of a single one, to annihilate them all, and not leave any traces* [author's italics].'[4]

One case where the above order appears to have been carried out to the letter concerns what happened to ninety mainly Dutch civilians, who were last seen alive boarding a Japanese submarine at the northern Javanese port of Cheribon in July 1945. Due to missing documents, the submarine concerned has never been properly identified, but one Javanese-speaking Dutch colonist managed to live long enough to explain what had occurred to his civilian internees far out at sea. The 90 men, women and children were internees from one of the many camps the Japanese had set up throughout the Netherlands East Indies and quite why they were killed so close to the end of hostilities has never been established. No paper trail exists, any relevant documents were probably destroyed by the Japanese themselves around the time of their surrender, and no Japanese service personnel were ever placed for trial for this war crime. We can probably surmise, however, that a good reason to kill the internees was the perceived waste of precious resources and guards in looking after the civilians. The military situation was so bad that it could have led to the Japanese rationalizing such a move. Of course, such an explanation does not explain why then, if things were so bad on Java for the Japanese, did they not murder all of their civilian internees? It may be that the massacre was simply the act of a single Japanese officer who was not acting under higher orders. Java was one of several places that were threatened with invasion, and the Japanese had orders to kill prisoners if it appeared that their liberation was imminent. A general order to this effect had been issued by Vice-Minister of War Shibayama on 11 March 1945. Shibayama's order read: 'The handling of prisoners of war in these times when the state of things is becoming more and more pressing and the evils of war extend to the Imperial Dominion, Manchuria and other places, is in the enclosed summary.' The summary stated: 'The Policy: With the greatest efforts prevent the prisoners of war falling into the hands of the enemy.' Preventing prisoners and internees from falling into Allied hands by killing them was the interpretation many army and navy commanders placed on Shibayama's rather vague order.

The internees boarded the submarine and were forced, due to their large numbers, to stand on the fore- and aft-decks where sailors armed with light machine guns guarded them. The submarine cast off at dusk and headed out into the open ocean for several miles. Probably fearing that they were going to be killed by gunfire from the conning tower, the prisoners, including several children, helpless and tormented by not knowing what was to become of them, stood and waited. Suddenly, the guards disappeared inside the submarine, hatches clanged shut, and without warning the ballast tanks blew and the submarine slid below the surface, pitching all 90 terrified Westerners into the dark ocean.

Many of the internees undoubtedly perished in those first horrible minutes, drowning in the black sea. The stronger swimmers gathered together and tried to help one another, for they had no lifejackets or any way of staying afloat once their strength was exhausted. Now began a slow death. Some people tired and drowned, but a far greater menace quickly appeared on the scene, attracted by the noise and splashing of the panic-stricken men, women and children. Within perhaps half an hour of the submarine submerging, sharks began to gather at the site, first devouring the bodies of the drowned, but soon moving on to the living. As the Japanese had intended, the sharks would finish the massacre begun by the navy. Over the next few hours hundreds of sharks congregated at the scene and the still night was rent by the screaming and crying of helpless civilians being eaten alive in the inky blackness.

By daybreak only one grievously injured man was still alive and, near to death, he was discovered and rescued by a small Javanese fishing boat. The crew pulled the man into the boat. The sharks had taken one of his arms and his right foot. Bleeding to death, the man told the Javanese what the Japanese had done, and then he died. The fisherman put his remains back into the sea; not wanting to come ashore with a European body in their boat, for the Japanese would have undoubtedly also killed them to protect the secret of the massacre they had perpetrated. In August 1945 the Javanese reported what had happened to the British occupation authorities, but an investigation was impossible owing to the 'cleaning' of Japanese files by naval officers *before* they were surrendered for inspection to the Allies. Ninety men, women and children were thus erased from history.

On the island of Borneo in July 1945, the Japanese Army massacred another group of prisoners-of-war and civilian internees, including dozens of children. About 100 members of the Netherlands East Indies Army, who along with their wives and children had been captured in March 1942, had not been imprisoned and had instead been permitted some limited freedom within the town of Samarinda. The Dutch POWs had provided technical assistance to the Japanese occupiers. However, all this came to an end on the morning of 30 July 1945, when the Dutch residents were suddenly rounded up by Japanese troops and taken before a senior officer. Without preamble, the officer declared that the entire Dutch population was forthwith sentenced to death. Families stood together in shock as the realization of their imminent death sank in. Shortly afterwards the hapless Dutch nationals were forced at gunpoint into trucks and driven to a mine at Loa Kulu just outside of the town. The Japanese did not intend to give the Dutch prisoners easy or quick deaths and in fact committed one of the most bestial atrocities of the entire Pacific War. Men and women had their hands tied behind their backs. The men were forced to their knees in a tight group to watch the execution of their wives and children. The Japanese soldiers attacked the women with swords and bayonets, quite literally hacking their victims to pieces in front of their distraught husbands. Then, demonstrating just how morally bankrupt the Imperial Army had become, the younger children and babies were thrown to their deaths down a 600-foot mine shaft by Japanese soldiers. Finally, Japanese officers beheaded each of the men in turn with swords, before the remains of the men and women were pitched unceremoniously down the same mine shaft where the broken bodies of their children lay. It was only several weeks after the war was over when the remains of the bodies were discovered by Australian troops, who had captured Borneo and begun a fruitless search for its missing European residents.[5]

The internees at Lunghwa Camp in Shanghai of course knew nothing of Japanese orders to kill prisoners, or of the terrible atrocities that had recently been committed by Japanese troops in the Netherlands East Indies. But they did at least *suspect* that the Japanese might have plans to kill them all before any surrender was contemplated. References had been made to a large brick factory located down the road from the camp and many of the internees believed that the Japanese would herd them into the factory, murder them, and then dispose of their bodies inside the kilns.

'People were getting really edgy,' recalled Rachel Bosebury of the last *tenko*. 'Its 7 in the morning and nobody came, and then time went by and nobody came and pretty soon people got bold and figured if everybody left the buildings at once they couldn't kill us all at the same time.' Gingerly, the hundreds of prisoners at Lunghwa walked cautiously out into the sunshine and discovered that the compound was empty of Japanese. 'There were no guards out there, and then the internees went and formed a bunch of men who decided to check the guardhouse. Not a soul. The guards had left in the night.'[6]

Teenaged internee Heather Burch was also nonplused by the sudden disappearance of the guards at Lunghwa. 'We knew that was it, but not what to do,'[7] she said of the confusion caused among the internees by their sudden freedom after so many years of fearful captivity. 'Internment was absolutely the reverse of everything that I had ever known,' wrote the author J.G. Ballard. Although the internees were free, it would take several weeks before the camp was entirely emptied of people. In the main, families and individuals began to drift back into Shanghai without any assistance, looking for friends and relatives, homes and businesses, and trying with varying degrees of success to re-enter their pre-war lives in a city that had been profoundly altered. 'We had no transport but somehow obtained bikes and made our way back to Shanghai. I remember my first hot bath at a friend's house after the war.'[8]

At Stanley Camp in Hong Kong, Katherine Anderson, head-mistress of the camp junior school, wrote in her end-of-war report that in her opinion the experience of internment had not been completely negative regarding the children. There had been some compensation. 'Freedom from the well-meaning but unintelligent attention of amahs should have made them self-reliant and saved them from the necessity of unlearning pidgin English. Also, hardships endured and difficulties overcome may in some ways have been a fitter preparation for life in a post-war world than the somewhat pampered and often over-stimulated life of the Hong Kong child.'[9]

At Batu Lintang Camp in Sarawak on 15 August, a group of emaciated male prisoners huddled over a small, hand-built radio receiver inside one of the barrack blocks. Through crackling static, the voice of a radio announcer carefully enunciated the news they had all been waiting to hear for so many years. Radio Chungking in Free China announced the surrender of Japan. Within a few minutes, the joyful news had spread throughout the male sections of the camp by word of mouth and even though most of the prisoners were extremely emaciated and many unable to even stand, broad smiles broke out across the thin faces. The Japanese guards were confused, for they had received no such news of surrender and as far as they were concerned the war would continue. The prisoners gathered together carefully built-up supplies of food and began preparing celebratory dinners. Later that day, the Japanese had scheduled a routine visit for the married men to their families and this was how the women and children discovered that they were at last free. The only problem was the Japanese, who remained in ignorance of their Emperor's decision to capitulate.

The reason why many of the prisoners held at Batu Lintang were suspicious of Japanese intentions towards them in the few days leading up to the end of the war was the behaviour of the medical officer, Lieutenant Yamamoto. Throughout the previous three and a half years, Yamamoto had deliberately withheld life-saving medicines from the camp hospital, refused to feed sick prisoners, and even personally assaulted prisoners who had begged for medicines to be provided. One day shortly before the Japanese surrender, Yamamoto told some prisoners that they were to be moved to a camp 'equipped with the best medical equipment obtainable ... there would be no working parties and food would be plentiful ... the sick men would be especially well cared for.' Considering what the military prisoners and the internees had been through at Batu Lintang, Yamamoto's fairy tale smacked of a Japanese plot. Lieutenant Colonel Tatsuji Suga, the camp commandant, had received written orders sometime before the surrender instructing him to kill all of the prisoners, including the women and children, on 17 August 1945. Japan surrendered on 15 August, but Suga and his men would remain in control of the camp until Australian troops arrived to take over on 11 September.

Elsewhere in Borneo at Sandakan, the Japanese murdered nearly 3,000 Australian and British POWs, whom they forced on to three separate death marches, and they were still killing prisoners over a week *after* the war's end. If he had so chosen, Suga could have butchered all his charges and still had a two-week head-start on war crimes investigators. Suga's orders outlined exactly how he was to kill the prisoners. The military prisoners-of-war and all male internees were to be marched to a camp at milestone 21 and then bayoneted to death. The sick men who were unable to walk were to be placed in the camp square at Batu Lintang and bayoneted to death by their guards. Finally, and perhaps even more horrifically, the women and children were to be locked inside their barrack block and the building set on fire – they were to be burned alive. All three massacres were to be deliberately cruel.

Later, revised orders were discovered in Suga's office that ordered the execution date to be changed to 15 September 1945, and the methods to be used were also revised. This time the women and children were to be given poisoned rice. The internee men were to be shot and their bodies burned. The POWs were to be marched into the jungle, shot and then burned, and the sick and those too weak from malnutrition to join the march were to be bayoneted to death in the hospital, following which the entire camp was to be burned down to obliterate all trace of the crimes.

Fortunately for the prisoners, they harboured only ill-formed suspicions of Japanese intentions towards them, unaware of the full dastardly truth. On 16 August, three Beaufighters of the Royal Australian Air Force roared over the camp and dropped leaflets whose headline ran 'JAPAN HAS SURRENDERED' in bold type. On 19 August, more leaflets fluttered down over the camp, announcing that troops of the Australian 9th Division were close by. On 24 August, Suga finally admitted that the war was over when he formally announced that Japan had indeed surrendered. He clearly also had no intention of carrying out the execution orders that he had received, for he ordered that all work parties cease operations and that his guards immediately stop beating prisoners. Suddenly, extra food was made available, and the hospital received bed chairs and mosquito nets as well as large amounts of medicine. Whether these gestures were some eleventh-hour attempt to curry favour with the prisoners and the rapidly approaching Australians is not known, but to his credit Suga remained at his post and did not scarper into the jungle as many Japanese officers did when their day of reckoning was upon them.

On 29 August, letters were dropped on the camp instructing Suga to make contact with the Australians using a code based on panel signs laid out on the ground, and the commandant readily agreed. Suga permitted the Australians to drop supplies to the camp, which came parachuting down in huge silver canisters known as 'storpedoes' because of their resemblance to naval torpedoes. The first storpedoes floated down on Batu Lintang Camp on 30 August. 'Today a plane dropped twenty parachutes with packages attached,' recalled Hilda Bates, a British civilian nurse internee. 'One fell outside our hut and was labelled "bread". Others contained flour, tinned rabbit, and other meat. The goods were collected by the Japs under the supervision of Australian Officers [POWs] who distributed them to the groups of internees. All sorts of what we had thought of as luxuries arrived; such as sugar, sweets, milk, bundles of clothing, and even fashion books.'[10] Daily drops were made until the arrival of elements of Brigadier Thomas Eastick's Kuching Force, part of the 9th Australian Division, on 11 September.

Eastick had first taken the surrender of Major General Hiyoe Yamamura's Japanese garrison aboard the Australian warship HMAS *Kapunda*, which was moored in Kuching harbour on the morning of 11 September. Later that day occupation forces landed, accompanied by a few US Navy officers. The 9th Division troops arrived at Batu Lintang Camp in the afternoon. At 5.00 pm the entire camp was assembled on the central square, where they witnessed Colonel Suga surrender his sword to Brigadier Eastick. Immediately after the ceremony, a group of prisoners that included Australian civil servant Ivan Quartermaine, approached the liberating troops and demanded weapons. They wanted to kill those guards who had abused and murdered their fellow prisoners. The Australian soldiers reluctantly refused this request.

Colonel Suga, Captain Nagata, Lieutenant Yamamoto and many other Japanese personnel from the several camps located on Borneo were detained and transported to Labuan Island, where they would await trial as war criminals. Suga circumvented his just punishment for the Sandakan Death March, and for all the death and suffering that had occurred in the camps under his control, by cutting his own throat with a razor. His batman finished him off by beating him to death with a water canteen half filled with sand. Many now believe that Suga had deliberately disobeyed his orders to kill the prisoners and destroy the camp and had therefore saved the lives of the internees and the remaining POWs. But Suga had also done nothing to alleviate the suffering inflicted throughout the war on the POWs, male and female internees, and on the children held at Batu Lintang by his sub-ordinate officers and men. For that reason, Suga chose suicide rather than the hangman's rope. His second-in-command Captain Nagata and the homicidal medical officer Yamamoto were placed before an Australian Military Tribunal at Labuan. Found guilty of war crimes, both officers were later hanged. Around 70 of the 120 guards at Batu Lintang were convicted of lesser offences against the prisoners and many of them served time in jail.

The freed internees and military prisoners at Batu Lintang began to leave the camp on 12 September. The most seriously ill were taken to the Kuching Civil Hospital for treatment. Those up to the journey were transported by Dakota or by ship to the 2/1st Australian Casualty Clearing Station on Labuan Island, and thence home.

For those internees released from the camps in Shanghai, their pre-war world had been seriously shaken up. The International Settlement and the French Concession in Shanghai were no longer foreign enclaves – a deal had been struck with the Chinese Nationalist leader Chiang Kai-shek in 1943 that had dissolved the separate foreign parts of Shanghai and the foreigners had lost their special legal protection. Shanghai was now a fully Chinese city and everyone in it was subject to Chinese law. But it was not a stable nation, for no sooner had Japan surrendered than Chiang's Nationalists and Communist forces led by Mao Zedong had begun a bloody civil war, struggling for control of the nation. Those Westerners who tried to take up their old lives would discover that only heartache lay ahead, as the clock inexorably ran down on the foreign enterprise in mainland China. Hong Kong would be a destination for some before the Communists seized power completely in October 1949, while many former internees elected instead for repatriation to an austere post-war Britain. For many of the internee children, it would be their first experience of their motherland.

At Ambarawa 8 Camp in central Java, Johan Rijkee and his mother and sister had no knowledge of the atomic bombing of Japan. 'We did not know what was happening in the world,' Johan recalled. An inkling that something was afoot began in mid-August 1945 when the 'food situation suddenly improved and my mother pulled through.' On 22 August, the commandant addressed the camp, and gave a speech in Indonesian. 'He told us that the Emperor of Japan had pleasure in telling us that he had decided to end the war. When the gate was opened there was a crowd of Indonesian people to welcome us. I was adopted by an Indonesian couple. They gave me extra food and I could have a shower every day.'[11] Johan was also reunited with his father, an engineer working for Royal Dutch Shell who had been interned for the duration of the war in another camp on Java.

Until British troops arrived to secure the Netherlands East Indies and disarm the Japanese occupation forces, a dangerous power vacuum existed. Into this gap stepped militant Muslim Indonesian groups who were keen to exterminate the remaining Western colonists still inside the internment camps and to declare Indonesia an independent Muslim state. 'They were forcing the Indonesian population to stop helping us,' recalled Johan Rijkee. 'The nationalist groups all had their own agenda and sometimes were fighting each other. It became very dangerous to leave the camp. Many people who did were kidnapped and murdered.'[12] The British had managed to parachute a few individual officers into the camps to take over from the Japanese, but until substantial British forces were landed on Java the situation remained extremely perilous. The solution was to order the Japanese guards to protect the camps from attack. Thus, in a strange role reversal, the internees now relied on the hated Japanese to protect them from the rebels and the Japanese actually performed this task very well, earning high praise from the British military for their efforts (one Japanese officer was even awarded the Distinguished Service Order for his bravery whilst leading his men alongside British troops in battle).

The Indonesian rebels organized themselves and launched concerted attacks on seven Japanese civilian internment camps around the town of Ambarawa. Even though British forces had begun to land on Java, they were unable to supply food by road to the camps that were still packed full of desperate and starving people, because the rebels had closed down the internal transport system. The British solution was to air drop supplies by Dakota until armoured spearheads could break through the rebels and relieve the camps. On 22 November a large band of rebels managed to break into Rijkee's camp. They 'herded the camp inmates with their arms above their heads, to the central area where they started shooting and throwing hand grenades into the crowd. A lot of people were killed or wounded but miraculously my family and I survived this attack without a scratch.'[13] The inmates were saved by the sudden arrival of a British armoured column led by Gurkhas of the British Indian Army. Fierce fighting raged for two days around the camp, and Major Kido, the Japanese guard commander, and his men, fought side-by-side with the British forces. 'The British caught one attacker [who had taken part in] the atrocity. He was placed in the middle of the field with bound hands and feet, where he was kicked by the camp inmates,' wrote Rijkee. 'For days on end heavy fighting went on all around us. Next to our building a British 25-pounder gun was continually firing.' The Indonesian rebels fired back with mortars and captured Dutch 75mm field guns. 'One day we had a direct hit,' recalled Rijkee. 'The roof caved in and you could see the blue sky. Again we were lucky and were only slightly wounded.'[14] In December, the British managed to open the road to the coast and the internees were evacuated in a heavily armoured convoy to Semarang. One of the enduring memories Rijkee recounted was a wonderful Christmas party that the British and Gurkha troops organized for all the internee children, many of whom were now orphans. 'I was given a Meccano set No. 1 which was overwhelming after years of suffering,' remembered Rijkee.[15]

At Kampong Makassar Camp in Java, the Japanese did not inform the 3,500 women and children internees that the war was over until 17 August 1945, two days after Japan had surrendered. The prisoners stayed put, unsure of what to do or where to go. 'We had no courage to flee the camp,' recalled Nel Halberstadt, who had a three-year-old daughter and realized that outside the camp rival gangs of Indonesian nationalists posed just as big a threat to life as the Japanese ever had. 'One day men arrived in search of their wives and children,' recalled Halberstadt. 'Oh, what a sad sight that was, all those skeletal-like men only clothed in a "jawat" (loin cloth). In their hundreds the women and children flew towards the gate to see whether their husband or father was amongst them.' Halberstadt's young daughter ran to her mother. 'Robke, loudly shrieking, came running into the hospital. "Mama, come quick. To the gate! Otherwise all the daddies will be gone!" What did she know what a daddy was. She had so often stood in the queue when something was handed out and thought we might miss out if we weren't there quick enough. That moment I felt like crying. I told her she already had a daddy, that the man in the photograph was her daddy.'[16] There was no happy reunion for Nel Halberstadt and her husband – he had already perished inside a Japanese prisoner-of-war camp.

When the first British officers arrived to take charge of the Japanese internment camps, they were stunned by what they found. In the Netherlands East Indies, the camps resembled the recently liberated Nazi concentration camps in Europe. After visiting Tjideng, Kramat and Strimsweg Camps, one British officer, Lieutenant Colonel Read-Collins, wrote of the internees: 'Their entire existence appeared to revolve around hunger and starvation. They were so conditioned to hunger by September 1945 that when adequate supplies of food arrived the women camp leaders could hardly be persuaded to issue them. They felt that it would be rash not to hoard them against some future shortage.'[17] The tendency to hoard scraps of food was just one aspect of the psychological wound the Japanese had inflicted upon the internees. All of the prisoners had become compulsive hoarders, with an urge to acquire and possess trivial things like string, cigarette packets and cellophane paper. When the internees in the Netherlands East Indies were sent home by ship to Holland, many carried old tins with them, and during the voyage they saved every scrap or crumb of food from each meal inside these containers.

Lieutenant Colonel Read-Collins noted that most of the women internees were listless and showed little or no emotion. The children in the camps, according to this British officer, were largely the same. All had suffered from dysentery and a multitude of other tropical diseases and they were all painfully thin. 'Many of the youngest boys and girls had not seen a white man for the better part of their life. They would not have recognized their fathers,' writes Gavan Daws. 'And their fathers would not have recognized them, little boys and girls grown older but no taller, with stick legs and the distended bellies of malnutrition, hardly knowing where they were or who they were.'[18]

The very worst camp was the Tjideng Ghetto in Batavia. By July 1945, the commandant, Captain Kenichi Sonei, had over 10,000 women and children confined in an area measuring only 1,000 square yards. The Japanese had taken away all the doors and windows from the Ghetto buildings and during the stifling heat of summer the inmates had suffered terribly. Women prisoners wandered about in thin cotton dresses over their painfully emaciated bodies, or just in their underwear. All had suffered from malaria, as well as oedema caused by a poor diet, and dysentery, beriberi and malnutrition. The husbands and older boys had been separated from the women years earlier and they were discovered in an equally poor physical condition at Struiswijk Camp located inside an old prison on the edge of Batavia. Many of the husbands and fathers had also died earlier in the war when the Japanese had forced them aboard rusting steamers, the intention being to ship them to other parts of the empire as slave labour. Some of these 'Hell Ships' had fallen prey to American submarines off the coast of Sumatra.

Outside Tijdeng Ghetto, the British discovered that there was no food shortage. Investigators found only well-fed Japanese soldiers and well-fed Indonesians, so the food shortages at the camp had been deliberately engineered by Captain Sonei and his superiors in order to further punish the civilian prisoners. Lieutenant Colonel Read-Collins discovered 1,200 patients in the camp hospital, around 10 per cent of the camp population, who probably would have died had liberation been delayed a week or so longer.

The surviving Allied internees originally imprisoned at Muntok Camp on Banka Island, who had been moved several times during the last year of the war, ended up at Loembok Linggan Camp in Sumatra. Incredibly, the Japanese had continued to run the camp as if the war was still going for over a week after Japan's capitulation, and had concealed the fact that the war was over from the internees. The only concession to reality made by the Japanese had been the sudden increase in the quantity and quality of the rations they distributed to the internees through the month of August. It appears to have been a rather late attempt by the Japanese authorities to develop better relations with the prisoners. When the surrender announcement was at last made, it was the commandant himself who stood on a table and addressed the entire camp. 'The war is over,' he announced to his dumbfounded audience. 'England won. Now we all friends.'[19]

Allied troops liberated the camp a week after the commandant's announcement and they discovered that the Japanese had been hoarding Red Cross food parcels sent to the internees, as well as stockpiling life-saving medicines. The Japanese had been using this illicit supply for their own purposes, in violation of the Rules of War. Undoubtedly, this cynical exploitation of resources intended to help prisoners led to countless deaths from starvation and disease. It was a common pattern throughout the Japanese camp system across Asia – everywhere Allied investigators discovered warehouses piled high with Red Cross parcels. Drina Boswell's mother was in such a bad way that Allied doctors reckoned that she would have perished had the war lasted another week. As it was, the surviving members of the Boswell family, in common with thousands of other devastated families who had endured the camps, required immediate hospitalization due to the state of their health. The Boswells were flown to Singapore by the Royal Australian Air Force in September 1945. On arrival at the airport their plane was met by Red Cross volunteers who were eager to distribute steaming mugs of tea and slices of cake. As Drina reached for a slice of cake, a strong hand clamped down on her shoulder, and an army doctor spoke to the volunteers. 'Nothing to this plane load of passengers,' said the doctor. 'They are too ill.'[20] The Allies had learned the lessons of Bergen-Belsen and Dachau concentration camps liberated a few months before in Europe. If severely malnourished prisoners were overfed, they died. In the case of Singapore, army doctors had to be cruel to be kind and so bad was Drina Boswell's health that it took a week in hospital before she could manage to eat a whole boiled egg. Drina also suffered another bout of malaria in the hospital. For many of the rescued former internees, the horrors of the camps continued to rack their bodies in the form of disease or parasites for decades after they had left the tropics, unpleasant reminders of the whole ordeal at Japanese hands.

12

The Lost Children

The Japanese tortured, murdered, raped and killed so many people, so many people, and nobody knows about it. Nobody cares. The Japanese Government would like people to believe that the war was a figment of our imagination and if there was a war, it was our fault anyway. They're trying to whitewash the whole thing as something we dreamed up, or at worst, something we started.

Rachel Bosebury Beck
British child internee, Shanghai 1943–45

'We spent three-and-a-half years in utter hell,' said Muriel Parham, who was aged five when her family was interned in Manila and is now a spokeswoman for the Association of British Civilian Internees Far East Region. 'We were all skeletons when we came out.' Parham's mother never recovered from the experience and committed suicide in 1960. 'Nobody spoke about it after we came out,' said Parham, 'and the Japanese have never even admitted it happened.'[1]

Eileen Harris, a British Eurasian who had been eleven years old when she was interned at Changi Prison in Singapore in early 1942, emerged an emaciated teenager from the Sime Road Camp in September 1945. Her family was reunited, but 'we were too ill to start living a normal life,' she recalled. The entire family was sent to a recuperation hospital in India. After that, they spent a further year in England before returning to Singapore. Her father resumed work as a prison warder at Outram Road Prison, 'but he was far from a fit man due to his ill-treatment and the appalling hardships and privations.' Harris's mother, Clara, 'was never fully well during the whole time of her captivity, was very ill and becoming weaker ...'[2] Eileen Harris's parents both died on the same day in 1949. Her brothers and sisters were fostered out to relatives in England, and her family was scattered to the wind. This typical pattern of family break-up and physical and emotional trauma was the result of Japan's failed quest for empire, and its race war against those who fell into its hands as civilian captives.

Arie den Hollander was just four and a half years old when he was released from an internment camp on Java. The Den Hollander family, mother, father and child, arrived in the Netherlands after an extensive period of convalescence in Singapore and moved in with an aunt's family. The experience of imprisonment had estranged Den Hollander's parents and they divorced less than two years after being liberated. 'My parents had grown apart from the effects of three and a half years of brutality and starvation at the hands of the Japs,' recalled Den Hollander. 'They were no longer the same people who had fallen in love with one another some years earlier.' Den Hollander was left with relatives in Amsterdam and his father returned to military duties in Sumatra. 'I was one of many kids who had been robbed of three and a half years of childhood behind the barbed wire of prison camps, where rules were many and pleasures didn't exist,' recalled Den Hollander. [3]

> We didn't talk about that miserable time. It was not the thing to do, and the countless shocking experiences were buried in our sub-consciousness. Consequently the people in the home country were not aware of what had actually happened. A striking example was a remark made by a kind soul who had spent the war in Holland under German occupation. 'We had to make do with ersatz coffee and margarine instead of butter, and everything like meat was rationed,' she moaned. 'You were well out of it!'[4]

One of the effects of prolonged incarceration in the camps was deep psychological damage to even very young children, as

Den Hollander remarks: 'Neither could people understand why I was such a weird child: timid, scared of every aircraft flying over, speaking politely in what was not much more than a whisper and positively terrified of anything approaching violence, even among children outside. If a crust of bread was left, or crumbs fell on the table, I would eat them or put them in my pocket for later, even though I was no longer hungry.'[5] Den Hollander was still a toddler when he arrived in Amsterdam. 'I, myself, had by now recovered enough to be able to get around without my legs trembling with the effort of standing up.' Home life was strained. 'At four and a half years old I should have had the benefit of a loving relationship, but less than two years later my parents were divorced, after the unhappy marriage was "blessed" with a second child.' With his family unit unravelled in Amsterdam, young Den Hollander found it difficult to come to terms with his earliest childhood memories, which were all of the camps in Asia. 'After the separation I, together with my little baby brother, were being cared for by people in Amsterdam I hardly knew, father having been posted back to Sumatra for another turn of military duty.'[6]

Many adults who were prisoners of the Japanese when they were children have spoken about their own strange behaviour, similar to that exhibited by Arie den Hollander, after they returned to Europe or America. It was ingrained reflexive behaviour that was also commonplace among the adult prisoners, both civilians and military POWs, who were released from Japanese camps, and it had been created by habituation to a terrifyingly unpredictable regime where even tiny infractions of the rules brought on extreme violence, and by living with disease and starvation as daily bed-fellows. Today, these survivors, children and adults, would be diagnosed with a form of Post-Traumatic Stress Disorder and sent for treatment. In the immediate postwar period, psychological treatment was not even considered – people were expected to consider themselves lucky to have survived and were encouraged to bury the past and to move on with their lives. 'If a crust of bread was left, or crumbs fell on the table, I would eat them or put them in my pocket for later, even though I was no longer hungry,' are the words of Arie den Hollander as we have seen above, and this was extremely common behaviour among all released prisoners. Even among Allied soldiers who fought the Japanese in appalling jungle campaigns in Asia, many recall food shortages that have led to compulsive behaviours in later life. My paternal grandfather never leaves a scrap of food on his plate after a meal; when I asked him once why he ate absolutely everything, he recalled the dire situation for those young British soldiers operating deep in the Burmese jungle in early 1945, where, wracked by malaria and dysentery and with inadequate supplies, he and his comrades battled against fanatical Japanese troops in conditions few of us could imagine in our worst nightmares.

Arie den Hollander remembered how normal childhood desires were absent from his life. 'Toys were a wonder to me and we received a few, though for a long time I never asked for any. This was something, I felt, one didn't need.'[7] Some children were forced to confront what had happened to them more directly, as families returned to the colonies after a few years rest and recuperation in home countries, with many fathers returning to jobs that they knew and locales that they were familiar with from before the war. Arie den Hollander was seven when he was shipped back to the Netherlands East Indies. 'The lady who cared for us married my father by proxy, and we boarded a steam ship to Belawan, Sumatra, to join him. After eighteen months as a family we received news that father's new posting was to be in Holland and the three of us moved into a transition camp for a month in Semarang, from where we could be easily transported to the port as soon as a ship became available.'[8] Being back inside a 'camp' was the event that broke down young Den Hollander's fragile composure. 'It was during this month in Semarang that nightmares I had suffered with from time to time suddenly increased in frequency. My father took me to see an army psychologist, who could not provide any answers.'[9] In later life Den Hollander realized the profound significance of the Semarang camp and its relationship with his earlier experiences of internment. 'It is, in retrospect, interesting to note that the transition camp, although comfortable and with plenty of food, was surrounded by a barbed wire fence and was guarded by armed military personnel to discourage any marauding Indonesian nationalists.'

Rose, who had been a child prisoner of the Japanese at Bandoeng and Kampong Makassar Camps in the Netherlands East Indies, found herself unwillingly transported back to internment in much later life. 'I had completely forgotten about the camp, until one fine summer day, some ten years ago, I tried to persuade a fat lazy fly to leave the room by waving a newspaper at it. Instead I killed it. The horror I felt was so disproportionate that it stayed with me for days. It was only when I read a book about our particular camp and the measures which the Japs had taken when the combination of open latrines and dysentery had caused the fly population to grow alarmingly, that I understood why. Handfuls of flies had to be handed in each day.' Standing in her living room in 1995, five decades after the events that had profoundly shaped her childhood, 'the sickly sweet smell came back, too. Horror upon horror.'[10]

Not only had Arie den Hollander's parents' marriage collapsed because of internment, and his own life been scarred by his experiences as a very young prisoner, but his relationship with his father became increasingly negative. In late 1950, the Den Hollander family moved back to the Netherlands and there took up lodgings with his stepmother's sister and her husband. 'My uncoordinated awkwardness would, at times, cause problems and my father, who had been hardened and twisted by the years under the Japs, was unable to restrain himself from becoming violent towards me. This caused a bit of friction with my step auntie and uncle. When we eventually moved to a home of our own, the relationship became more strained as I grew towards puberty and it was decided that I should spent a few years with another family in another town.'[11] Arie den Hollander cut short his education and joined the merchant navy, working the North Sea coasters, and eventually he and his father became good friends.

The psychological trauma and damage caused to the children of the Japanese wartime camps is a subject which has only just begun to be seriously studied – but it demonstrates how internment shaped the lives of children unlucky enough to experience it, and how the emotional baggage of that experience remains with the survivors, now all pensioners, to this day.

13

Blood Link

Where my parents and grandparents were born has nothing to do with my Britishness, nor anyone else's.

Rebecca Neufeld, Former child internee
Lunghwa Camp, Shanghai

Some of the released internees ended up virtually penniless back in Britain after surviving the camps. Joan Bulley, four years old when her family was interned by the Japanese, recalled what happened when her mother took her children back to Britain after liberation, homeless and widowed. 'She wrote to the War Department to say she was penniless, but they did not put her in touch with any organisation which could help. She was widowed at 39, she worked until she retired, and when she went into an old people's home she had to live off income support.'[1] Bulley confirmed that the experiences of Japanese internment deeply affected the children who were thrown into the camps. 'I still suffer from depression. I think we all buried it. You were told not to talk about it, and if you did talk about it, people didn't understand.'[2]

Fifty-five years after British internees were released from the camps, the British government finally granted the survivors, many of whom had been children at the time of their captivity, a paltry compensation for their sufferings. The money had to come from the British taxpayer because none of the former Allied governments has managed to win proper and fair compensation from Japan and they never will.

The convoluted and inglorious story of individual compensation for both military prisoners and civilian internees captured by the Japanese has brought little credit to either Japan or the Allied nations that defeated her in 1945, and this stands in direct contrast to the attitude of Germany. The Germans have paid out a staggering US$45 billion in reparations to the nations and individuals affected by Hitler's empire building and the events of the Holocaust. Japan, on the other hand, though equally culpable for all the death and destruction it caused between 1937 and 1945, has not paid its victims even one tenth of the German figure. The reason why the Japanese have paid virtually nothing is political expediency and geopolitics. Even before Japan surrendered in August 1945, the attention of the Western Allies had turned to the reoccupation of lost territories and how best to counter the growing threat of the Soviet Union to the United States and Britain. This ideological conflict quickly became the paramount concern for American and British leaders as Japan's defeat became inevitable once nuclear weapons had entered the battle.

The United States recognized soon after Japan's defeat that the nation could be used as a bulwark against the spread of communism within Asia. By creating a democratic and economically strong Japan, America and its close ally Britain would checkmate Moscow's exportation of Marxism and protect the free world. It is no coincidence that this policy of creating a strong Japan was proved right within only five years of the Japanese surrender, when American and British troops were fighting in Korea. Japan was the main base for United Nations forces in Korea and a new policy of entente with the Japanese was politically desirable. Talking about 'the war' to the Japanese was actually counter-productive and was likely to erode pro-Western goodwill, just when the Americans and British desperately needed Tokyo's cooperation.

The state of war that existed between Japan and the Western Allies was formally ended with the San Francisco Treaty in 1951. The American government deliberately softened its approach to the Japanese, particularly over the issue of reparations payments to former prisoners, fearing that forcing the Japanese to pay huge sums in compensation to nations and individuals who had suffered at the hands of the Emperor's army would have seriously weakened the Japanese economy at a critical juncture. Japan's economy was just beginning to recover from the devastation wrought by the American strategic air offensive and submarine campaign, helped by massive injections of mainly American capital; jeopardizing this, as well as Japanese goodwill towards General Douglas MacArthur's Army of Occupation, was seen by many Western politicians as a negative strategy. The fear of communist encroachment appeared very real in the first few years after the Second World War, and America and Britain had watched with horror as China, formerly their wartime ally, had become a People's Republic under Mao Zedong in October 1949.

Everyone recognized that some symbolic gesture towards compensation had to be made by Japan to appease the bad press the nation was receiving in the West. The 1951 treaty did this, even as it made sure that Japan was protected from having to pay crippling reparations. The by-product of this 'softly-softly' approach was that it would later encourage successive Japanese governments, and many of its ordinary citizens, to temper their memories of Japanese wartime behaviour, and in some cases to entirely rewrite history to portray Japan as a victim of the war, rather than as a prime aggressor. It would also encourage a revisionist culture in Japan whereby wartime atrocities, such as the infamous Rape of Nanking in 1937–38, have either not been taught to successive generations of schoolchildren or, and perhaps worse, are portrayed as 'communist propaganda' emanating from China.

An important effect of the 1951 treaty was the limiting of the legal rights of former Western prisoners-of-war and civilian internees to make claims for compensation against the Japanese government. Some payments were made from seized Japanese assets shortly after the war ended, and, for example, the British government made *ex gratia* payments that totalled 1.5 million pounds to former British employees of the Shanghai and Tientsin Municipal Councils in China who had been interned. Former British POWs received a one-off payment of £76 10s to cover their entire horrific detention, worth today only about £1,200. Civilian internees had received even less, just £48 10s. Even by the living standards of the day such sums were paltry. The Americans, who led the 1951 treaty negotiations, decided that these payments would be the absolute limit of the Japanese government's responsibility to its wartime victims, and they inserted into the San Francisco Treaty the statement that 'all reparations claims of the Allied Powers, other claims of the Allied Powers, and their nationals arising out of any actions taken by Japan and its nations in the course of the prosecution of the War' be waived. In plain English, this meant that never again would Japan have to pay a penny to a single former British POW or civilian internee. The slate of Japanese responsibility was to be wiped clean at San Francisco, and the hand holding the eraser was American. There was, however, sufficient resistance to this high-handed American decision from nations such as the Netherlands and the Soviet Union, that John Foster Dulles, the American chief negotiator, drafted a new article that was inserted into the treaty to appease the outrage of many other Allied governments. Article 26 stated that 'should Japan make a peace settlement or war claims settlement with any State granting that State greater advantages than those provided by the present Treaty, those same advantages shall be extended to the parties to the present Treaty'. Article 26 has never been invoked by the American or British governments, because from the very beginning it was kept secret from the people it was meant to help – the victims of Japanese imperialism. In the case of the British government, they have always stated that the issue of compensation was settled under the 1951 *ex gratia* payments scheme, and Article 26 of the 1951 Treaty was never used on behalf of British citizens. The British government deliberately suppressed victims' access to legal compensation by hiding the files in the National Archives at Kew, under a closure order that remained in force for decades. In 1951, the Marquess of Reading, Joint Parliamentary Under-Secretary of State for Foreign Affairs, had written across the front of the secret file the following statement: 'We are at present unpopular enough with the Japanese without trying to exert further pressure which would be likely to cause the maximum of resentment for the minimum advantage.'[3]

It was only in 1998 that historians stumbled across documents at Kew that had been routinely declassified, and which provided insights into the cover-up perpetrated by Sir Winston Churchill's Conservative Government in 1951. Once the press got wind of this find, it was widely reported, and it reinvigorated veterans' efforts to apply pressure on the government of the day to reopen the case for compensation from Japan. It was embarrassing for the British government that Canada swiftly agreed to pay compensation to all its former prisoners and internees of the Japanese and this decision by a fellow Commonwealth nation added further pressure on the British to do likewise.

Led by the Royal British Legion, and the Association of British Internees Far East Region (ABCIFER), as well as gaining from some renewed public and press interest in internment, Prime Minister Tony Blair came to an agreement on compensation in November 2001. The so-called 'Debt of Honour' *ex gratia* scheme was created by the government to settle once and for all the issue of compensation. The British government agreed to pay all living former POWs and civilian internees of the Japanese, and the living spouses of those who perished in the camps, the sum of £10,000 each. This money would originate from the British taxpayer, and not from the Japanese government, prompting one former British POW and Chairman of the Japanese Labour Camp Survivor's Association, Arthur Tithrington, to remark: 'Better late than never ... The British Government has shown that it has fully understood the importance of these issues to today's society. My only disappointment is that the real culprit, that is the Japanese Government, has got away scot-free.'[4]

The British government estimated in November 2000 that 16,700 claims would be made under the scheme, including 3,700 former civilian internees or their surviving spouses. This would prove a considerable underestimation, as by February 2005, 29,288 claims had been submitted and 23,963 payments made. It was estimated that the total number of claims to be made by surviving spouses would eventually be over 15,000. Unfortunately, the scheme was not well-run from the beginning, leaving it open to legal challenges and investigations, and it was further undermined when, three weeks into the payments being made, the government suddenly introduced the 'blood link' criterion. To be eligible under the scheme, a person had to have been born in Britain, or had to have a parent or grandparent born in Britain. At a stroke, hundreds of applicants suddenly were not eligible, even though they had been imprisoned by the Japanese precisely because they were 'British'. This ruling led to legal proceedings being enacted by many of those who suddenly found themselves disqualified from the scheme. The High Court, in its ruling, expressed sympathy 'for those who were British enough to be interned by the Japanese in the Second World War because they were British citizens at the time ... but do not have a sufficient blood link connection to qualify for an ex gratia payment under the scheme.'

An investigation launched by the Parliamentary Ombudsman discovered that the payments made in the new scheme were based to a significant extent on evidence of payment of compensation made under the 1951 scheme. The Ministry of Defence, which ran the new scheme, recognized in May 2001 that eligibility for the 1951 payments had been widened during the 1950s to include persons who had been married to British citizens, wherever the spouse had been born. Therefore, in early 2001 the government had no way of knowing, without a detailed scrutiny of all the papers in each case, whether a recipient under the 1951 scheme had a blood link to Britain for the purposes of the current scheme. Eligibility for the 1951 scheme had been based on being a British national normally resident in the United Kingdom prior to internment and who had also lived in Britain *after* the war. Under the legislation then in force, however, being a 'British national' at that time and being resident in the United Kingdom, would give no indication as to whether that person had a blood link to Britain – this was not a requirement when those applications were made. Thus, eligibility for the 1951 scheme was an insufficient basis on which to assess eligibility in 2001. Blair's government had already made 14,000 payments under the new scheme, before they suddenly introduced the blood link requirement.

The whole business appeared ill-conceived and rushed. Officials had been given only two weeks to design the scheme before it was announced in the House of Commons. This did not give the government sufficient time to iron out the details properly, leading to a lack of clarity and a lot of very angry former internees. The Court of Appeal commented in its judgement that the Prime Minister had been 'unwise' to have announced the scheme 'when it was apparent that the details still had to be worked out.' It had given a misleading impression to prospective applicants, because at the time no mention was made of any blood link criterion. The Parliamentary Ombudsman considered this lack of clarity to 'signal a departure from standards of good administration to the extent that it constitutes maladministration.'[5] The Court of Appeal said that the ministerial announcement 'was less clear than it should have been' and 'many civilians had their hopes of compensation raised by Dr. Moonie's announcement' only to be 'extremely disappointed, and indeed angered.'[6]

The conclusion of the Parliamentary Ombudsman was scathing. He stated that the way in which the scheme had been devised, announced and operated constituted maladministration. He also concluded that the scheme constituted an injustice to the survivors of Japanese prison camps, based on his examination of several cases where applicants who had devoted their lives to the service of the United Kingdom had been refused compensation based on the blood link criterion. For example, there was Squadron Leader 'X', who had been repatriated to Britain shortly after the war as a civilian internee and had then been conscripted for National Service in the RAF. He had pursued a permanent career in the RAF, and retired at fifty-five years of age. Also, Doctor 'Y', who had spent his whole life following his internment by the Japanese working at the government's Royal Aircraft Establishment at Farnborough, and had been elected a Fellow of the Royal Society. 'These are people who have given public service to the UK,' commented the Ombudsman in his report to Parliament in 2005. 'Many others who are ineligible under the clarified terms of the scheme can also demonstrate a close link with the UK: by having taken up UK citizenship, through long residence here, or by having brought up a family here.'[7]

Another pertinent example of the way in which the blood link criterion has caused an injustice is the case of Diana Elias. She came from a very prominent Iraqi-Jewish family famous as traders in the Far East and her father was a close friend of Sir Victor Sassoon, whose enduring legacy of fine buildings can be seen throughout Shanghai and whose company, Sassoon's, was one of the leading foreign-owned businesses operating in China before the war. Elias's father was also friendly with the fabulously wealthy Kadoorie clan, a family that still owns the famous Peninsula Hotel in Hong Kong. Elias's father and grandfather held British citizenship, as did Diana herself, though none of them had been born within the United Kingdom. Diana Elias, aged seventeen when the war in Asia started, along with her entire family, were judged British enough to be roused from their beds one night in December 1941 by bayonet-toting Japanese soldiers and sent to Stanley Internment Camp in Hong Kong for the duration of the war. The MOD, based on the fact that only those who had at least one parent or grandparent born in Britain would be deemed eligible, ruled that Diana Elias was not British enough to be compensated. In response, she launched a legal action against the British government. 'I do feel bitter about my treatment by the British government,' said the 83-year old in an interview in 2006. 'It has taken six years for me to prove that I was not a second-class British citizen, yet I have still not even received so much as the courtesy of a written apology.'[8] The Elias family, no matter how wealthy they may have been before the war, nonetheless had their lives shattered by the experience of Japanese internment. 'My mother had a nervous breakdown and was never the same again,' said Diana Elias. 'She just could not cope with the stress of trying to fend for her children. My father spent much of the time in hospital with dropsy, beriberi, typhoid and diphtheria.'[9] Elias's father died soon after liberation, aboard a hospital ship that was steaming its way to Australia.

The blood link criterion has been a particularly misguided piece of legislation, for it ignores the basic realities of Britain during the Second World War. The size of the British Empire meant that in some cases whole generations of British citizens were born, lived and died outside of the mother country, in colonies like Hong Kong or Singapore. It did not mean that these expatriate Britons felt any less 'British' than their compatriots who lived in London or Manchester, and in many cases the opposite was true. 'We had pictures of the King and Queen on the wall and we were all very conscious of the fact that we were British and proud of it.'[10]

Rebecca Neufeld emerged from Lunghwa Internment Camp in Shanghai aged six, after she and her family had been incarcerated for the duration by the Japanese. She possessed a British birth certificate that had been issued by the Consul-General in Shanghai in 1938. Her father was a British citizen, but he had been born in Bombay in India. Her mother was Russian. Neufeld's paternal grandfather was also British, though he had been born in Baghdad in Iraq. The family moved to Britain in 1949, after the communist takeover of China. Her family history was typical of many 'British' families living in Shanghai before the war, where residence in the United Kingdom had not occurred, but citizenship had been proudly maintained. In a similar case to Diana Elias, Rebecca Neufeld found herself ineligible for compensation in 2001, deemed not 'British' enough under the blood link regulations. 'How British do I have to be?' asked the 62-year-old Neufeld in 2001. 'I have lived in Britain for 52 years, paid taxes to the state all my working life. My husband was born and bred in London and I have lived in London since I got off the boat from Shanghai.' An angry Neufeld echoed the sentiments of many other former internees, a considerable number of whom were children during their confinement, when she commented: 'We were in Lunghwa precisely because we were British ... Where my parents and grandparents were born has nothing to do with my Britishness, nor anyone else's.'[11]

The courts in England ruled that the actions of the Blair government were incorrect. In 2006, the Court of Appeal in London ruled in favour of Diana Elias's case, undermining the government's position. Lord Justice Mummery said that the MOD's actions were in breach of Section 41 of the Race Relations Act. 'For those concerned with sound standards of administration, prudence in the handling of taxpayers' money and State compliance with principles of equal and fair treatment of individuals, some aspects of this affair are troubling.'[12] Lord Justice Mummery continued: 'The result of inadequate preparation has been an embarrassing administration and legal muddle, personal pain, charges of incompetence, costly litigation and political apologies, accompanied by inquiries, investigations, reports, hearings and reviews.'[13] Mummery awarded £3,000 compensation to Elias, and although initially the government rejected the court's ruling and appealed against the decision, ministers eventually realized that they had to change the blood link criterion. In 2006, the MOD duly abandoned the blood link rule, and replaced it with a rule that said that only applicants who had been resident in the United Kingdom for 20 years would be eligible for compensation under the scheme. This change, although it allowed many applications to be processed and compensation paid out to thousands more people who would otherwise have been denied anything, has not resulted in a complete resolution of the issue. Hundreds of people interned as 'British' by the Japanese still do not qualify for compensation under the new 20-year residence rule because they moved to other settler colonies, like Canada and Australia, after the war. It is expected that further costly legal actions and campaigns by veterans' groups are likely to attempt to create full equality in the scheme.

So far, the scheme has cost the public finances over 250 million pounds – and the Japan government not a single yen. British taxpayers have, in effect, been paying for Japanese aggression and war crimes, while the British government's main priorities regarding Japan include not antagonizing a country whose businesses employ so many people throughout the United Kingdom. In much the same way that geopolitical and economic concerns prevented the victorious Allied powers from properly punishing the Japanese for their conduct when the war ended in 1945, so the means taken to resolve the compensation issue now appear to be designed to appease Japan, rather than force it to face up to its global responsibilities in a manner similar to that of postwar Germany.

Appendix A

Chronology of the Asia-Pacific War

1936
25 November   Japan signs the Anti-Comintern Pact with Germany

1937
7 July   Japan invades China
13 December   Start of the 'Rape of Nanking'

1939
May–August   Japanese and Soviet forces fight the Battle of Nomonhan on the Manchurian-Mongolian border and Japan is defeated
1 September   **Germany invades Poland**
3 September   **France, Britain and the Commonwealth declares war on Germany**

1940
22 June   **France falls to the Germans**
Japan invades and occupies French Indochina
26 June   United States places an embargo on iron and steel imports to Japan
27 September   Japan signs the Tripartite Pact with Germany and Italy

1941
10 January   Thailand invades French Indochina
22 June   **Germany invades the Soviet Union**

26 July	United States places an oil embargo on Japan
7 December	Japanese bomb Pearl Harbor, Wake Island, Midway Island and the Philippines
8 December	Japanese invade British Malaya, Thailand and Hong Kong
9 December	China declares war on the Axis Powers
10 December	Japan sinks the British capital ships HMS *Prince of Wales* and HMS *Repulse* off Malaya and begins landings on the Philippines
14 December	Japan invades Burma
16 December	Japan invades Borneo
20 December	Japan attacks the Netherlands East Indies
24 December	Japan occupies Wake Island after a bitter battle with US forces
25 December	Hong Kong surrenders to the Japanese

1942

3 February	Japanese forces begin landing in the Netherlands East Indies Japanese aircraft attack Port Moresby, New Guinea
15 February	British forces surrender to the Japanese in Singapore Japanese aircraft attack Darwin in Australia
27 February	Japanese Navy wins the Battle of the Java Sea
8 March	Japanese invade New Guinea
6 April	Japanese invade the Admiralty and British Solomon Islands
9 April	US forces in the Bataan Peninsula, Philippines, surrender to the Japanese
18 April	The Doolittle Raid is launched on Tokyo
1 May	Japanese forces capture Mandalay, Burma
6 May	US forces on Corregidor Island, Philippines, surrender to the Japanese
7 May	Battle of the Coral Sea
23 May	British withdrawal from Burma completed
4 June	Japanese attack Midway Island
6 June	Japanese invade the Aleutian Islands US Navy is victorious at The Battle of Midway

7 August	US forces land on Guadalcanal in the British Solomon Islands
9 August	Japanese Navy victorious at the Battle of Savo Island
12 August	Japanese land at Buna, New Guinea
18 September	Australian forces begin advancing down the Kokoda Trail, New Guinea
11–12 October	Japanese Navy defeated at the Battle of Cape Esperance
17 October	British forces advance into the Arakan, Burma
26 October	Japanese Navy victorious at the Battle of Santa Cruz

1943
2 February	**Soviet Union wins the Battle of Stalingrad**
13 February	British launch the first Chindit expedition into Burma
2 March	Battle of the Bismarck Sea
20 June	US forces invade New Georgia
3 September	**Allied forces land in Italy**
20 November	US forces land on Tarawa

1944
31 January	US forces land in the Marshall Islands
2 March	British launch second Chindit expedition into Burma
15 March	Japanese invade India at Imphal and Kohima
22 April	US forces land at Hollandia, New Guinea
31 May	Japanese begin withdrawing from Kohima
4 June	**Allied forces capture Rome**
6 June	**D-Day landings in Normandy, France**
15 June	US forces land on Saipan
19 June	Commencement of the Battle of the Philippine Sea
18 July	Japanese forces begin withdrawing from Imphal
15 September	US forces land on Peleliu
20 October	US forces land on Leyte, Philippines
24–25 October	Battle of Leyte Gulf
December	British 14th Army enters Burma

1945

9 January	US forces land on Luzon, Philippines
11 January	British forces cross the Irrawaddy River, Burma
19 February	US forces land on Iwo Jima
2 March	British forces capture Meiktila, Burma
20 March	British forces capture Mandalay, Burma
1 April	US forces land on Okinawa
12 April	**President Roosevelt dies**
30 April	**Hitler dies in Berlin**
3 May	British forces enter Rangoon, Burma
8 May	**Germany surrenders**
26 July	**Churchill resigns as British Prime Minister**
6 August	Atomic bomb dropped on Hiroshima, Japan
8 August	Soviet Union declares war on Japan and invades Manchuria
9 August	Atomic bomb dropped on Nagasaki, Japan
15 August	Japan announces its surrender
26 August	Soviet invasion of Manchuria complete
2 September	Formal surrender of Japan

Appendix B

Asia: Then and Now

Former Name	Present Name
Batavia	Jakarta
Chapei (Shanghai district)	Zhabei
Chungking	Chongqing
Lunghwa (Shanghai district)	Longhua
Netherlands East Indies	Indonesia
Nanking	Nanjing
Peking	Beijing
Pootung (Shanghai district)	Pudong
Tientsin	Tianjin
Weihsien	Weifang

Appendix C

British and Commonwealth Dead Shanghai and Yangzhou 1941–45

As an example of the suffering inflicted upon Allied civilians who were interned by the Japanese in Asia during the Second World War, detailed below is a list of British and Commonwealth citizens who perished in Shanghai. The city of Shanghai is an excellent example of the experience of internment, boasting as it did a large pre-war expatriate community, who were sent to a large number of internment camps by the Japanese. Throughout China (and excluding Hong Kong), about 1,500 children under the age of sixteen were interned by the Japanese during the war. Reading the list indicates the diverse nature of those who were interned, their ages, occupations and camps. Thousands more perished in other areas of China, Hong Kong, the Netherlands East Indies and Japan, and the names listed below are but an example of the fate of Allied civilian men, women and children all across Asia. Notice how few children perished in the Shanghai camps (highlighted in bold), testament to J.G. Ballard's comment that 'our parents starved themselves for us.'

British Citizens
1. ABRAHAM, Civilian, DAVID EZEKIEL JOSHUA. Age 80. 27 May 1945. Husband of Moselle Abraham, of 310 Avenue Foch, Shanghai. Died at Lincoln Avenue Internment Camp, Shanghai.

APPENDIX C

2. ABRAHAM, Civilian, JULIAN. Age 66. 31 March 1945. Died at Lincoln Avenue Internment Camp, Shanghai.
3. ACKERMAN, Civilian, ELIZABETH. Age 56. 20 September 1943 at Lunghwa Internment Camp, Shanghai.
4. AIERS, Civilian, MAGGI. Age 59. 19 January 1945, Died at Lincoln Avenue Internment Camp, Shanghai.
5. ASHDOWNE, Civilian, WALLACE CHARLES GEORGE, Dr. Age 79. 13 August 1944. Died at Yangchow C Internment Camp, Yangzhou.
6. AUSTIN, Civilian, PERCY JOHN. 9 May 1945. Age 48. Son of Frank Thomas Austin and Charlotte Austin, of 1 Palamos Road, Leyton, Essex; husband of Winifred Austin, of Thanes, Brands Hill Avenue, High Wycombe, Buckinghamshire. Died at Haiphong Road Internment Camp.
7. BAKER, Sister, GERTRUDE. Age 66. 7 July 1943 at St. Joseph's Hospital, Shanghai.
8. BALL, Civilian, ESTHER MARIE. Age 34. 10 September 1944. Wife of James Ball, of 35 Duke Street, Wigan, Lancashire. Died at Country Hospital, Shanghai.
9. BARRY, Civilian, JAMES JOSEPH, M.M. 7 March 1943. Age 47. Superintendent, Shanghai Municipal Police. Son of John and Mary Barry, of Ballyman, Co. Dublin, Republic of Ireland; husband of Margaret C. Barry, of Shanganagh, Shankill, Co. Dublin, Republic of Ireland. Died at Shanghai Police Hospital.
10. **De Sa HOPE**, Civilian, **Sheila May**, 1943, age 2. Daughter of G.B. de sa Hope. Died at Ash Camp.
11. BELL, Civilian, LAWSON. 10 March 1943. Husband of Mary C. Bell, of 49 Kingwailing Road, Glasgow. Died at Shanghai Police Hospital.
12. BLANCKENSEE, Civilian, ALFRED STEPHEN. 17 August 1945.Age 68. Son of the late Aaron and Elizabeth Blanckensee husband of Gen Blanckensee, of 24 Kwen Ming Lee, 941 Dixwell Road, Shanghai. Died at St. Luke's Hospital, Shanghai.
13. BLANDFORD, Civilian, EDWARD JOHN, age 83. March 1943, Chapei Camp.
14. BOURNE, Civilian, MARGARET HELENA. Age 63. 4 December 1944. Wife of H. L. Bourne. Died at Lunghwa Internment Camp.

15. BOYES, Civilian, GEORGE MASON. Age 68. 28 August 1943. Died at Yangchow A Internment Camp, Yangzhou.
16. BROOMFIELD, Civilian, GEORGE. 23 December 1944. Age 51. Shanghai.
17. BROWN, Civilian, ANNIE. Age 55. 11 February 1945 at Shanghai General Hospital.
18. BROWN, Civilian, THOMAS. 21 May 1945. Age 62. Died at Great Western Road Camp, Shanghai.
19. BRUCE, Civilian, WILLIAM PETER. Age 53. 30 December 1944. Husband of Edith Augusta Bruce, of 9 Grove Avenue, York Road, Doncaster, Yorkshire. Died at Shanghai General Hospital.
20. BURNS, Civilian, NORMAN. 26 September 1943. Age 39. A.M.I.E.E. Son of Mary Jane Burns, of Fairmont, Butts, Stanhope, Bishop Auckland, Co. Durham, and of the late Jacob Burns; husband of Margaret Burns, of 7 Claremont South Avenue, Gateshead, Co. Durham. Died at Pudong Internment Camp.
21. BUTTERFIELD, Civilian, SHEILA KATHLEEN MARY. 5 October 1943. Age 32 of Hankow Club, Hankow (Hankou). Daughter of W. G. Hare, of 154 Penstone Road, Waterloo, Huddersfield, Yorkshire; wife of Henry Samuel Butterfield. Died at Yu Yuen Road Internment Camp, Shanghai.
22. BYRNE, Civilian, ERNEST GODFREY. Age 68. 10 June 1943. Husband of S. M. K. Byrne. Died at Country Hospital, Shanghai.
23. CHAMBERLAIN, Civilian, LILIAN MABEL. 30 August 1943. Age 56 of 60 New Street, Castle Bromwich, Birmingham. Daughter of Mabel Brazier, of 1355 Stratford Road, Hall Green, Birmingham; wife of A. H. Chamberlain. Died at Country Sanatorium, Shanghai.
24. COOK, Civilian, JOHN ALEXANDER. Retired Shanghai Municipal Police Officer. Age 71. Died 8 February 1944 at Shanghai Police Hospital.
25. COVENEY, Civilian, ALEXANDER HENRY. 17 September 1944 at Isolation Hospital, Shanghai.
26. CRAFTER, Chief Engineer Officer, EARNEST RICHARD, S.S. Marie Moller (Shanghai), Merchant Navy, 1 July 1943, aged 64. Son of Richard Andrew Crafter, O.B.E., and Catherine

Crafter; husband of Lily Mary Crafter, of Lancaster. Died at Shanghai.

27. CUMMING, Civilian, KENNETH MENZIES. 26 November 1944. Age 57 of Shanghai. Died at Shanghai General Hospital.

28. DAVID, Civilian, HABABA SHALONE. Age 82. 19 July 1945 at St. Luke's Hospital, Shanghai.

29. DAVIDSON, Civilian, A R. 15 September 1943. Shanghai.

30. DAVISON, Civilian, LEA AUGUSTA. 3 November 1944. Age 33. Wife of William R. Davison. Died at Shanghai General Hospital.

31. DAVIES, Civilian, HENRY WILLIAM. Age 63. 13 December 1943. Husband of L.M. Davies. Died at Shanghai General Hospital.

32. DAWSON, Civilian, ADELAIDE BLANCHE. 15 September 1943. Age 78 at Shanghai General Hospital.

33. DUNBAR, Stoker 1st Class, JAMES (C/KX 87890), HMS *Peterel*, Royal Navy, died 11 December 1941, Shanghai.

34. DUNCAN, Civilian, ANNIE MCBEAN LOW. Age 42. 16 September 1945. Wife of George Duncan. Died at Shanghai General Hospital.

35. DUNSTAN, Civilian, MABEL CORNELIA. 21 March 1945. Age 56 of Shanghai. Died at St. Luke's Hospital, Shanghai.

36. EABRY, Civilian, ERNEST JOHN, aged 54. 22 May 1945 at St. Luke's Hospital, Shanghai.

37. ENGLEY, Civilian, ERNEST RICHARD. Age 59. 14 October 1944 at Shanghai Isolation Hospital.

38. ETHERINGTON, Civilian, JOSEPH BURTON. 11 February 1943. Age 52 of 52a Tynsin Road. Son of the late L. and R. Etherington; husband of Marjorie Etherington. Died at Japanese *Kempeitai* Military Police Headquarters, Jessfield Road, Shanghai.

39. FABIAN, Civilian, SYDNEY PHILIP. Age 69. 10 January 1945. Husband of A. N. Fabian, of 59 Edinburgh Road, Shanghai. Died at Lunghwa Internment Camp, Shanghai

40. FINCH, Civilian, GEORGE THOMAS. 28 January 1945. Age 71. Husband of Marie Bennett Finch. Died at Shanghai General Hospital.

41. FLEMING, Civilian, DOUGLAS. 30 November 1942. Age 63 of 961 Avenue Foch, Shanghai. Son of the late Richard and

Louise Fleming, of 98 Mundania Road, Honor Oak, London; husband of Amy Julia (Doree) Fleming. Died at Shanghai General Hospital.

42. **FOX**, Civilian, **CHRISTOPHER DAVID EDWARDS**. 7 July 1943. Aged 6 months. Son of Samuel John Henry and Rosemary Edwards Fox, of 400 Avenue Haig, Apartment 33, Shanghai. Died at Shanghai General Hospital.

43. FOX, Civilian, ELIZABETH MARY. 11 July 1945. Aged 10 months. Daughter of Samuel John Henry and Rosemary Edwards Fox, of 400 Avenue Haig, Apartment 33, Shanghai. Died at Shanghai General Hospital.

44. **FRANCIS**, Civilian, **MARGARET HEATHER**. 20 June 1945. Aged 1 month. Daughter of Mr. and Mrs. Robert Francis. Died at Shanghai General Hospital.

45. FROST, Civilian, JOE. Age 68. 30 July 1945 at Lunghwa Internment Camp, Shanghai.

46. GIBSON, Civilian, MAY VICTORIA KATHERINE. Age 66. 11 February 1944 at Country Sanatorium, Shanghai.

47. GOULBOURN, Civilian, WILLIAM HENRY. Age 61. 8 October 1943. Husband of A. M. Goulbourn. Died at Yu Yuen Road Internment Camp, Shanghai.

48. GREENFIELD, Civilian, JAMES ALBERT. 10 September 1944. Age 58. Husband of E. Greenfield. Died at Shanghai General Hospital.

49. HAMMOND, Civilian, WILLIAM. Age 77. 1 May 1945. Died at Lincoln Avenue Internment Camp, Shanghai.

50. HANSON-KAHN, Civilian, JOSEPH. 19 June 1944. Age 47. Son of A. Hanson-Kahn; husband of Susan Hanson-Kahn, of 21 Harbin Road, Shanghai. Died at Country Hospital, Shanghai.

51. HARRAP, Civilian, LESLIE AUSTIN. 19 October 1945. Age 55 of 512 Embankment Buildings, Shanghai. Son of Charles and Elizabeth Harrap, of 33 Engayne Gardens, Upminster, Essex; husband of Mary Louise Harrap. Injured August 1943, in Yangchow C.A.C.; died at Chapei Internment Camp, Shanghai.

52. HARRIS, Civilian, ELSIE MILDRED. 31 December 1943. Age 48. Wife of F. D. Harris. Died at Shanghai Isolation Hospital.

53. HARTOPP, Civilian, EDWARD LIDDELL. 16 October 1942. Husband of Emmy Hildred Charlotte Elizabeth Hartopp. Died at Country Hospital, Shanghai.
54. HICKEY, Civilian, ARTHUR WILSON. Age 65. 1 July 1944. Died at Lincoln Avenue Internment Camp, Shanghai.
55. HOLTAM, Civilian, SIDNEY HARRY. 8 July 1943. Age 34. Sub-Inspector of Shanghai Municipal Police. Son of Sydney Harry Holtam, of Tonyrefail, Glamorgan; husband of Galina Holtam, of 65 Great West Road, Shanghai. Died at Shanghai Isolation Hospital.
56. HOPE, Civilian, RICHARD IRVING. 12 November 1942. Age 43 of Shanghai. Husband of Sonia Hope. Died at Country Hospital, Shanghai.
57. HUBER, Civilian, MARTHA HELEN. Age 65. 1 September 1944 at Lunghwa Internment Camp, Shanghai.
58. HUNTER, Civilian, JACK LEICESTER. 17 August 1945. Age 49 of 532 Avenue Haig, Shanghai. Son of the late Leonard and Jeanette Hunter, of 153 Burton Road, West Didsbury, Lancashire; husband of Helen Margaret Hunter. Died at Shanghai.
59. HUTCHISON, Civilian, VERA. Age 71. 25 June 1945 at St. Luke's Hospital, Shanghai.
60. HUTTON, Civilian, WILLIAM. 15 August 1943. Age 43. Chief Inspector of Detectives in Shanghai Municipal Police. Son of William and Elizabeth Hutton, of 24 Abbot Street, Craigie, Perth, Scotland; husband of Anna Hutton, of 310 Carlton Apartments, 65 Park Road, Shanghai. Died under torture, *Kempeitai* Military Police Office, Jessfield Road, Shanghai.
61. HUXLEY, Civilian, GRACE STELLA. Age 49. 17 March 1944 at Lunghwa Internment Camp, Shanghai.
62. INCH, Captain, JAMES EDWIN. Pilot. Age 74. 2 November 1944 at Shanghai General Hospital.
63. INCH, Civilian, T. 10 April 1944. Shanghai.
64. JEUNE, Captain, FRANCIS HERBERT. Ship's Pilot. Age 62. Died 22 June 1945. Husband of C. M. Jeune. Died at Shanghai Police Hospital.
65. JOHNSTON, Civilian, ELIZABETH HENRIETTA. 9 October 1944. Age 76. Daughter of Mr. and Mrs. James Johnston, of

Dumfries, Scotland. Died at Lincoln Avenue Internment Camp, Shanghai.

66. JOHNSTON, Civilian, MATTHEW. Age 29. Died 8 November 1944 at Yu Yuen Road Internment Camp, Shanghai.
67. JONES, Civilian, RUTH. 20 June 1945. Age 57. Wife of Robert Ernest Jones, of 5 Widcombe Crescent, Bath, Somerset. Died at Lincoln Avenue Internment Camp, Shanghai.
68. KALE, Civilian, EWART. Age 65. 20 September 1943. Died at Yangchow C Internment Camp, Yangzhou.
69. LEDBURY, Civilian, JOSEPH THOMAS. Age 68. 19 February 1945. Died at Lincoln Avenue Internment Camp, Shanghai.
70. LEE, Civilian, MARY JANE ELIZABETH. 19 November 1943. Age 56. Died at Shanghai General Hospital.
71. LIVESSEY, Civilian, LUCY. Age 56. 22 September 1945. Died at Lincoln Avenue Internment Camp, Shanghai.
72. LOWRY, Civilian, HENRY WILLIAM. Age 55. 21 March 1945. Husband of T. N. Lowry, of 148 Avenue du Roi Albert, Shanghai. Died at Pudong Internment Camp, Shanghai.
73. MACDONALD, Civilian, RANALD GEORGE. Age 61. 13 September 1943. Died at Yangchow A Internment Camp, Yangzhou.
74. MACKENZIE, Civilian, Albert Raymond, age 23. Killed 8 November 1943, Wayside, Shanghai from Ash Camp.
75. MANLEY, Civilian, GEOFFREY RONALD. Age 18. 3 September 1945. Died at Yangchow C Internment Camp, Yangzhou.
76. MARR, Civilian, ADA MAUDE. 9 February 1945. Age 50. Wife of F. B. Marr, of 374 Kiangse Road, Apartment 44, Shanghai. Died at Great Western Road Camp, Shanghai.
77. MASON, Master, CECIL, S.S. Kathleen Moller (Shanghai), Merchant Navy. Died 3 June 1944, age 56. Son of William James Mason and Jessie Mason, of Liverpool; husband of Florence Mason, of Great Crosby, Liverpool. Died at Shanghai.
78. McDONALD, Civilian, RONALD GEORGE. Husband of M. McDonald, of 301 Route Cohen, Shanghai.
79. McKEE, Civilian, JOHN MATTHEWS. 23 August 1944. Husband of A. M. McKee, of 148 Route Amiral Courbet, Shanghai. Age 59. Died at Shanghai General Hospital.

Appendix C

80. McTAVISH, Civilian, JANET. 3 May 1945. Age 67. Daughter of the late Mr. and Mrs. Archibald McTavish, of Whitehouse, Tarbert, Argyllshire. Died at Lunghwa Internment Camp, Shanghai.
81. MELLIN, Civilian, GRAHAM MURRAY. 9 January 1945. Age 34. Son of G. L. Mellin, of 87 Calton Avenue, Dulwich, London, and of the late Madge Marion Mellin. Died at Shanghai General Hospital.
82. MENNIE, Civilian, DONALD. Age 60. 10 January 1944 at Country Sanatorium, Shanghai.
83. MERECKI, Civilian, HARRY ALBERT. 24 September 1945. Age 70. Son of Jan and Rebecca Merecki; husband of Martha Merecki, of 10 Millicent Road, West Bridgford, Nottingham. Died at St. Marie Hospital, Shanghai.
84. MILES, Civilian, ALFRED JOHN. 28 March 1945. Age 17. Son of Robert Henry and Sarah Miles, of 35 Overchurch Road, Upton, Wirral, Cheshire. Died at Shanghai Isolation Hospital.
85. MILNER, Civilian, FRANCIS. 10 April 1943. Age 69 of Avenue Petain, French Concession, Shanghai. Son of the late William Milner, of Bridlington, East Yorkshire; husband of Alice Maud Milner, of 21 Eber's Road, Mapperley Park, Nottingham. Died at Shanghai General Hospital.
86. MOIR, Civilian, SALLY BLACK. 22 December 1944. Age 58. Hong Kong Auxiliary Nursing Service; of Cornhill, Quarry Bay, Hong Kong. Daughter of the late James Glover, of Kincubbin, Co. Down, Northern Ireland, wife of Archibald Black Moir. Died at Shanghai.
87. MOLLOY, Civilian, HENRY PATRICK. Age 47. 15 January 1944, Haiphong Road Camp, Shanghai.
88. MONK, Civilian, WILLIAM JOHN. Age 62. 23 March 1943 husband of Jane Monk. Died at Haiphong Road Camp, Shanghai.
89. MURPHINE, Civilian, SHEPLEY. 25 June 1945 of Shanghai. Age 43. Son of Annie Murphine, of 171 Henshaw Street, Oldham, Lancashire; husband of Zofja Murphine. Died at Shanghai General Hospital.
90. NASH, Civilian, ROBERT HENRY. Age 83. 26 January 1945. Husband of F. F. Nash, of 1522/42 Bubbling Well Road, Shanghai. Died at Shanghai General Hospital.

91. NOBLE, Civilian, JAMES. 22 November 1944. Age 74. Husband of Agnes May Noble, of 854 Kiangsu Rad, Shanghai. Died at Shanghai General Hospital.

92. NORMAN, Civilian, RUTH. Age 82. 11 February 1945 at Shanghai General Hospital.

93. NORRIS, Civilian, THE REVD. FRANCIS LUSHINGTON. 2 July 1945. Age 82. D.D.; Bishop in North China. Son of the late Ven. J. P. Norris (Archdeacon of Bristol) and Edith Grace Norris. Died at Lincoln Avenue Internment Camp, Shanghai.

94. OLIVER, Civilian, ARTHUR HENRY. 4 April 1943. Age 74 at Shanghai Police Hospital. Son of Philip Jacob and Emma Fowler Oliver, of Bromley, Kent.

95. ORCHIN, Civilian, PAMELA ALFREDA. 16 December 1944. Age 23 of Tsingtao, North China. Daughter of A. C. and A. Orchin. Died at Shanghai General Hospital.

96. PAYNE, Civilian, HOWARD. 3 December 1942. Age 65 of Yenching University, Peking. Husband of Alice Mary Payne. Died at Country Hospital, Shanghai.

97. PEACOCK, Civilian, HENRY KARTCHKEL. Age 60. Died 11 September 1943 at Pudong Internment Camp, Shanghai.

98. PEARSON, Civilian, GODFREY. 22 June 1944. Age 53. Son of the late Lars and Elna Hultgren. Died at Country Hospital, Shanghai.

99. PERRY, Civilian, LILLIAN CLARA. Age 42. Died 1943 at Lunghwa Internment Camp, Shanghai.

100. RAEBURN, Civilian, PETER DUNCAN. Age 83. 6 April 1945 at Shanghai General Hospital.

101. REEKS, Civilian, HUGH ARTHUR. Age 55. Death date unknown, Haiphong Road Internment Camp, Shanghai.

102. **REES**, Civilian, **JOHN ALFRED**. Age 13. 22 June 1943. Died at Yangchow C Internment Camp, Yangzhou.

103. REEVES, Civilian, MARY. Age 84. 30 August 1944 at Shanghai General Hospital.

104. REID, Civilian, ANNIE, age 70. 5 July 1945 at St. Luke's Hospital, Shanghai.

105 **ROBB**, Civilian, **DONALD KEITH**. 10 May 1944. Aged 7 weeks. Son of Douglas and Militza Robb. Died at Country Hospital, Shanghai.

106. ROGERS, Civilian, ANNA JENSINE. Age 56. 9 July 1944. Died at Yangchow C Internment Camp, Yangzhou.
107. ROUSE, Civilian, HELEN MARY. 10 June 1945. Age 76 of 16 Kelmscott Gardens, Avenue du Roi Albert, Shanghai. Widow of Edward Henry Rouse. Died at Lunghwa Internment Camp, Shanghai.
108. RUCHWALDY, Civilian, MABEL AUGUSTA. Age 67. 8 January 1945 at Shanghai General Hospital.
109. SALMON, Civilian, ROBERT EVANS. 21 October 1943. Age 57 at Shanghai General Hospital.
110. SHEPHERD, Civilian, GEORGE CLIFFORD. 15 June 1943. Age 44 of 1790 Avenue Joffre, Shanghai. Son of Granville Keith Shepherd, of Taly-Bont, Ruan Lanihorne, Truro, Cornwall; husband of Gladys Bolen Shepherd. Died at Haiphong Road Camp, Shanghai.
111. **SHEREVERA**, Civilian, **DMITRY CONSTANTINOVICH**. 8 June 1944. Age 7. Son of Mrs. L. H. Sherevera, of 230 Route Vallon, Shanghai. Died at Chapei Camp, Shanghai.
112. SHIRAZEE, Civilian, MAHOMED CAZIN. 16 November 1944. Age 69 of 472 Kiangoo Lee, Edinburgh Road, Shanghai. Died at Shanghai General Hospital.
113. SIMOES, Civilian, MARIO MIGUEL. 2 October 1944. Age 27. Son of Charles Pereira Simoes and Marie Therese Simoes, of Shanghai. Died at Shanghai.
114. SINCLAIR, Civilian, ARCHIBALD. Age 82. 13 December 1944. Died at Lincoln Avenue Internment Camp, Shanghai.
115. SLOAN, Civilian, ANNIE. Age 80. Died 1945 at Pudong Internment Camp, Shanghai.
116. SMITH, Civilian, ISABELLA. 24 April 1944. Age 65. Daughter of the late John Fleming Smith and Janet Tweedie Smith. Died at Lunghwa Internment Camp, Shanghai.
117. SMITH, Civilian, LOUISE. Age 58. Died 1944 at Lincoln Avenue Internment Camp, Shanghai.
118. SMITH, Civilian, VIVIAN. Age 65. 22 January 1945. Died at Yangchow C Internment Camp, Yangzhou.
119. SOUZA, Civilian, JOHN JOSE DA SILVA. Age 59. 7 February 1945 at Shanghai General Hospital.
120. STEPHEN, Civilian, A. 17 August 1945, at Shanghai.

121. STRUTH, Master, JAMES BARKER, S.S. Kaiping (London), Merchant Navy. Died 26 June 1944, age 51. Son of James Struth, Master Mariner, and Mary Ann Struth; husband of Margaret Sinclair Struth of Edinburgh. Died at Shanghai.

122. SYMONS, Civilian, RICHARD SAMUEL, August 1944. Age 73, Died at Chapei Camp, Shanghai.

123. TAIT, Civilian, EDWIN GARLAND. 31 January 1945. Age 66 of 20 Verdun Terrace, Shanghai. Died at Pudong Internment Camp, Shanghai.

124. THOMSON, Civilian, WILLIAM . Age 85. September 1944. Died at Lincoln Avenue Internment Camp, Shanghai.

125. TOON, Civilian, ARTHUR JAMES, M.M. Superintendent, Shanghai Municipal Police. 28 September 1944. Age 47 of 173 Seymour Road, Shanghai. Husband of Dorothy Corona Toon. Died at Country Hospital, Shanghai.

126. **TUCK**, Civilian, **SHARON ANNE**. 28 September 1944. Aged 10 months. Daughter of Thomas W. C. and Annah Raphael Tuck. Died at Country Hospital, Shanghai.

127. VITTE, Civilian, ALEXANDER. Age 64. 23 March 1943. Died at Yangchow B Internment Camp, Yangzhou.

128. VON BRADKE, Civilian, LEO NICHOLAS. Shanghai Municipal Police Officer. Age 48. 15 December 1944 at Shanghai General Hospital.

129. WARDELL, Civilian, MATTHEW MORRISON. 25 September 1945. Age 37. Husband of Ann Harland Wardell, of Stranton, Thorpe Road, Easington Village, Co. Durham. Died at Radium Institute, Shanghai.

130. WATSON, Civilian, MARGARET BROWN MCKAY. Age 50. 6 July 1945. Wife of John Watson. Died at St. Luke's Hospital, Shanghai.

131. WATSON, Civilian, WINIFRED MAY FLORENCE. 20 August 1945. Age 42. Wife of Capt. E. C. Watson, of 14 War Crimes Team, H.Q. Land Forces, Hong Kong. Died at Shanghai General Hospital.

132. WEILL, Civilian, MAURICE BERNARD. 30 March 1944. Age 36 of Shanghai. Son of Mrs. R. Weill, of 132 Pokfulam, Hong Kong; husband of Esther Weill, of the same address. Died at Shanghai General Hospital.

133. WHITE, Civilian, DOMINIC. 12 September 1944. Husband of A. H. White, of 120 Jinkee Road, Shanghai. Died at Shanghai General Hospital.

134. WHITE, Civilian, WILLIAM AUGUSTUS. 20 February 1945. Age 77. Son of the late William Augustus White; husband of Clara White, of 213a Grosvenor Gardens, Rue Cardinal Mercier, Shanghai. Died at Lincoln Avenue Internment Camp, Shanghai.

135. WHITEHEAD, Civilian, CHARLES CECIL. 7 April 1943. Age 53 of High Street, Melbourn, Cambridgeshire. Son of Thomas and Mary Stockbridge Whitehead, of Royston, Hertfordshire; husband of Mabel Whitehead. Died at Shanghai.

136. **WILLIAMSON**, Civilian, **HEATHER**. Age 1. 27 September 1944. Daughter of E. E. Williamson. Died at Country Hospital, Shanghai.

137. WILSON, Civilian, CHARLES CYRIL WAGSTAFFE. Age 67. 23 December 1942. Died at Haiphong Road Internment Camp, Shanghai.

138. WOODS, Civilian, ARTHUR. 18 December 1943. Age 63 of Shanghai. Son of the late Robert and Elizabeth Woods. Died at Shanghai Police Hospital.

139. WORLEY, Civilian, JANE. Age 35. 29 July 1943. Wife of Sidney Worley. Died at Country Hospital, Shanghai.

140. WYATT, Civilian, HAROLD, 29 March 1945. Age 68. Chapei Camp, Shanghai.

141. YATE, Civilian, THOMAS MOORE. Age 73. 21 August 1944 at Shanghai Isolation Hospital.

Australian Citizens

1. MACFARLANE, Civilian, ALICE. Age 80. 1 March 1945. Died at Lunghwa Internment Camp, Shanghai.

2. ROBJOHNS, Civilian, DOROTHY ELIZABETH. 30 March 1944. Age 36. B.A. Daughter of the late Mr. and Mrs. J. A. Haslam, of King's College, Kensington Park, South Australia; wife of Dr. Henry Collin Robjohns, of 128 Glen Osmond Road, Parkside, Australia. Died at Great Western Road Internment Camp, Shanghai.

3. ROSS, Civilian, ALFRED JOHN. Age 73. 11 January 1945. Died at Yangchow C Internment Camp, Yangzhou.
4. WYATT, Civilian, HAROLD. 29 March 1945. Age 67. Son of John and M. Wyatt, of Sydney, Australia; husband of Annie Wyatt, of 1032/43 Yu Yuen Road, Shanghai. Died at Shanghai General Hospital.

Canadian Citizens
1. DAY, Civilian, GORDON GEORGE. Age 48. Died on release August 1945, Yangchow C Internment Camp, Yangzhou.
2. MAYNE, Civilian, GEORGE EDWARD OTWAY. Age 57. 15 May 1945. Son of Mrs. Mayne, of Suite 2, Park Plaza, 1140 W. Pender Street, Vancouver, Canada, and of the late Blair Edward Otway Mayne; husband of Geraldyn P. L. Mayne. Died at Lunghwa Internment Camp, Shanghai.
3. ROSS, Civilian, ROBERTA SUSAN. Age 50. 9 March 1945. Died at Chapei Internment Camp, Shanghai.
4. WALKER, Civilian, MARY ELLEN. Age 72. 22 January 1945. Died at Lincoln Avenue Internment Camp, Shanghai.

Notes

Introduction

1. Colin Smith, *Singapore Burning: Heroism and Surrender in World War II* (London: Penguin Books Ltd, 2005), 488

Chapter 1 – School's Out

1. Shanghai – Longhua Camp, from an interview with Rachel Bosebury Beck, Shanghai High School International Division
2. Bernice Archer, *The Internment of Western Civilians under the Japanese, 1941–1945* (Routledge, 2004), 178
3. Ibid.
4. Ibid.
5. Shanghai – Longhua Camp, from an interview with Rachel Bosebury Beck, Shanghai High School International Division
6. 'Heather Burch remembers Lunghwa CAC', interview, Shanghai High School International Division
7. Lieutenant Commander Stephen Polkinghorn was awarded the Distinguished Service Cross for his courage in resisting the Japanese. One crewman of the *Peterel*, a petty officer radio operator, was ashore at the time of the attack and he joined the Chinese underground in Shanghai, surviving for over three years.
8. Valerie Kinghorn interviewed by Dani Garavelli, *The Sunday Times*, 12 February 2001
9. J.G. Ballard interviewed by Martin Amis, *The Observer Magazine*, 2 September 1984
10. Valerie Kinghorn interviewed by Dani Garavelli, *The Sunday Times*, 12 February 2001
11. Shanghai – Longhua Camp, from an interview with Rachel Bosebury Beck, Shanghai High School International Division

12. 'Life in Occupied Shanghai – 1941' by Norman Douglas Shaw, *WW2 People's War*, Article ID: A3913382, BBC History, http://www.bbc.co.uk/history, 18 April 2005, accessed 22 January 2010
13. Ibid
14. Shanghai – Longhua Camp, from an interview with Rachel Bosebury Beck, Shanghai High School International Division
15. 'My Memories of Leaving Singapore by Catherine Butcher', Children of Far East Prisoners of War Association, www.cofepow.org, accessed 14 January 2009
16. 'A Toddler in Singapore at the Outbreak of WW2' by Roger Eagle, Bemerton Local History Society, *WW2 People's War*, Article ID: A3998334, BBC History, 3 May 2005, accessed 15 January 2010
17. Ibid.
18. 'Taken Prisoner: 'The March' from Katong House to Changi Jail Singapore – 12th February to 8th March 1942' by Robert Brooks, Children of Far east Prisoners of War Association, www.cofepow.org, accessed 15 January 2010

Chapter 2 – Evacuation

1. 'My Memories of Leaving Singapore' by Catherine Butcher, Children of Far East Prisoners of War Association, www.cofepow.org, accessed 14 January 2009
2. Ibid.
3. Ibid.
4. 'My Memories of Being a Child Civilian Internee' by Eileen Page (nee Harris), Children of Far East Prisoners of War Association, www.cofepow.org, accessed 5 January 2009
5. 'A Lost Youth' by greyladies, *WW2 People's War*, Article ID: A8049378, BBC History, http://www.bbc.co.uk/history, 26 December 2005, accessed 1 May 2010
6. HMS *Giang Bee* – Researched Passenger List, Children of Far East Prisoners of War Association (COFEPOW), www.cofepow.org, accessed 6 May 2010
7. Ibid.
8. 'A Lost Youth' by greyladies, *WW2 People's War*, Article ID: A8049378, BBC History, 26 December 2005, accessed 1 May 2010

Chapter 3 – New Masters

1. 'Taken Prisoner: 'The March' from Katong House to Changi Jail Singapore – 12th February to 8th March 1942' by Robert Brooks,

Children of Far East Prisoners of War Association, www.cofepow. org, accessed 15 January 2010

2. Colin Smith, *Singapore Burning: Heroism and Surrender in World War II* (London: Penguin Viking, 2005) 554

3. R. M. Horner, *Singapore Diary: The Hidden Journal of Captain R. M. Horner* (London: Spellmount Publishers Ltd, 2007), 12

4. *Diary of Brigadier Eric Whitlock Goodman, DSO, MC*, 17th February 1942, Far East Prisoners of War Association (FEPOW), http://www. britain-at-war.org.uk/WW2/Brigadier_EW_Goodman/

5. 'Taken Prisoner: 'The March' from Katong House to Changi Jail Singapore – 12th February to 8th March 1942' by Robert Brooks, Children of Far East Prisoners of War Association, www.cofepow. org, accessed 15 January 2010

6. Ibid.

7. Ibid.

8. Ibid.

9. Ibid.

10. 'My Tenko Quilt: The 78-year-old reunited with the quilt she made secretly in Japan camp' by Elizabeth Sanderson, *The Mail on Sunday*, 20 March 2010

11. Noel Barber, *Sinister Twilight: The Fall of Singapore* (London: Cassell Military, 2002), 243

12. 'Taken Prisoner: 'The March' from Katong House to Changi Jail Singapore – 12th February to 8th March 1942' by Robert Brooks, Children of Far East Prisoners of War Association, www.cofepow. org, accessed 15 January 2010

Chapter 4 – Internment

1. 'My Memories of Being a Child Civilian Internee' by Eileen Page (nee Harris), Children of Far East Prisoners of War Association, www.cofepow.org, accessed 5 January 2009

2. Ibid.

3. Bernice Archer, *The Internment of Western Civilians under the Japanese, 1941–1945: A patchwork of internment* (Routledge, 2004), 177

4. Ibid: 184

5. Ibid.

6. Ibid: 186

7. Ibid: 186

8. Ibid: 186

9. Ibid: Author to add page number

10. Ibid: 187

11. Ibid: 188
12. Ibid: 190
13. Ibid: 190
14. Ibid: 190
15. Ibid: 192
16. Ibid: 192
17. Ibid: 192
18. Ibid: 192
19. Frances B. Cogan, *Captured, The Internment of American Civilians in the Philippines, 1941–1945* (Athens, University of Georgia Press, 2000), 2
20. Ibid: 246
21. Bernice Archer, *The Internment of Western Civilians under the Japanese, 1941–1945: A patchwork of internment* (Routledge, 2004), 181
22. Lyn Smith, *Young Voices: British Children Remember the Second World War* (London: Viking, 2007), 293–4
23. Bernice Archer, *The Internment of Western Civilians under the Japanese, 1941–1945: A patchwork of internment* (Routledge, 2004), 184
24. Lyn Smith, *Young Voices: British Children Remember the Second World War* (London: Viking, 2007), 293–4
25. Ibid: 294
26. Ibid: 299–300
27. Bernice Archer, *The Internment of Western Civilians under the Japanese, 1941–1945: A patchwork of internment* (Routledge, 2004), 187
28. Lyn Smith, *Young Voices: British Children Remember the Second World War* (London: Viking, 2007), 300
29. Bernice Archer, *The Internment of Western Civilians under the Japanese, 1941–1945: A patchwork of internment* (Routledge, 2004), 192
30. C. Hudson Southwell, *Uncharted Waters* (Calgary: Astana Publishing, 1999), 165
31. Peter Firkins, *Borneo Surgeon: A Reluctant Hero* (Western Australia: Hesperian Press, 1995)

Chapter 5 – City of Terror

1. Ralph Shaw, *Sin City* (London: Warner Books, 1973), 207
2. 'Life in Occupied Shanghai – 1941' by Norman Douglas Shaw, *WW2 People's War*, Article ID: A3913382, BBC History, http://www.bbc.co.uk/history, 18 April 2005, accessed 22 January 2010
3. Ibid.
4. Ibid.
5. Ibid.

6. 'Japanese Internment Camp in China' by Moira Barbara, *WW2 People's War*, Article ID: A4038220, BBC History, 9 May 2005, accessed 21 January 2010

7. Valerie Kinghorn and Ronald Calder interviewed by Dani Garavelli, *The Sunday Times*, 12 February 2001

8. Ibid.

9. 'Japanese Internment Camp in China' by Moira Barbara, *WW2 People's War*, Article ID: A4038220, BBC History, 9 May 2005, accessed 21 January 2010

10. Ibid.

11. Bernard Wasserstein, *Secret War in Shanghai: Treachery, Subversion and Collaboration in the Second World War* (London: Profile Books Ltd, 1998), 140

12. 'Heather Burch remembers Lunghwa CAC', interview, Shanghai High School International Division

13. Shanghai – Longhua Camp, from an interview with Rachel Bosebury Beck, Shanghai High School International Division

14. Lyn Smith, *Young Voices: British Children Remember the Second World War* (London: Viking, 2007), 294

15. Valerie Kinghorn interviewed by Dani Garavelli, *The Sunday Times*, 12 February 2001

16. Lyn Smith, *Young Voices: British Children Remember the Second World War* (London: Viking, 2007), 295–6

17. Shanghai – Longhua Camp, from an interview with Rachel Bosebury Beck, Shanghai High School International Division

18. Ibid.

19. Lyn Smith, *Young Voices: British Children Remember the Second World War* (London: Viking, 2007), 295

20. Shanghai – Longhua Camp, from an interview with Rachel Bosebury Beck, Shanghai High School International Division

21. Ibid.

22. Ibid.

23. 'Heather Burch remembers Lunghwa CAC', interview, Shanghai High School International Division

24. Lyn Smith, *Young Voices: British Children Remember the Second World War* (London: Viking, 2007), 295

25. 'Heather Burch remembers Lunghwa CAC', interview, Shanghai High School International Division

26. Valerie Kinghorn and Ronald Calder interviewed by Dani Garavelli, *The Sunday Times*, 12 February 2001

27. Shanghai – Longhua Camp, from an interview with Rachel Bosebury Beck, Shanghai High School International Division

28. Valerie Kinghorn interviewed by Dani Garavelli, *The Sunday Times*, 12 February 2001
29. Lyn Smith, *Young Voices: British Children Remember the Second World War*, (London: Viking, 2007), 296
30. Ibid: 296
31. Ibid: 299
32. 'Heather Burch remembers Lunghwa CAC', interview, Shanghai High School International Division
33. 'Nel's Story: Part II: Internment – Kares-E and Kota Paris' by anak-bandung, *WW2 People's War*, Article ID: A2796942, BBC History, http://www.bbc.co.uk/history, 30 June 2004, accessed 22 January 2010
34. Ibid.
35. J.G. Ballard interviewed by Martin Amis, *The Observer Magazine*, 2 September 1984
36. J.G. Ballard interviewed by Claire Tomalin, *The Sunday Times*, 9 September 1984
37. Lyn Smith, *Young Voices: British Children Remember the Second World War* (London: Viking, 2007), 299
38. Shanghai – Longhua Camp, from an interview with Rachel Bosebury Beck, Shanghai High School International Division
39. 'Heather Burch remembers Lunghwa CAC', interview, Shanghai High School International Division
40. Courtesy of David Parker, OBE, Director of Information and Secretariat, Commonwealth War Graves Commission, in a letter to the author, 14 March 2008

Chapter 6 – Hell's Waiting Room

1. *Michel's Musings*, http://members.iinet.net.au/~vanderkp/michel.htm, accessed 14 January 2010
2. 'Tjideng – A Prison Camp for Woman: Riet Remembers', Children of Far East Prisoners of War (COFEPOW), www.cofepow.org, accessed 20 January 2010
3. Ibid.
4. 'Tjideng Camp – 1942 to 1945 (a women and children's internment camp in Batavia) Hetty's Story', Children of Far East Prisoners of War (COFEPOW), www.cofepow.org, accessed 13 January 2009
5. Ibid.
6. Ibid.
7. Ibid.
8. 'Hardy's memories of life in Tjideng Camp – 1942 to 1945', Children of Far East Prisoners of War (COFEPOW), www.cofepow.org, accessed 15 January 2010

9. 'Tjideng Camp – 1942 to 1945 (a women and children's internment camp in Batavia) Hetty's Story', Children of Far East Prisoners of War (COFEPOW), www.cofepow.org, accessed 13 January 2009

10. Gavan Daws, *Prisoners of the Japanese: POWs of the Second World War* (London: Pocket Books, 1994), 59

11. 'Tjideng Camp – 1942 to 1945 (a women and children's internment camp in Batavia) Hetty's Story', Children of Far East Prisoners of War (COFEPOW), www.cofepow.org, accessed 13 January 2009

12. 'Hardy's memories of life in Tjideng Camp – 1942 to 1945', Children of Far East Prisoners of War (COFEPOW), www.cofepow.org, accessed 15 January 2010

13. *Michel's Musings*, http://members.iinet.net.au/~vanderkp/michel.htm, accessed 20 January 2010

14. 'Tjideng Camp – 1942 to 1945 (a women and children's internment camp in Batavia) Hetty's Story', Children of Far East Prisoners of War (COFEPOW), www.cofepow.org, accessed 13 January 2009

15. Ibid.

16. Ibid.

17. 'Hardy's memories of life in Tjideng Camp – 1942 to 1945', Children of Far East Prisoners of War (COFEPOW), www.cofepow.org, accessed 15 January 2010

18. Ibid.

19. *Michel's Musings*, http://members.iinet.net.au/~vanderkp/michel.htm, accessed 20 January 2010

20. Ibid.

21. 'Hardy's memories of life in Tjideng Camp – 1942 to 1945', Children of Far East Prisoners of War (COFEPOW), www.cofepow.org, accessed 15 January 2010

22. Ibid.

23. Ibid.

24. *Michel's Musings*, http://members.iinet.net.au/~vanderkp/michel.htm, accessed 20 January 2010

25. Ibid.

26. Ibid.

27. Ibid.

28. 'Tjideng Camp – 1942 to 1945 (a women and children's internment camp in Batavia) Hetty's Story', Children of Far East Prisoners of War (COFEPOW), www.cofepow.org, accessed 13 January 2009

29. 'Tjideng – A Prison Camp for Woman: Riet Remembers', Children of Far East Prisoners of War (COFEPOW), www.cofepow.org, accessed 20 January 2010

30. Ibid.
31. Ibid.
32. Ibid.
33. 'Tjideng Camp – 1942 to 1945 (a women and children's internment camp in Batavia) Hetty's Story', Children of Far East Prisoners of War (COFEPOW), www.cofepow.org, accessed 13 January 2009
34. 'Hardy's memories of life in Tjideng Camp – 1942 to 1945', Children of Far East Prisoners of War (COFEPOW), www.cofepow.org, accessed 15 January 2010
35. Ibid.
36. 'Tjideng Camp – 1942 to 1945 (a women and children's internment camp in Batavia) Hetty's Story', Children of Far East Prisoners of War (COFEPOW), www.cofepow.org, accessed 13 January 2009
37. Hardy's memories of life in Tjideng Camp – 1942 to 1945', Children of Far East Prisoners of War (COFEPOW), www.cofepow.org, accessed 15 January 2010
38. 'Tjideng Camp – 1942 to 1945 (a women and children's internment camp in Batavia) Hetty's Story', Children of Far East Prisoners of War (COFEPOW), www.cofepow.org, accessed 13 January 2009
39. Hardy's memories of life in Tjideng Camp – 1942 to 1945', Children of Far East Prisoners of War (COFEPOW), www.cofepow.org, accessed 15 January 2010
40. 'How I lost My Best Friend' by sonnyjim/Mike Nellis, WW2 People's War, Article ID: A2859276, BBC History, accessed 20 November 2008
41. 'My Experiences in Japanese Concentration Camps on Java, Indonesia' by Johan Rijkee, WW2 People's War, Article ID: A4180169, BBC History, accessed 3 January 2009
42. Ibid.
43. 'How I lost My Best Friend' by sonnyjim/Mike Nellis, WW2 People's War, BBC History, Article ID: A2859276, accessed 20 November 2008
44. Ibid.
45. Ibid.
46. Ibid.
47. Lyn Smith, Young Voices: British Children Remember the Second World War (London: Viking, 2007), 295
48. 'My Experiences in Japanese Concentration Camps on Java, Indonesia' by Johan Rijkee, WW2 People's War, BBC History, Article ID: A4180169, accessed 3 January 2009
49. Ibid.
50. Ibid.
51. Ibid.

Notes

Chapter 7 – Hard Times

1. Bernice Archer, *The Internment of Western Civilians under the Japanese, 1941–1945, A Patchwork of Internment* (Routledge, 2004), 197
2. Ibid: 197
3. Ibid: 198
4. Ibid: 200
5. 'My Memories of Being a Child Civilian Internee' by Eileen Page (nee Harris), Children of Far East Prisoners of War Association, www.cofepow.org, accessed 5 January 2009
6. Ibid.
7. Ibid.
8. Bernice Archer, *The Internment of Western Civilians under the Japanese, 1941–1945, A Patchwork of Internment* (Routledge, 2004), 198
9. Ibid: 199
10. Ibid: 203
11. 'My Tenko Quilt: The 78-year-old reunited with the quilt she made secretly in Japan camp' by Elizabeth Sanderson, *The Mail on Sunday*, 20 March 2010
12. Ibid.
13. Lyn Smith, *Young Voices: British Children Remember the Second World War* (London: Viking, 2007), 299
14. 'Three Years In A Prison Camp' by Ada N. Hayes, *The Hampton Union*, May 10, 1945
15. Ibid.
16. Lyn Smith, *Young Voices: British Children Remember the Second World War* (London: Viking, 2007), 298
17. Ibid.
18. 'Three Years In A Prison Camp' by Ada N. Hayes, *The Hampton Union*, May 10, 1945
19. Lyn Smith, *Young Voices: British Children Remember the Second World War* (London: Viking, 2007), 298
20. Ibid.
21. 'Three Years In A Prison Camp' by Ada N. Hayes, *The Hampton Union*, May 10, 1945
22. Lyn Smith, *Young Voices: British Children Remember the Second World War* (London: Viking, 2007), 298
23. Bernice Archer, *The Internment of Western Civilians under the Japanese, 1941–1945, A Patchwork of Internment* (Routledge, 2004), 205
24. Ibid: 205
25. Ibid: 205
26. Ibid: 205–6

27. Ibid: 191
28. Ibid: 191

Chapter 8 – Comfort Girls

1. Lyn Smith, *Young Voices: British Children Remember the Second World War* (London: Viking, 2007), 295
2. Bart van Poelgeest, *Report of a Study of Dutch Government Documents on the Forced Prostitution of Dutch Women in the Dutch East Indies during the Japanese Occupation*, Unofficial Translation, 24 January 1994
3. Ibid.
4. Lyn Smith, *Young Voices: British Children Remember the Second World War* (London: Viking, 2007), 296
5. Ibid.
6. *The Forgotten Ones*, transcript of television documentary on Australian Story, produced by Margaret Parker, Australian Broadcasting Corporation, http://www.abc.net.au/auhistory/transcripts/s351798.htm
7. Ibid.
8. Ibid.
9. Ibid.
10. Ibid.
11. *The Forgotten Ones*, transcript of television documentary on Australian Story, produced by Margaret Parker, Australian Broadcasting Corporation, http://www.abc.net.au/auhistory/transcripts/s351798.htm

Chapter 9 – God Save the King

1. Shanghai – Longhua Camp, from an interview with Rachel Bosebury Beck, Shanghai High School International Division
2. Lyn Smith, *Young Voices: British Children Remember the Second World War* (London: Viking, 2007), 297
3. Shanghai – Longhua Camp, from an interview with Rachel Bosebury Beck, Shanghai High School International Division
4. Ibid.
5. Valerie Kinghorn and Ronald Calder interviewed by Dani Garavelli, *The Sunday Times*, 12 February 2001
6. 'God Save the King!' by Mrs K.S. Snuggs, *WW2 People's War*, Article ID: A2350135, 26 February 2004, BBC History, http://www.bbc.co.uk/history, accessed 21 January 2010
7. Ibid.

8. Ibid.
9. Lyn Smith, *Young Voices: British Children Remember the Second World War* (London: Viking, 2007), 294
10. Ibid: 294

Chapter 10 – The Final Stretch

1. Keat Gin Ooi, *Japanese Empire in the Tropics: Selected Documents and Reports of the Japanese Period in Sarawak, North West Borneo, 1941–1945*, Ohio University Center for International Studies, Monographs in International Studies, SE Asia Series 101, 1998
2. 'Tjideng Camp – 1942 to 1945 (a women and children's internment camp in Batavia) Hetty's Story', Children of Far East Prisoners of War (COFEPOW), www.cofepow.org, accessed 13 January 2009
3. 'How I lost My Best Friend' by Mike Nellis, *WW2 People's War*, Article ID: A2859276, BBC History, http://www.bbc.co.uk/history, accessed 20 November 2008
4. Shanghai – Longhua Camp, from an interview with Rachel Bosebury Beck, Shanghai High School International Division
5. Lyn Smith, *Young Voices: British Children Remember the Second World War* (London: Viking, 2007), 296
6. Ibid.
7. Ibid.
8. 'One Suitcase, No Toys' by Rose of Java, *WW2 People's War*, Article ID: A3712231, BBC History, 24 February 2005, accessed 19 March 2010
9. Ibid.
10. Ibid.
11. 'Nel's Story: Part III: Internment in Work Camp Kampong-Makassar' by anak-bandung, *WW2 People's War*, Article ID: A2797338, BBC History, , 30 June 2004, accessed 22 January 2010
12. Ibid.
13. Ibid.
14. 'Tjideng Camp – 1942 to 1945 (a women and children's internment camp in Batavia) Hetty's Story', Children of Far East Prisoners of War (COFEPOW), www.cofepow.org, accessed 13 January 2009
15. 'A Lost Youth' by greyladies, *WW2 People's War*, Article ID: A8049378, BBC History, 26 December 2005, accessed 1 May 2010
16. 'Phyllis Briggs's War – Life in the Dutch Houses [P. Thom : Part 5]' by Bournemouth Libraries, *WW2People's War*, Article ID: A3478179, BBC History, accessed 27 November 2008
17. Ibid.

18. Ibid.
19. 'Prisoner of War Memories' by Cassandra Jardine, *Daily Telegraph*, 29 November 1997
20. Ibid.
21. Ibid.
22. Lyn Smith, *Young Voices: British Children Remember the Second World War* (London: Viking, 2007), 294
23. Ibid: 295
24. Ibid.
25. 'Tucsonan Recalls POW Ordeal after Japan Captured Corregidor' by Bonnie Henry, *The Arizona Daily Star*, http://www.azstarnet.com, accessed 15 May 2008
26. Max Hastings, *Nemesis: The Battle for Japan, 1944-45* (London: Harper Perennial, 2008), 247
27. 'Japanese Internment Camp in China' by Moira Barbara, *WW2 People's War*, Article ID: A4038220, BBC History, 9 May 2005, accessed 21 January 2010
28. Ibid.
29. Ibid.
30. Ibid.
31. Keat Gin Ooi, *Japanese Empire in the Tropics: Selected Documents and Reports of the Japanese Period in Sarawak, North West Borneo, 1941-1945*, Ohio University Center for International Studies, Monographs in International Studies, SE Asia Series 101, 1998, 332
32. Ibid: 391

Chapter 11 – The Last *Tenko*

1. 'Shanghai – Longhua Camp', from an interview with Rachel Bosebury Beck, Shanghai High School International Division
2. Ibid.
3. *War Ministry to Commanding General of Military Police, Taiwan, 1 August 1944*, Document No. 2710, Record Group 238, Box 2015, (National Archives and Records Administration (NARA), Washington D.C.)
4. Ibid.
5. *George Duncan's Historical Facts of World War II: Massacres and Atrocities of World War II*, Pacific (including Dutch East Indies) http://members.iinet.net.au/~gduncan/massacres_pacific.html# Pacific
6. *War Ministry to Commanding General of Military Police, Taiwan, 1 August 1944*, Document No. 2710, Record Group 238, Box 2015, (National Archives and Records Administration (NARA), Washington D.C.)

7. 'Heather Burch remembers Lunghwa CAC', interview, Shanghai High School International Division
8. Ibid.
9. Bernice Archer, *The Internment of Western Civilians under the Japanese, 1941–1945, A Patchwork of Internment* (Routledge, 2004), 206
10. Author to supply ref for Bates at proof.
11. 'My Experiences in Japanese Concentration Camps on Java, Indonesia' by Johan Rijkee, *WW2 People's War*, Article ID: A4180169, BBC History, http://www.bbc.co.uk/history, accessed 3 January 2009
12. Ibid.
13. Ibid.
14. Ibid.
15. Ibid.
16. 'Nel's Story: Part III: Internment in Work Camp Kampong-Makassar' by anak-bandung, *WW2 People's War*, Article ID: A2797338, BBC History, 30 June 2004, accessed 22 January 2010
17. Lord Russell of Liverpool, *The Knights of Bushido: A Short History of Japanese War Crimes* (London: Greenhill Books, 2005), 210
18. Gavan Daws, *Prisoners of the Japanese: POWs of the Second World War in the Pacific* (London: Pocket Books, 2006), 350
19. 'A Lost Youth' by greyladies, *WW2 People's War*, Article ID: A8049378, BBC History, 26 December 2005, accessed 1 May 2010
20. Ibid.

Chapter 12 – The Lost Children

1. 'British PoWs vow to fight on', BBC News, 26 November 1998, http://www.bbc.co.uk/news, accessed 10 January 2009
2. 'My Memories of Being a Child Civilian Internee' by Eileen Page (nee Harris), Children of Far East Prisoners of War Association, www.cofepow.org, accessed 5 January 2009
3. 'Lost' by Arie den Hollander, Children of Far East Prisoners of War Association, www.cofepow.org, accessed 10 January 2009
4. Ibid.
5. Ibid.
6. Ibid.
7. Ibid.
8. Ibid.
9. Ibid.
10. 'One Suitcase, No Toys' by Rose of Java, *WW2 People's War*, Article ID: A3712231, BBC History, 24 February 2005, accessed 19 March 2010

11. 'Lost' by Arie den Hollander, Children of Far East Prisoners of War Association, www.cofepow.org, accessed 10 January 2009

Chapter 13 – Blood Link

1. 'Britain to pay debt of honour to Japanese PoWs' by Michael Smith and Andy McSmith, *Daily Telegraph*, 19 June 2001
2. Ibid.
3. 'Japanese PoWs uncover cash timebomb' by Tim Butcher, *Daily Telegraph*, 24 April 1998
4. 'PoWs to receive "debt of honour"', BBC News, 7 November 2000, http://www.bbc.co.uk/news, accessed 9 January 2009
5. *A debt of honour: the ex gratia scheme for British groups interned by the Japanese during the Second World War*, The Parliamentary Ombudsman, Parliamentary and Health Service Ombudsman, http://www.ombudsman.org.uk, 2005
6. Ibid.
7. Ibid.
8. 'Subjects of rough justice', *The Standard* (Hong Kong), 28 October 2006
9. Ibid.
10. Ibid.
11. '£10,000 PoW payments delayed' by Philip Johnstone, *Daily Telegraph*, 12 June 2001
12. 'Victory at last for war camp widow snubbed by MoD' by Philip Johnstone, *Daily Telegraph*, 10 October 2006
13. Ibid.

Selected Sources and Bibliography

Archives

1. MacMillan Brown Library, University of Canterbury, Christchurch, New Zealand

Imperial Japanese Army, Box 263, Exhibit 1978, Document No. 1114-B: *Regarding the outline for the disposal of Prisoners of War according to the change of situation, a notification, Army-Asia-Secret No. 2257, by the Vice War Minister*, 11 March 1945

2. National Archives and Records Administration (NARA), Washington D.C.
1. *Chief Prisoner of War Camps Tokyo to Chief of Staff, Taiwan Army, 20 August 1945*, Document No. 2697, Record Group 238, Box 2011
2. *War Ministry to Commanding General of Military Police, 1 August 1944*, Document No. 2710, Record Group 238, Box 2015

Published Sources

Allan, Sheila, *Diary of a Girl in Changi, 1941–45*, Simon & Schuster Australia, 3rd Edition, 2004

Archer, Bernice, *The Internment of Western Civilians under the Japanese 1941–45: A Patchwork of Internment*, Hong Kong University Press, 2008

Arthur, Anthony, *Deliverance at Los Banos*, New York: St. Martin's Press, 1985

Bayly, Christopher & Harper, Tim, *Forgotten Armies: Britain's Asian Empire & the War with Japan*, Penguin Books, 2005

Chang, Iris, *The Rape of Nanking: The Forgotten Holocaust of World War II*, Penguin Books, 1998

Cogan, Frances B., *Captured: The Internment of American Civilians in the Philippines, 1941–1945*, University of Georgia Press, 2000

Colijn, Helen, *Song of Survival: Women Interned*, White Cloud Press, 1998

Daws, Gavan, *Prisoners of the Japanese: POWs of the Second World War*, Pocket Books, 1994

Emerson, Geoffrey, *Hong Kong Internment, 1941–1945: Life in the Japanese Civilian Camp at Stanley*, Hong Kong University Press, 2008

Felton, Mark, *The Coolie Generals: Britain's Far Eastern Military Leaders in Japanese Captivity*, Pen and Sword Books Limited, 2008

—— *Japan's* Gestapo: Murder, Mayhem and Torture in Occupied Asia, Pen & Sword Books Limited, 2009

—— *The Real Tenko: Extraordinary True Stories of Women Prisoners of the Japanese*, Pen and Sword Books Limited, 2009

Firkins, Peter, *Borneo Surgeon: A Reluctant Hero*, Hesperian Press, 1995

Hastings, Max, *Nemesis: The Battle for Japan, 1944–45*, Harper Perennial, 2008

Kaminski, Theresa, *Prisoners in Paradise: American Women in the Wartime South Pacific* University Press of Kansas, 2000

Keith, Agnes, *Three Came Home: A mother's ordeal in a Japanese prison camp*, Eland Publishing Ltd (New Edition), 2002

Lord Russell of Liverpool, *The Knights of Bushido: A Short History of Japanese War Crimes*, Greenhill Books, 2002

Lindsay, Oliver, *The Battle for Hong Kong 1941–1945: Hostage to Fortune*, Spellmount Publishers Ltd, 2005

Lucas, Celia, *Prisoners of Santo Tomas: Civilian Prisoners of the Japanese, Based on the Diaries of Mrs. Isla Corfield*, Leo Cooper, 1975

Oronato, Michael P., *Forgotten Heroes: Japan's Imprisonment of American Civilians in the Philippines, 1942–1945 – an Oral History*, Meckler, 1990

Smith, Colin, *Singapore Burning: Heroism and Surrender in World War II*, Penguin Books Ltd, 2005

Smith, Lyn, *Young Voices: British Children Remember the Second World War*, Viking, 2007

Southwell, C. Hudson, *Uncharted Waters*, Astana Publishing, 1999

Papers

Keat, Gin Ooi, *Japanese Empire in the Tropics: Selected Documents and Reports of the Japanese Period in Sarawak, North West Borneo, 1941–1945*, Ohio University Center for International Studies, Monographs in International Studies, SE Asia Series 101, 1998

Poelgeest, Bart van, *Report of a Study of Dutch Government Documents on the Forced Prostitution of Dutch Women in the Dutch East Indies during the Japanese Occupation*, Unofficial Translation, 24 January 1994

Selected Sources and Bibliography

Newspapers and Periodicals

The Daily Mail
The Sunday Times
The Observer

Websites

Australian Broadcasting Corporation, http://www.abc.net.au/auhistory
BBC History *WW2 People's War*, http://www.bbc.co.uk/history
Brave Women of Oceania, http://www.angellpro.com.au
Children of Far East Prisoners of War Association, http://www.cofepow.org
Dutch Resistance Museum, http://www.verzetsmuseum.org
Far East Prisoners of War Association, http://www.fepow-community.org.uk
Singapore Ministry of Education, http://www1.moe.edu.sg
Veterans Affairs Canada, http://www.vac-acc.gc.ca

Index